Mile-High Fever

Mile-High Fever

*Silver Mines, Boom Towns, and
High Living on the Comstock Lode*

DENNIS DRABELLE

St. Martin's Press   New York

A portion of this book first appeared in *American History* magazine.

www.stmartins.com

Library of Congress Cataloging-in-Publication Data

Drabelle, Dennis.
  Mile-high fever : silver mines, boom towns, and high living on the Comstock Lode / Dennis Drabelle.—1st ed.
      p. cm.
  Includes bibliographical references and index.
  ISBN-13: 978-0-312-37947-6
  ISBN-10: 0-312-37947-1
  1. Comstock Lode (Nev.) 2. Virginia City (Nev.)—History. 3. Silver mines and mining—Nevada—Comstock Lode. 4. Mines and mineral resources—Nevada—Virginia City—History. I. Title.
  F849.V8D726 2009
  979.3'56—dc22

                                                                2009007636

First Edition: July 2009

10   9   8   7   6   5   4   3   2   1

For Mike

❧ CONTENTS ❧

❧ ACKNOWLEDGMENTS ❧

This book began as an article on Big Bill Stewart, and I thank Jim Doherty, then with *Smithsonian* magazine, for making the assignment. Rachel Hartigan Shea, a native Nevadan and longtime colleague of mine (first at the late, lamented *Civilization* magazine and now at *The Washington Post Book World*), gave me valuable advice and helped with Comstock logistics. Meredith Shedd-Driskel, law curator at the Library of Congress, went out of her way to make "her" rare books useful. In Berkeley, Steve Weissman and Laura Mahanes came through with hospitality and support at multiple stages of the work; and on the other side of San Francisco Bay, Chris Bull kindly put me up while I visited Comstock-related sites in San Francisco. Ron James, who is both Nevada's state historic preservation officer and *the* expert on all things Comstockian, was kind enough to include me in his class's tour of Virginia City and later to read and critique my first draft (even so, the standard disclaimer that any errors are my own applies). Mitchell Waters, my agent, saw the project through with his customary brio. Michael Flamini, my editor at St. Martin's, was a joy to work with, as was assistant editor Vicki Lame. And Mike Bell, my partner, to whom I dedicate *Mile-High Fever*, gave me peerless support throughout, including the kind of painstaking read-through that only a natural-born editor can provide.

For two decades, the 1860s and 1870s, the Comstock Lode may have been the most fascinating site in America. True, you could mix with more people and enjoy a higher level of culture in New York, Philadelphia, St. Louis, and a few other metropolises. But the Comstock capital of Virginia City, Nevada, was boozy, bawdy, well-stocked with luxury goods, and pasted onto a desiccated mountainside—a Babylon of the Great American Desert.

The town's hard-playing population worked hard, too, under the direction of capitalists on fire with risk-taking bravado and so intent on using new technology to solve problems that the mining district came to resemble an unofficial World's Fair. In addition to marveling at Virginia City's reason for being—its mines—a visitor there could preview the machinery and organizing principles of America's industrial future.

For those unable to make the trip, the Comstock held the allure of an investment opportunity: even when the mines themselves were in the doldrums, shrewd speculators could clean up in the stock market. And if you were content simply to sit back and read about the place, a tribe of local journalists, supplemented by visiting reporters and disseminated by the wire services, was at your service.

In the end, however, the most unforgettable thing about Virginia City may have been its tip-of-the-iceberg existence. Here was a thriving community whose sole purpose was to preside over the extraction of untold quantities of silver and gold from the ground beneath its own streets and buildings, a town where people got rich on what could be taken out of their collective basement.

The Comstock quickstepped through phases of Western history. A chaotic rush. A war with Native Americans. A period of bonanza and high living. A takeover by outside forces that went on to impose a series of interlocking monopolies. Hard times and recovery. A coup that transferred control to a new group of entrepreneurs.

By 1880, however, the drama had just about run its course. In an early staging of the classic Western boom-and-bust cycle, Virginia City and environs went into a punishing decline. Yet even as the Lode itself languished, the Comstock stayed in the news as swindles by its principal players came to light, along with scandals embroiling their wives, mistresses, children, and legacies. By the mid-twentieth century, the local population had shrunk to fewer than a thousand, but they'd learned to sustain themselves on past glory. The trick was to play up the remnants of a frontier boomtown fixated on round-the-clock drinking, gambling, whoring, and brawling, an image that crystallized in the TV Western *Bonanza*.

Layers of mythology may have obscured the truth about the Comstock, but trends started there continued to affect American life long after the rush itself had cooled. The Comstock helped open the gap (which has since widened to a chasm) between the super-rich and the rest of us: at the height of the Big Bonanza, miners were earning $4 a day, and although that was a handsome wage for its time, each of the four Comstock Bonanza Kings was clearing $40,000 or more a week. More benignly, innovations created for Comstock mines were adapted to the skyscraper, helping to shape the modern American skyline.

The Comstock also extended its influence in less tangible ways. At a time when it didn't cost a fortune to buy a press and start a newspaper, the region was crawling with scribes. Mark Twain trained there; he arrived in 1861 as Sam Clemens, left in 1864 bearing the soon-to-be most famous pseudonym in American literature, and in between learned a lot from his talented colleagues. In particular, Twain imitated and improved upon the printed ruses by which local papers kept readers entertained when the only hard news to speak of was another day's record tally at the mines. His knack for raising the Western tall tale to an art form launched one of the most illustrious careers in American letters. His zest for the slang of Virginia City inspired him to trade in the refined diction of his predecessors for an earthy style reflecting American English as it was actually spoken. But Twain had a dark side, and the Comstock nurtured that, too, infecting him with a letch for easy money that led him to make a series of cockamamie investments, go bankrupt, and pick up the "pen warmed up in hell" with which he wrote his last, grim stories.

Another personage, less imaginative but also quite gifted, got his start on the Comstock: the lawyer and politician William Morris Stewart, who in a series of courtroom battles drove home the truth that the Lode was just that: a single ore formation, not a collection of atomistic deposits. But along with proving his abilities as an advocate and leader of men, Stewart picked up bad habits in Nevada: a yearning for wealth and a bullheaded refusal to rein in men (such as himself) willing to do almost anything to get it. Stewart acted upon his corrupt values by peddling his influence to wealthy backers, joining schemes to bilk investors, and using his political power to extend throughout the West the grab-the-resources-and-run mentality that had both made and unmade Virginia City.

The Comstock, then, was a laboratory for much that is great (and much, too, that is problematic) about America. In an aerie more than a mile above sea level, engineers built the grandest, most up-to-date industrial complex the world had ever seen; businessmen set in motion financial mechanisms by which they became grotesquely and unfairly rich; a brilliant, avaricious attorney entered into a frame of mind that was to shape the development of the American West; and a gifted young writer widened the scope of literature and revitalized the vocabulary that could be used to express it. Inventions, commerce, political philosophy, literature, even fraud: New Yorkers and Bostonians might have scoffed at the idea, but if you wanted to be on top of new developments in those fields, the Comstock Lode was the place to be.

❧ A NOTE ON PRECIOUS ❧
METALS

When the returns were all in, the Comstock had yielded ore valued at about $300 million, in a ratio of fifty-seven percent silver to forty-three percent gold (the California Gold Rush produced only $200 million more in value). But it was silver that set off the Comstock rush, silver that dominated the gab in saloons and on stock exchange floors, silver that figured in the tall tales, silver that broke the hearts. To put it another way, the Bonanza Kings were also referred to as the Silver Kings, but nobody ever called them the Golden Boys. Gold will make a number of appearances in the following pages, but the star of the Comstock drama was silver.

Silver also played a role in wider political battles. The issue had been joined in 1873, when Congress passed the Mint Act, which tied the U.S. monetary system almost exclusively to gold. The demonetization of silver, as it was called, caused little anguish on the Comstock at first; people were too busy exclaiming over the Big Bonanza, discovered the same year. Later, as hard times hit, being able to sell silver to the government became a crusade in Nevada and beyond (adopting a bimetal standard, the reasoning went, would devalue money and thus lend a hand to overextended farmers and other debtors trapped in economic stagnation).

In 1890 a compromise went through: the Sherman Silver Purchase Act, which committed the federal government to buying a fixed dollar amount of silver each month. Nevada's congressional delegation pressed for more: a free silver amendment, by which the government would buy all the silver offered it. But the Panic of 1893 reinforced Eastern traditionalists' devotion to the gold standard, and the Sherman Silver Purchase Act was repealed. William Jennings Bryan's Cross of Gold speech and his nomination as the 1896 Democratic presidential candidate gave the pro-silverites renewed hope, until Bryan lost in the general election. Although the free (unlimited) coinage of silver continued to stir passions in Nevada for some time afterward, the idea gets little attention in this book because by the time the silver controversy was grabbing headlines, the Comstock Lode had gone from boom to bust and was edging into the realm of legend.

Mile-High Fever

ONE

The Perfect Monster

The Comstock rush began as an outlet for the California gold fields, where too many prospectors were trying to strike it rich at the same time. In 1850, restless 49ers heard that gold had been discovered east of the Sierra Nevada, forty miles from Lake Tahoe, in a part of Utah Territory called Washoe after a local Native American tribe. On reconnoitering, they found deposits in Gold Canyon, a gulch in Sun Mountain (soon to be renamed Mt. Davidson), about five miles from the Carson River.

The setting was hardly the kind that halts pioneers in their tracks, eliciting cries of "Let's build a town here." The mineralized area wasn't much to look at: dry and drained of most colors other than blue (sky), brown (dirt), and gray (rock). Nor was the weather accommodating: aridity combined with the thin, high-altitude air to deliver hot, piercingly sunny days followed by deeply cold nights, with strong winds sharpening the extremes. Before the region could be mined profitably, its remoteness would have to be overcome and its safety assured from Native Americans, not, as it turned out, the namesake Washoes but the more formidable Paiutes. But such challenges lay in the future. For now, the prospects looked good enough to warrant a gamble: some miners began dividing their time, laboring in the Sierra Nevada foothills during the winter to finance summer forays to Gold Canyon.

Among the sojourners were two brothers, Hosea and Ethan Allen Grosh, who deserved far better than what life had in store for them. The sons of a Universalist minister in Pennsylvania, the Groshes were

> . . . of medium height, slight in figure, good-looking, fairly well educated, very quick of observation, ready with expedients [i.e., resourceful], gifted (especially Allen) with exceptional powers of original thought, thoroughly honest and honourable, absolutely devoted to each other, industrious, persevering, chaste, sober, and, above all, "filled with that genuine religion of the heart which is the salt of the earth."

The exemplary young men had gone through a lot simply to reach the West, traveling to Mexico by ship and crossing that country on horseback only to get stranded eighty miles from the Pacific when the fellow handling their transportation ran out of funds. To secure passage to San Francisco, they sold their horses and gear. When they landed in California in August of 1849, Hosea, the younger brother, was suffering from dysentery, and Ethan had to nurse him back to health before they could set out for gold country. The brothers shook off these setbacks and joined other 49ers in California's El Dorado County.

On a visit to Gold Canyon in 1853, the Groshes spotted a vein of silver. Setting themselves the goal of "get[ting] a couple of hundred dollars together for the purpose of making a careful examination," they based their plans on a fundamental difference between the mining of gold and silver. In the classic scenario, a 49er with a mule, a grubstake, and a few tools would work placer deposits: loose gold that he isolated by using a pan to scoop up sand from a streambed, then giving the pan a flipping motion to separate out lighter detritus from heavier "color," or specks of gold. With luck, he would be able to follow these specks upstream to the mother lode from which they had eroded. Having "located" (put boundaries to) a claim that embraced the lode, he would stake it, record it with the local registrar of claims next time he went to town, start excavating, and give the resulting mine a name. He might also go so far as to build himself a rocker (a wooden trough with ridges on the bottom to capture gold nuggets carried along with the sand and water sluicing through), but even with that extra, the process was what we would now call low-tech.

Not so the mining of silver. The claiming process was the same, but how you got to that point was quite different. Silver tends to occur in compounds called sulphurets and is often trapped in silicon dioxide, or quartz, which must be broken down before the precious metal can be extracted. Comstock silver generally took the form of silver chloride, appearing as blue-gray rock or blue-black sand, and streams were not in the habit of pointing the way to it. When other prospectors at Gold Canyon uncovered this foreign matter mixed in with the gold they were chipping out of lodes, they dismissed it as that "damned blue stuff," but the Groshes knew better and kept returning to Gold Canyon. On November 3, 1856, they wrote home to announce the discovery of two veins of silver, one of which they rated "a perfect monster."

What the Groshes didn't realize was that they had stumbled upon only the monster's tip, which lay above and at the edge of a subterranean zone where the foot of Sun Mountain came into contact with strata of uplifted rock. There volcanic forces had forced molten material containing gold and silver up into fissures, where it had slowly cooled and solidified, leaving a broad belt of ore that stretched for two miles, roughly north–south, although interspersed with sections of worthless rock called "horses." (The horses were to cause much trouble in Comstock country, by delaying recognition of a basic truth: the ore formed a more or less continuous vein or ledge rather than a cluster of discrete deposits.) But the Groshes were pleased enough with what little they could see. The following summer, counting on funds promised by a cattle-trader in the Carson Valley, they were trying to master the complexities of silver mining when they learned that their would-be benefactor had been murdered.

They pressed on anyway until, on August 19, 1857, Hosea swung a pick carelessly, puncturing his foot just below the ankle. Ethan applied poultices, but gangrene set in, and two weeks later Hosea was dead. Ethan wrote pitiably to his father:

> In the first burst of my sorrow I complained bitterly. . . . I thought it most hard that he should be called away just as we had fair hopes of realizing what we had labored for so hard for so many years. But when I reflected . . . what a debt of gratitude I owed God in blessing me for so many years with so dear a companion, I became calm and bowed my head in resignation. "O Father, Thy will, not mine, be done."

Another letter, sent a few days later, shows that despite his strong faith, Ethan was inconsolable: "I feel very lonely, and miss Hosea very much—so much that at times I am strongly tempted to abandon everything and leave the country forever, cowardly as such a course would be. But I shall go on. . . . We have, so far, four veins. Three of them promise much."

In addition to his emotional loss, Ethan was in the hole for the expenses of Hosea's funeral. By the time he'd worked enough to pay off the debt, it was late in the year to be trekking back to California. Accompanied by a friend, a young Canadian prospector named Richard M. Bucke (the author of the above tribute to the brothers' "exceptional powers," etc.), Ethan set out on November 20. A snowstorm hit as the pair neared Lake Tahoe. Conditions became so dire that they killed and butchered their donkey for food and, when their wet matches fizzled out, lit a fire with the powder flash from their gun. A second storm followed, their gun wouldn't fire anymore, and they sought warmth at night by burrowing into the snow. By day, they staggered along the middle fork of the American River. Bucke wanted to "lie down and die," but Ethan rallied him.

By December 6, the two men were so weak that they spent a good part of the day on their hands and knees. As Eliot Lord related in his *Comstock Mining and Miners*, "From daybreak till noon they had crawled less than a mile and their eyes were closing from overmastering faintness, when they heard the bark of a dog and saw a thin wreath of smoke in the air." They were taken in by miners at a camp fittingly called Last Chance. It came too late for Ethan, though: twelve days later, he died. Bucke survived, but at the cost of having one foot and part of the other amputated. He also lost his taste for prospecting. After recovering, he returned to Canada, where he became a distinguished physician, later the superintendent of a madhouse, and the source for Lord's account of the 1857 ordeal.

Despite failing to realize their dream, the Groshes occupy a pivotal spot in Comstock lore. It's not quite right to credit them with discovering the Lode (when Hosea died, they were homing in on a tributary deposit that never amounted to much) but they were the first to recognize that this was primarily silver country, in which a new and more complex kind of mining would be required.

What happened next marks the difference between sentimental fiction and callous reality. In a novel written by Horatio Alger or Zane Grey, the energetic, loving brothers would have been the ones to put the great silver deposit—the Grosh Bonanza, as it might have been called—on the map. Instead, the founders were a couple of characters remembered as lowlifes. The first was Henry "Pancake" Comstock, a man so peculiar that he was reputed to be a half-wit (his nickname came from his habit of frying up pancakes because he was in too much of a hurry to bake bread). In fact, however, he seems to have been a scheming blowhard. In January of 1859, he happened upon two placer miners in another cleft in the side of Mt. Davidson, Six Mile Canyon, a mile or so north of Gold Hill, the settlement that had grown up above Gold Canyon. The miners were one party out of many working the area, but Comstock liked what he could see of their chosen terrain. In what was probably a bold-faced lie, he asserted that they were trespassing on property he'd already claimed as a "ranch." Unless you mean to raise reptiles, it's hard to imagine a site less suitable for ranching than that barren slope. But the pair couldn't prove him wrong, so they did what might be expected of men who live for luck and aren't looking for trouble: they shrugged and let him in on the action.

The nascent mine was called the Ophir, after a bountiful gold mine in the Bible, but in an early American example of how the bold shall inherit the earth, the loquacious Comstock made it inseparable from himself. "When visitors came, it was always *my* mine and *my* everything," a local newspaperman wrote of Comstock's egotism. By sheer persistence, the loquacious Comstock got his name attached to the whole mining district that sprang up around the claim.

The other alleged good-for-nothing to make a lasting impression was a prospector named James "Old Virginia" Finney, who named the new town that evolved out of the camp thrown together above Six Mile Canyon. Perched about halfway up the mountainside at 6,200 feet above sea level, the site at first went by the utilitarian handle "Ophir Diggings." According to a story told by Pancake himself, " 'Old Virginia' was out one night with a lot of the 'boys' on a drunk, when he fell down and broke his whisky bottle. On rising he said—'I baptize this ground Virginia.' " With the added "City," this is how the town sitting on top of some of the Comstock Lode's richest ore has been known ever since. (The name "Virginia" also stuck to the mountain range of which Mt. Davidson is the highest peak.)

Traces of these founding worthies can still be found among the records of the Storey County Courthouse. (Virginia City became and remains the county seat whereas the more conveniently located Carson City won out as state capital.) Notice Book C consists of loose pages gathered into a binder and protected by plastic sleeves, but the handwritten entries were originally made in a blank book shelved behind a bar. An 1859 notice refers to "the supposed Quartz Vein discovered by Mr. Pancake Comstock & Co.," although in another entry, a deed of sale, the flapjack-lover styles himself "H. Comstock." On October 21, 1859, Finney signed a notice of sale with an X, described as "his mark"; the man was obviously illiterate. A barroom was a handy place to file records—too handy, as it turned out. Miners liked to take the book down and fiddle with the boundaries of their claims to reflect what they'd learned by following ore deeper underground. That second-guessing contributed to the chaos that provoked an infamous series of Comstock lawsuits.

With Comstock himself yakking on the sidelines, the gold miners worked their and his claim for several weeks, discarding pieces of gray-blue rock as they went along. (The Groshes had confided their opinion that this was silver-bearing ore to a few friends, but it wasn't general knowledge.) Not until July did the truth come out. A visiting rancher walked off with a chunk of the dark rock, which he passed on as a curiosity to a judge in Placerville, California. The judge took the stone to a local assayer, who put a value of $876 per ton on its gold content, and $3,000 on its silver. Although His Honor meant to keep the find a secret, he couldn't contain himself. Word flew up and down the Sierra foothills: the "damned blue stuff" commingled with the gold being chipped out of Six Mile Canyon wasn't so accursed after all. It was late in the season to be striking out for high country, but a small mob of fortune-hunters reached Gold Hill in time to extract $275,000 worth of gold before winter set in.

Such a robust number whetted appetites back west, and the following spring the rush resumed in full spate, a lengthy queue of humanity wending its way from California gold country and beyond.

Writing for *Harper's Monthly Magazine*, an indefatigable traveler named J. Ross Browne gave an eyewitness report of the tumult in progress:

> An almost continuous string of Washoeites stretched "like a great snake dragging its slow length along" as far as the eye could reach. . . . Irishmen wheeling their blankets, provisions, and mining implements on wheel-barrows; American, French, and German foot passengers, leading their heavily-laden horses, or carrying their packs on their backs, and their picks and shovels slung across their shoulders; Mexicans, driving long trains of pack-mules, and swearing fearfully, as usual, to keep them in order; dapper-looking gentlemen, apparently from San Francisco, mounted on fancy horses; women, in men's clothes, mounted on mules or "burros"; Pike County specimens, seated on piles of furniture and goods in great lumbering wagons; whiskey-peddlers, with their bar-fixtures and whiskey on mule-back, stopping now and then to quench the thirst of the toiling multitude; organ-grinders, carrying their organs; drovers, riding, raving, and tearing away frantically through the brush after droves of self-willed cattle designed for the shambles; in short, every imaginable class, and every possible species of industry, was represented in this moving pageant . . . all stark mad for silver.

Browne himself had made the trip mostly on foot, walking more than one hundred miles on soupy roads and potholed trails from Placerville to Carson City, where he caught a stagecoach that took him the last few miles to the Comstock. Traveling conditions were so daunting that suppliers could charge outlandishly high prices for their wares. A fellow named Moore got hold of some pack mules and loaded them up with what he thought miners would want. He guessed right: reaching Virginia City on March 31, 1860, he "sold two hundred dollars worth of drinks before nightfall. Forty men paid him a dollar apiece per night for the use of blankets and space enough in his tent to sleep in. Moore refused eight thousand dollars for his goods, which had cost him less than one fifth as much." The men (and some women) kept pouring in, day after day, month after month; two years later, a San Francisco newspaper estimated that nine hundred fifty wagon teams regularly brought in freight to serve the townspeople's needs. A year after that, the number of teams had tripled.

Despite having got the jump on this human flood, neither of the region's namesakes managed to parlay his early luck into durable wealth. Finney sold his Gold Canyon interests and moved to nearby Dayton, where in July of 1861 he got drunk and tried to ride a bucking mustang. The animal threw him, and he fractured his skull. Within hours he was dead, leaving a mere $3,000 behind. Comstock sold his Ophir claim for just under $10,000, took a wife but couldn't keep her, ran a store that failed, and returned to prospecting. Unable to duplicate his Mt. Davidson success, he went slowly insane and committed suicide in Montana in 1870.

He and Finney weren't the only pioneers left behind. A survey conducted seventeen years later showed that of the original Comstock claimants, "half of them were dead, most of the remainder were living in reduced circumstances, and none were rich." Some prominent mines were obviously named after human beings—the Gould & Curry, for example, and the Hale & Norcross—but few could remember who they were. Yet Finney, Comstock, and the others weren't necessarily chumps for selling out. As Lord noted, they were placer miners who "knew nothing of underground mining or of the methods of reduction of silver ores, and were too poor or too impatient to undertake any systematic course of exploration. . . . Weighing the chances of gain and loss as they stood in 1859, the prospectors had no cause to reproach themselves for lack of foresight." Which is to say that silver mining is apt to be a complex and capital-intensive endeavor, and the Comstock was saving most of its bonanzas for an oligopoly of speculators and managers who could pool resources, share risks, trade inside information, and finance far-reaching technological innovations. It was a rush tailor-made for the big-time capitalism of The Gilded Age.

The influx of fortune-seekers and their suppliers gave Virginia City and environs a population of 3,000 in the 1860 census, but it was less a human settlement than a glorified prairie dog town wedged into the steep face of Mt. Davidson, where the streets were laid out parallel to the slope and named A,B,C, and so on. The immediate setting was desolate. Mark Twain, who was there from 1861 to 1864, said it looked "something like a singed cat, owing to the scarcity of shrubbery," and another journalist, Alf Doten, on hand starting in the summer of 1863, groused about the surrounding landscape: "[mining] is all this Territory is good for—not worth living in." As noted earlier, the very atmosphere was hostile. The town's mile-plus elevation left it prey to penetrating sunlight by day and deep chills at night. Strong westerlies, called Washoe Zephyrs, cuffed residents even on clear summer days; in winter, the gales could be savage.

A no-nonsense observer described the zephyr's effects as follows: "Such a wind rips boards, shingles, and sheets of tin from buildings, tumbles stovepipes and chimney pots down the gulches, and fills the air with flying gravel." To the irrepressible Twain, however, the zephyr was a gas. Here is his spoof of the blustery havoc it wreaked in Carson City (elevation a mere 4,730 feet): "hats, chickens, and parasols sailing in the remote heavens; blankets, tin signs, sagebrush, and shingles a shade lower; door-mats and buffalo robes lower still; shovels and coal scuttles on the next grade; glass doors, cats, and little children on the next," all the way down to "a scurrying storm of emigrating roofs and vacant lots." One can only imagine the kind of debris with which he might have stocked the air layers above loftier Virginia City.

As for the scruffy, embryonic town through which the zephyr

blew, the aghast Browne went on to describe it for *Harper's* readers, with special emphasis on the impromptu housing occupied by its pioneers:

> On a slope of mountain [i.e., Mt. Davidson] speckled with snow, sagebrushes, and mounds of upturned earth, without any apparent beginning or end, congruity or regard for the eternal fitness of things, lay outspread the wondrous city of Virginia. Frame shanties, pitched together as if by accident; tents of canvas, of blankets, of brush, of potato-sacks and old shirts with empty whiskey-barrels for chimneys; smoky hovels of mud and stone; coyote holes in the mountain side forcibly seized and held by men; pits and shafts with smoke issuing from every crevice; piles of goods and rubbish on craggy points, in the hollows, on the rocks, in the mud, in the snow, everywhere, scattered broadcast in pell-mell confusion, as if the clouds had suddenly burst overhead and rained down the dregs of all the flimsy, rickety, filthy little hovels and rubbish of merchandise that had ever undergone the process of evaporation from the earth since the days of Noah. The intervals of space, which may or may not have been streets, were dotted over with human beings of such sort, variety, and numbers, that the famous ant-hills of Africa were as nothing by comparison.

The sizable number of men (and a few women) huddling in those primordial shanties becomes all the more striking when you consider how hard it was to get to the Comstock. From San Francisco you had to travel by boat, train, and stagecoach, and the time consumed could be as much as a week. You could hike to Virginia City from California gold country, but only if you were hardy and patient. Best take the stagecoach if you could afford to, although it was obliged to follow sinuous trails through terrain noted for its ruggedness even in the mountainous West. San Francisco, the main source of supplies, was two hundred miles away, and in May of 1860 teamsters were charging $600 to haul a wagonload of goods, at an average weight of 3,500 pounds, to the Comstock from Placerville, which was only half as far. Consumer prices were correspondingly high: in a memoir of her Comstock years, an enterprising housewife and author challenged readers who might shake their heads at her claim to have sold eggs in Virginia City for a dollar a dozen, more than ten times the going price back East. "Nevertheless," she assured them, "it is true."

With a flood of newcomers and no decent place to put them, Virginia City came into being as a tough town. Revisionist historians argue that its reputation for wildness was exaggerated: there may have been a good deal of fighting and whoring early on, they admit, but Virginia City soon evolved into a settlement of hardworking, amiable souls. Maybe so, but the impression left by Doten's journals, which chronicle daily Comstock doings almost nonstop from 1863 to 1903, is one of frequent shootings, brawls, duels, and suicides, many of them occasioned by liquor working upon a community-wide hypersensitivity to the slightest insult. (If Virginia City is any guide, the Old West's signature personality trait was touchiness.)

Twain's blasé treatment of a bloody incident from 1863 seems telling. The young reporter was writing a letter home when a fracas outside caused him to jot a postscript: "I have just heard five pistol shots down the street—as such things are in my line, I will go and see about it." Several hours later, he inserted another p.s.: "The pistol did its work well—one man—a Jackson County, Missourian, shot two of my friends (police officers,) through the heart—both died within three minutes. Murderer's name is John Campbell." *Ho-hum*, you can almost hear Twain adding to himself, *just another night on the Comstock*. Old-timers assured him that violence had been even more pervasive as Virginia City was taking root. "The first twenty-six graves in the Virginia cemetery were occupied by *murdered* men," he wrote in *Roughing It*, his 1872 memoir of his years in the American West. "So everybody said, so everybody believed, and so they will always believe." That last sentence shows the fledgling town setting the tone for a regional habit still with us today: painting history in epic strokes. John Ford and his writers might have had that cemetery in mind when they inserted a memorable line into his film *The Man Who Shot Liberty Valance*: "This is the West, sir. When the legend becomes fact, print the legend."

Young Virginia City also fits the pattern of the Wild West town as we think we know it by virtue of its heavy drinking and gambling. Drawing on contemporary newspaper stories, Lord noted how in the winter of 1860 nearly everyone would leave his unheated hovel to congregate in saloons and gambling dens, which provided warmth, fellowship, and diversion:

> Little stacks of gold and silver fringed the monte tables and glittered beneath the swinging lamps. A ceaseless din of boisterous talk, oaths, and laughter spread from the open doors into the streets. The rattle of dice, coin, balls, and spinning-markers, the flapping of greasy cards and the chorus of calls and interjections went on day and night, while clouds of tobacco smoke filled the air and blackened the roof-timbers, modifying the stench rising from the stained and greasy floors, soiled clothes, and hot flesh of the unwashed company. Sometimes the sharp crack of a pistol would bring the players to their feet and the doorway would be choked with a wild rush of all except the two who were settling a trifling dispute by an effective Washoe duel across a table.

Both inside and outside the dens, Lord added, another form of gambling "raged without check": speculation in shares of the very things that had lured those stinkers to this God-forsaken mountainside: the mines.

One episode from early Comstock days, however—the Pyramid Lake War—undermines a cherished tenet of Wild West mythology: white superiority. You might call it a splendid little war—splendid, that is, for the Northern Paiute Native Americans and their allies. Their warriors fought with distinction, if not always with airtight discipline. Their war chief practiced astute generalship, taking advantage of local geography in ways that anticipated Lee and Jackson in the imminent Civil War, and the first battle in particular is still studied for its strategic value. Ultimately, of course, the white settlers prevailed. But the Pyramid Lake War not only stymied them for a time (reading about the war's first phase in the newspapers, residents of other states must have wondered if the national Destiny was quite as Manifest as they'd been led to believe); it also left the Paiutes with a grip on their homeland which they have retained to this day. Taken as a whole, the episode serves as a cautionary tale of impetuosity and hubris.

The Comstock rush had heightened already existing tensions between whites and Native Americans in Utah Territory. The newcomers looked upon the area's natural resources as theirs for the squandering. They diverted and consumed scarce water, caught fish and game as they pleased, turned their livestock loose on grassland, and felled whole forests, all with little regard for the Native Americans' prior use and occupancy. The tree-cutting—for fuel and housing and mine timbers—hit the Paiutes especially hard, for pinyon pine nuts were a staple of their winter diet.

The noted pathfinder Peter Lassen, after whom a number of California features are named (Lassen Peak, Lassen County, Lassen Volcanic National Park), was killed in the spring of 1859 en route to Comstock country, perhaps by a renegade band of Paiutes; what mattered was that the settlers blamed the Native Americans, stoking an animosity that already smoldered on both sides. Later that year, residents of the Great Basin experienced an unusually harsh winter, and by early 1860 both whites and Native Americans were short-tempered. In March and April, Bannocks and Shoshones, tribes related to and allied with the Paiutes, joined them at Pyramid Lake, about fifty miles north of Virginia City, for discussions on what to do about the Anglo influx. Numaga, the Northern Paiute war chief, questioned the wisdom of waging war against a people whose swelling numbers had no apparent end. "They will come like the sand in a whirlwind," he warned, "and drive you from your homes. You will be forced among the barren rocks of the north, where your ponies will die; where you will see the women and old men starve, and listen to the cries of your children for food."

Numaga's caution might have carried the day if not for the tendency of some white men to treat Native American women as one more exploitable resource: an instance of such criminality seems to have set off the conflict. (In another version, the precipitating factor was the grazing of white-owned cattle on Native American land; to make a point, Native Americans butchered and ate a few head, whites shot the "rustlers," and the Native Americans struck back in kind.) Whatever the cause, news of the effect hit Virginia City in an electrifying way, carried by a Pony Express messenger on May 7, 1860: five white men, two of them brothers, had been killed by Bannocks at Williams Station, a stagecoach stop twenty miles away. "Horrid massacre . . . ," the *Sacramento Union* screamed, "shocking butchery." Left unmentioned by a third, surviving, brother was the likelihood that the killings were in retaliation for the kidnapping and rape of two Native American girls about twelve years of age: in this account, the one believed by present-day Paiutes, the Native Americans had attacked the station to rescue the girls.

Rumors fed the settlers' rage: the Paiutes and their allies, five hundred strong, were on the warpath. Not quite, but the Native Americans *were* considering their options, with even Numaga coming around. "There is no longer any use for counsel," he was reported to have said; "we must prepare for war, for the soldiers will now come here to fight us."

Men from the Comstock and nearby mining camps formed a

one-hundred-five-man posse under the leadership of U.S. Army Major William Ormsby, who was also an innkeeper in Carson City. Their mission, endorsed by nearly every miner and settler, was made explicit by the *Union*: "teaching the red devils a lesson." The ranks included a promising young lawyer named Henry Meredith, a member of a Virginia City firm whose guiding light, William Morris Stewart, was one of the most prominent men in the territory. Stewart had tried unsuccessfully to dissuade his junior partner from volunteering. As Stewart pointed out, these "soldiers" were a passel of amateurs, untrained and poorly equipped. They also tended to find their courage in the bottle, leading a reporter for San Francisco's *Daily Alta California* to observe: "There has been a vast deal of talk, noise, and confusion, collection of rifles, muskets, revolvers, and knives, and an immense punishment of whiskey. Could the Indians be as effectually consumed, peace would soon be restored."

On May 9, the makeshift army marched toward Williams Station in a mixed mood of arrogance, wrath, and adventurism. Firm believers in white superiority, they vastly underestimated the enemy and regarded the endeavor as, in the words of a local reporter, Dan De Quille, "a sort of pleasure excursion"; their war cry was "An Indian for breakfast and a pony to ride." Finding no Native Americans at the station, they made for Pyramid Lake, a favorite gathering place for the Northern Paiutes and neighboring tribes, on a trail marked by hoofprints and litter. (Savvier vigilantes might have noted how exceptionally easy to follow this trail was, and drawn appropriate conclusions.) Meanwhile, cold weather had settled in, topped off by an unseasonable snowfall.

Led by that reluctant warrior, Numaga, the mass of seasoned Native American warriors awaited Ormsby's army on the Truckee River southeast of Pyramid Lake, a great blot of cerulean blue out of which rises the shapely island that gives its name to the whole. Numaga knew the area well and deployed his forces brilliantly. Keeping his men out of sight, he lured the whites toward a kind of basin, bordered by a bluff to the west, high ground to the east, a ridge to the south, and more high ground to the north. The mounted Native Americans were so keen on delivering a surprise that they pinched their horses' nostrils shut to keep them from neighing. At a key moment, Numaga had some of his warriors show themselves on a ridge, not attacking but simply posing there on horseback, drawing the whites onward. One Native American carried what some observers identified as a white flag, although others insisted it was a battle-axe. The battle-axe theory won out, and a white officer ordered his men to fire. At a sign from Numaga, the Native Americans on the ridge dismounted and fired back.

Ormsby played into Numaga's hands by ordering an uphill charge. The soil was damp, the footing was rough on the horses, and suddenly the untried soldiers were taking fire from the sides, too, by Native Americans deployed in sagebrush. It dawned on the whites that they'd better get the hell out of this bowl, but when they tried to do so, Numaga sprang the last element of his trap: another detachment of Native Americans moved in to block the rear. As an early Nevada historian put it, Ormsby and company "had charged through an open gate into an Indian corral."

The volunteers fell back in haste and disorder toward a grove of cottonwood trees. Three hundred feet short of that, they reached a ravine, where they tried to make a stand. But the ridgeline warriors had come down to chase them, other Native Americans had invaded those same cottonwoods, and both these groups were firing muskets and rifles, whereas most of Ormsby's men had only short-range pistols and shotguns. Ormsby was wounded, and Meredith became separated from his mount. While his fellow soldiers looked on, Meredith ran out to retrieve the animal and was shot from behind. Before a rescue could be attempted, Ormsby took an arrow in the mouth. He yanked it out and turned the command over to someone else, urging that the men be directed "to cut their way through and get away." But the army had disintegrated to the point where orders were futile; it was every man for himself.

With victory certain, Numaga was no more eager to extend the carnage than he'd been to attack in the first place. But now *his* men, too, were deaf to orders. They kept firing on the whites, some of whom had finally taken over the cottonwood grove to put up a defense. Although he'd been wounded at least four times, Ormsby led a retreat toward a narrow pass where he'd posted a rearguard in the event that just such an exit became necessary. Astride a mule, with Native Americans riding hard behind him, Ormsby reached the pass only to find it empty. His intended saviors had deserted, and there was nothing left for him but to make a last stand.

When the Native Americans caught up, Ormsby was on foot, a helpless target. Some Paiutes knew and liked him, and according to an almost too-noble-to-be-true account written by an educated Paiute named Sarah Winnemucca, her brother Natchez raised his bow and arrow and cried out in English that Ormsby had only one chance: "Drop down as if dead when I shoot, and I will fire over you." But Ormsby either didn't hear or didn't understand this. Before Natchez could loose an arrow, another Native American shot Ormsby with a bullet, then with an arrow, and shoved his lifeless body into a ravine. Meredith, too, was among the estimated seventy white fatalities. There might have been no survivors at all if it hadn't been for the coming of night, which gave cover to the fleeing soldiers.

News of the battle horrified the mining towns' inhabitants. A physician on his way to Virginia City reported meeting "trains of people and stock on their way to California flying from the Indians." The residents of nearby Silver City built a stone fort at Devil's Gate, a pass between the Carson Valley and the Comstock, in which they mounted a cannon made of a hollowed-out pine log and loaded with "pieces of scrap iron, bits of chain, and the like." (De Quille described what happened after the war ended and someone thought to test-fire the homemade cannon: "When the explosion finally came, the air was filled in all directions, for many rods, with pieces of scrap iron, iron bands, and chunks of wood. Had [the cannon] ever been fired in the fort, it would have killed every man near it.")

While waiting for the invasion that never came, the region's white people consoled themselves by praising the valor of their fallen soldiers. A young merchant named Adolph Sutro, in the vicinity to scout out business opportunities, interviewed survivors and echoed popular sentiment in an article he wrote for the *San Francisco Bulletin*: "Amongst the killed are Major Ormsby of Carson City, who fought nobly to the last; Henry Meredith of Nevada, esteemed and honored by all who knew him—he was too proud to retreat, and he was cut to pieces. . . . Many more could be named who have acted nobly in the engagement."

Californians reacted to news of the battle with indignation. Rabble-rousers threw in anti-Mormon prejudice for good measure: the Saints were known to have perpetrated a massacre at Mountain Meadows in 1857, and now they were accused of inciting Native Americans to wage war on Gentiles. The California governor sent arms, the federal government dispatched regular troops, local militia units joined in, and the Carson Valley Expedition was born. The Battle of Pyramid Lake had taught a lesson all right, although to white men, not red: the settlers were not about to underestimate their opponents again. The new army topped out at eight hundred men, who trained and drilled and attained a semblance of cohesive professionalism before heading out for Pyramid Lake.

This time the Anglos even had a strategy. It was, in fact, almost the mirror image of Numaga's: entice the Native Americans into the open and make them fight where the topography didn't favor them. Numaga stuck to his proven approach, and skirmishing at Big Meadows ended in stalemate. The following day, June 2, Numaga surprised a contingent of Anglo cavalry on the old battleground. But their training stood these soldiers in good stead; refusing to panic, they held out until the rest of the army could ride up and support them. The battle might turn on whether the whites could take Pinnacle Mount, a formation from which Native American sharpshooters had them pinned down. Night fell with the position untaken, but the whites were satisfied with their performance so far, especially because, as a reporter traveling with the army noted, "The Indians were admirably posted, while our own men were without cover." Come morning, there was no sign of the Native Americans, who had fallen back to Pyramid Lake.

Feeling confident, the Carson Expeditionary Army pushed on toward the lake, referred to by an accompanying reporter as "the Jerusalem of our crusade [which was] hailed with delight, for here we hoped to witness the last act of the tragedy." That last act was an anticlimax. The Paiutes had already sent their women and children off to the desert, and now the warriors slipped away, too, leaving the whites to claim the advantage: they hadn't exactly won the Battle of Pinnacle Mount, but they had induced the Native Americans to retreat. The Carson force stayed put through the rest of June and into the beginning of July before falling back to build a fort nearby.

Sporadic fighting continued between regular army soldiers and the Paiutes, and in August Numaga agreed to discuss peace, although not before putting his counterpart, Colonel Frederick Lander, in his place. "I will look hard at you first," Numaga stated. "When the sun is low, we will talk." When finally delivered, Numaga's remarks featured a recital of promises made to reservation Native Americans over in California, and then broken. "Is it not better to fight while the whites are few in our country?" he asked. "I am sorry for the women and children who starve in the mountains, but if they all die, why not die before they are shut up by the whites and their arms taken from them?" These may have been rhetorical questions; Lander, in any case, had no answers. Numaga finished up with a conditional promise: he would see that peace was kept for a year, maybe two, but in return the whites must help the Paiutes learn to farm and to survive on a reservation. The Paiutes were allowed to return to Pyramid Lake and environs, and soon a number of them moved to the mining camps, looking for work and handouts.

How faithfully the whites upheld the peacemaking bargain varied with the Native American agent assigned to the Paiutes; they had a good one for a while, but then he was transferred, and his replacement proved to be corrupt. Overall, the Paiutes must have had a tough time of it after the war. In an article written many years later, journalist Alf Doten recalled an October 1863 visit by Numaga and a dozen or so "braves" to the town of Como, Nevada, about twenty miles southeast of Virginia City. Numaga, Doten wrote, was "rather a fine looking Indian, of about thirty-five years, full average height, straight and dignified, face painted brick red, a few eagle feathers stuck in his hair, and he wore shoes, pants and a gray blanket, but no hat." He and his men had come to lodge a familiar protest: please don't chop down the pine nut trees. The whites "were welcome to use all the dead timber which strewed the hillsides, for firewood, but they must not cut the live trees. Those trees were the 'Indians orchard.'" Bringing the story up to date (1883), Doten noted: "The Indians' orchards about Como are not there now. Nobody quit cutting the timber as long as there was any left to haul to market." (A few years later, not even Como was there; it had joined the ranks of Nevada's ghost towns.)

In 1874, President Ulysses Grant had set aside Pyramid Lake and environs as a reservation for the Paiutes, but in the meantime most of them had relocated to the more fertile Pacific Northwest. After a series of wanderings and confinements on reservations in Oregon and Washington, the Paiutes returned to their old Nevada homeland in 1883. There they hung on, partly thanks to the adaptability of their women, who took advantage of Comstock prosperity by hiring themselves out as servants to middle-class Virginia City families and by persuading greengrocers to give them day-old fruits and vegetables. The Paiutes appear to have drawn strength from renewing ties with their ancestral land. As archaeologist Eugene M. Hattori has pointed out, they "became willing participants in the Euro-American economy, yet they maintained their social distance and preserved elements of their pre-contact culture."

Ben Aleck, collections manager for the Pyramid Lake Paiute Museum, made a similar point when I visited the reservation in the summer of 2007. "We're one of the few tribes that are still where we traditionally were," he said. "We were a big enough tribe to hold off aggression, not only Ormsby's army, but other settlers, too. We tell our young people that if it wasn't for our elders standing up for us and fighting, we probably wouldn't be here." Outside the museum, Pyramid Lake still shimmers deep-blue and pristine, but it doesn't take much imagination to visualize its fate if the Paiutes had been routed. In the hands of white developers, its shores would have been converted into a playground (à la Lake Tahoe) or an urban site (à la Salt Lake City); dozens of Western cities have risen on less favorable spots.

After leaving Pyramid Lake, I got to thinking about the most famous Paiute of all, Wovoka. He was the visionary and prophet who, three decades after the Pyramid Lake War, led the messianic Ghost Dance movement, which gave hope to dejected Native Americans throughout the West. Wovoka came from another branch of the Northern Paiutes, those who now occupy the Walker River Reservation. But his people, too, had managed to keep the core of their land, and he undoubtedly grew up hearing accounts of the war. An indication of its importance to him can be gauged from his reply to a leadoff question from anthropologist James Mooney, who interviewed Wovoka in 1892. "He said that he was about 35 years of age," Mooney wrote, "fixing the date from a noted battle between the Paiutes and the whites near Pyramid lake, in 1860, at which time he said he was but the size of his little boy, who appeared to be of about 4 years."

So Wovoka might well have had the old war chief and his victories in mind when he declared that Native Americans could immunize themselves to the whites' bullets by dancing the Ghost Dance, and could obliterate the whites themselves by being virtuous and putting their trust in the Great Spirit. Hadn't Numaga and his braves twice met whites in battle without being defeated? Wasn't it reasonable to consider the unsinkable Paiutes a kind of New World Chosen People, capable of turning out a prophet such as Wovoka himself?

His creed appealed particularly to the Sioux, who in early 1890 sent a delegation to Nevada to learn more about it. But ignorant U.S. officials classified the new religion as a pagan nuisance and wrongly imputed aggressive tendencies to its pacifist adherents. (Wovoka preached dancing and piety only; in his creed, Native Americans need not lift a hand against the whites; the Great Spirit would take care of everything.) The visiting Sioux took the Ghost Dance back with them to the Dakotas, where it flourished until the whites set out to quash the movement, with force if necessary. That misguided campaign led to the horrific slaughter at Wounded Knee Creek on December 29, 1890, and with it the end of Native American resistance to the "civilizing" of the West.

In addition to fleeing, dithering, and building an unsafe cannon, the Comstock's white settlers reacted to Ormsby's Last Stand by placing a moratorium on the filing of mining claims. Had the Battle of Pinnacle Mount gone the other way, there might have been a mass exodus from Virginia City and Gold Hill, with the Comstock left to be developed some other time. But on the strength of an outcome just good enough to be entered in the victory column, mining resumed (if a bit nervously at first), and the U.S. Army built forts throughout western Utah Territory to ensure that such a thing would never happen again. In the end, Numaga's "sand in a whirlwind" remark proved accurate: after the Pyramid Lake War, Native Americans no longer posed an obstacle to the mining and settling of the Comstock.

But such an outcome wasn't at all clear in 1860. Indeed, the war caused a number of participants in the previous spring's rush to wonder what the hell they were doing there. They'd shown up in a 49er frame of mind, ready to sift precious metal out of the gravel in virgin streams. But silver-bearing Comstock quartz was like nothing they'd handled in California, the capital required to mine and process it was beyond most men's ability to raise, and for the time being there were still Native Americans to worry about. An under-capitalized fellow could always go to work in somebody else's mine, but that wasn't the dream they'd been nurturing. Some of them reckoned they might as well head back to California, even though their old standby, one-man-one-pan mining, was hardly being practiced there anymore. (With streambeds cleaned out of easily accessible gold, Californians had turned to hydraulic mining, a capital-intensive method that entailed damming rivers, building flumes, and using hoses to wash hillsides away.) In any case, as De Quille noted dryly, "The Indian troubles greatly assisted many of these men in a speedy arrival at the conclusion that Washoe was no good country in which to abide."

~ TWO ~

Heavy Metal

With the Native Americans subdued (or at least pushed to the sidelines) and faint-hearted miners retreating to California, it was time for Virginia City to throw off its squatters'-colony rags and put on the garb of a real town. The tents and coyote holes gave way to wooden structures: a reporter for the *San Francisco Bulletin* counted one hundred buildings, exclusive of residential cabins, going up on October 13, 1860. Among these were twenty-five saloons, ten laundries, and one each of bathhouse, music hall, and theater. The town's remoteness and the weather's vagaries made everyday items hard to come by, and therefore expensive: $9 for a dozen tin plates in the spring of that year and $1 for a pound of butter. To help workers cope with such prices, wages were correspondingly high, $8 a day for masons and $4 a day for miners.

It didn't take long for those miners to exhaust the easily accessible gold and silver. Working with pick and shovel, they were engaged in a precursor to open-pit mining, but the native rock was friable, and after a while the pit would collapse. The future obviously lay in following the ore underground by sinking shafts and cutting lateral drifts. As deeper passages were carved out, the traditional method of removing ore and waste rock (in buckets dangling from ropes that wrapped around windlasses) became increasingly clumsy. The better mines introduced an elevator system, in which a steam-driven hoisting engine raised and lowered iron-frame cages, usually open on at least two sides, to transport cars full of ore and the men who excavated it. (Before the introduction of elevators, miners had entered and exited the Ophir via a four-hundred-foot-long series of hacked-out steps.)

At lower depths, good ventilation was a necessity, but the first attempts to provide it were crude and makeshift, as explained by Dan De Quille:

> . . . wind-sails were used to carry air down into the shafts. This is a contrivance of cotton cloth, and is a cross between a sail and a bag. The mouth of the baggy sail is turned to the wind, and when it fills, air is forced down a tube that leads from its lower end. Sometimes air was forced into a shaft by means of a common blacksmith's bellows—slow and hard work. When water and a proper amount of fall can be obtained, a water-blast is sometimes used. In this the water falling through a tube carries down with it and forces into the shaft or mine a certain amount of air.

Those methods sound like warm-ups for the cartoonist Rube Goldberg, and the sails and cascades were soon replaced by Cornish pumps and fans. But these could push air only so far; they were followed, in turn, by jumbo forty-five-horsepower models. Another way to improve air circulation was to connect your shafts with your neighbors', and mining companies routinely entered into agreements to do so. Pumps and pipes were also used to pull something out of the mines: water. Perversely, the Comstock had little water on the surface but plenty of it down below, nearly all of it scalding hot and undrinkable. Over the years, as the miners went deeper, the pumps got bigger and bigger: the flywheel of a giant pump installed in 1879 reached a diameter of forty feet and a weight of one hundred ten tons.

The above measures relied on adapting available technology. Other problems, however, could not be solved without innovations. Fortunately, these arrived in timely fashion during the rush's first few years and then spread quickly to other Western mines. If the Sierra Nevada gold country had been the schoolhouse of precious-metal mining, the Comstock was considered the graduate school. More than that, it was a way station in the industrialization of the West, an early invasion by the kind of highly complex, technologically sophisticated processes, run by skilled labor, that characterized manufacturing in the country's eastern half but were previously unknown west of St. Louis. By the late 1860s, knowledgeable observers would rate deep mining on the Comstock as the most heavily industrialized operation in human history so far.

Comstock miners were lucky in that as a rule its silver ore was not associated with base metals (such as lead, zinc, and copper) and thus did not have to be subjected to the costly technique of smelting. Amalgamation (the process of alloying a precious metal with mercury) would do the job of separating Comstock silver from its ore, after which the amalgam was distilled in order to release the precious metal. Before being treated chemically, ore had to be pulverized, but existing methods were crude and laborious. A traditional combination process, introduced by Mexican miners, was to tether mules to a post and drive them around and around a patio covered with an ore and mercury mixture, which they turned over with their hooves to induce a chemical reaction with the aid of the sun's heat.

Many miners shared a hunch: that a streamlined process involving mercury supplemented by other chemicals could successfully reduce Comstock ore to pure silver. But it was unclear which chemicals these should be. In the tradition of patent medicine men, entrepreneurs set up makeshift laboratories and toyed with various recipes; one try involved making tea out of sagebrush and pouring this into amalgamation pans. De Quille cracked that "the object with many inventors of 'processes' appeared to be to physic the silver out of the rock, or at least make it so sick that it would be obliged to loose its hold upon its matrix and come out."

While waiting for better combinations to be found, Almarin B. Paul, a mill owner who'd come over from California, built a new, steam-powered mill to reduce ore in a highly mechanized fashion and on a large scale. His method, which evolved into the widely used Washoe pan process, fed ore to an array of twenty-four hammers, or "stamps," which crushed the ore to a powder. In that form it was placed in pans, where it was treated with water, mercury (also known as quicksilver), and other chemicals, then subjected to revolving blades called mullers, which churned the mixture. The silver and gold bound with the mercury, and the resulting amalgam settled to the bottom of the pan, where it could be retrieved. Paul's chemical blend worked better on gold than silver, but fortunately in the early going there was enough gold coming out of the ground to keep his mill running until better formulas could be developed.

Other capitalists built similar mills, and their presence brought down transportation costs: instead of raw ore, with its excess tonnage of worthless rock, wagons were now toting valuable bullion west to San Francisco, where most of it ended up at the U.S. mint. The advent of onsite milling speeded up the Comstock's transformation into an industrial zone, with shedlike buildings sprawling over the hillsides and smokestacks reaching into the sky and the drumbeat of ore being pulverized morning, noon, and night. In the early days, residents of Virginia City had hearkened to the charming clink of picks in the mines beneath their feet; now their ears were assailed by the din of pounding stamps.

The greatest technological coup, however, was not so much an invention as a pattern of deceptive originality. About one hundred seventy-five feet down, workers in the Ophir mine had run across large formations of ore so soft that it crumbled, dislodging pillars that had been driven into the shaft's floor to hold up the roof. "The dilemma was a curious one," wrote Lord in his governmental report. "Surrounded by riches, [the miners] were yet unable to carry them off."

An Ophir trustee got hold of Philip Deidesheimer, a German-born engineer who had graduated from the prestigious Freiburg School of Mines and was now working over in El Dorado County. When told that he would be consulting on quartz formations up to sixty feet wide, Deidesheimer said he'd never heard of such a thing. But he crossed the Sierra, studied the problem, and decided that traditional drift-set timbering (which resembled a doorframe, with a pole embedded on either side of a shaft and a board joining them at the top) was wrong for Comstock geology. Instead he came up with square-set timbering: think of four doorframes assembled into a skeletal box or room, six or seven feet tall and four to six feet wide, each set (called, not quite accurately, a "cube") identical to the next, so that they could be piled atop one another or installed sideways and bolted together. This solution not only counteracted soft ore by distributing the load; it also resisted the tremendous overhead pressure encountered in deep mining. For even greater stability, selected cubes could be filled with waste rock. With the stacking of enough cubes, a cavity of almost any size could be filled and worked, and cave-ins became rare. Deidesheimer opted not to seek a patent, and his timbering style became ubiquitous on the Comstock and, eventually, in mines around the world. (The unlucky engineer could have used the revenue from that missed patent; later in life, he made some bad mining investments and went bankrupt.)

I used the term "deceptive originality" for Deidesheimer's idea because modular cubes are so familiar nowadays that we tend to think they've always been around. But before Deidesheimer there was no such building form. Some Comstock journalists likened

piling up square-set cubes to erecting a Gothic cathedral underground, but De Quille drew a secular analogy: "Imagine [the mine]
hoisted out of the ground and left standing upon the surface. [The
viewer] would then see before him an immense structure, four or
five times as large as the greatest hotel in America." In other words,
the viewer would see the framework of the modern skyscraper; De
Quille was marveling at nothing less than the bone structure of
urban America. Over the next two decades, insights drawn from
innovations such as square-set timbering allowed architects to dis-
card the old way of putting up imposing buildings, which relied on
massive bases of stone or masonry and stout walls to bear loads, in
favor of slender steel beams placed at regular intervals.

Another Comstock contribution to the high-rise was originally
designed to improve safety in mines. Old-style cables for mine elevators tended to fray and break if made of rope or to kink and snap
while wrapping around the hoisting spool if made of steel wire. Alfred Doten published a harrowing account of descending into the
Imperial mine, with the cage being jerked up and down by the operator as he tried from above to maneuver it past obstructions. At
times the rope "was strained like a fiddle string," and it jerked the
cage's passengers around "like peas in a hot skillet."

In 1863, an engineer and manufacturer named Andrew Smith
Hallidie came out to the Comstock from his San Francisco factory,
sized up the problem, and invented flat, braided steel cables, which
when installed greatly reduced the accident rate. Halladie's brainchild proved to be highly adaptable. On its way to urban skylines,
the new, improved cable made an intermediate stop beneath the
hills of San Francisco, where it became the eponymous cord pulling the city's cable cars. Once the cables were adapted to office
buildings, two sine qua nons of the skyscraper were in place: the
skeleton, composed of metallic versions of Deidesheimer's cubes,
and the blood vessels, elevators that relied on Hallidie's cables to
make the building's higher floors accessible. It's not much of an

exaggeration to say that Comstock ingenuity gave us the modern American metropolis.

Inevitably, square-set timbering jacked up the already high demand for wood. In all, Lord claimed, "Fully 600,000,000 feet of timbers [were] buried in the mines, an amount sufficient to build a town of nearly thirty thousand two-story frame houses . . . which would comfortably shelter 150,000 inhabitants." What little the Virginia Range could offer in the way of trees went first, leaving the Sierra Nevada forests as the nearest appreciable source. Loggers stripped the lower Sierra slopes, then, as they went higher, cleared paths down which they could skid logs to wagons waiting at the bottom or built raised flumes to keep logs from getting tangled in brush and stumps on the ground. But logs tended to clog up the flumes' U-shaped courses until a lumberman named J. W. Haines came up with an improvement: the V-flume. He nailed two boards into a right-angled V, followed by two more and so on, all of them overlapping in such a way that they were tight enough to hold water and float wood. The beauty of the V shape was that if a log got stuck, water would back up behind it and lift it loose. This was another Comstock innovation that became an industry standard.

Harnessing these far-flung natural resources, summoning up new inventions, and installing them in the mines—all this called for heavy capital expenditures. But the most visible sign of the grand scale that came to typify the Comstock was the series of mills built there in the early 1860s. Onsite milling was the logical next step: sending ore elsewhere and having it reduced by outsiders was expensive, and speculators could point to the large profits being racked up by existing mills elsewhere in the West. And so in the Comstock's charged atmosphere, mills became the subject of their own rush. Soon local roads and trails were crowded with wagons bearing heavy machinery forged in California foundries, and by the end of 1861 the region was awash in mills, seventy-six in all, housing over a thousand stamps, with more under construction. (Examples of the old hardware used in mills can be seen outside the Chollar Mine and at the Way It Was Museum, both in Virginia City.)

But as milling technology improved, the process, like mining itself, grew costlier. Having bought, imported, and installed the pulverizing stamps at great expense, you needed hands to run the ore through the works, and they were getting from $4 to $6 a day. Nor, at first, was there enough ore to justify all the mill-building. By the spring of 1862, only twenty-three of those seventy-six mills were still operating.

Yet even as many of them were failing, mine owners were beginning to see what later became an article of Comstock faith: thanks to certain principles of accounting and the cabals organized to take advantage of them, the biggest profits were to be made not in mining ore but in processing it. (We'll see this phenomenon exemplified in the behavior of the Bank Ring and the Bonanza Kings, in Chapters 5 and 6.) And so in that giddy year 1861, trustees of the Gould & Curry had started building the mill to end all mills, about two miles east of Virginia City. It took "the form of the Greek cross, 250 feet long, with arms 75 feet in length and 50 feet in width. The lower story and foundations were constructed of massive stone blocks supporting a heavy frame superstructure of finished wood, adorned with broad verandas, and painted inside and out." That this edifice perched on a steep hillside only added to its aura of power. The whole thing had to be overhauled in 1864 to accommodate Almarin Paul's now-standard Washoe pan process, and the combined cost of the original construction and the rehab totaled $1.5 million. Only a bonanza could have justified such a heavy investment, and the Gould & Curry miners didn't find one. The great G&C mill closed in 1866, "to stand for years [as] a decaying monument to Comstock prodigality." It didn't take long, though, for the prodigal monument to be overshadowed by two larger mills serving the Consolidated Virginia and California mines.

Open or closed, the giant mills stood almost as rebukes to owners of modest means. *Look on my works, ye paltry, and despair*, they seemed to taunt. At the same time, the mining itself was getting more difficult with each drop in the level at which it occurred. Deep mining threw up challenges—foul air, high temperatures, hot water, flooding, and logistics—that virtually froze out mom-and-pop operations. As evidence, consider the contrasting fates of three Comstock pioneers: George Hearst and Sandy and Eilly Bowers.

Hearst was one 49er who showed up with mining credentials. Back home in Missouri's Meramec Valley, he'd overcome a fragmentary education (it added up to only two-and-a-half years in the classroom, snatched between long stretches of working for his father's livestock business) by calling upon a knack for locating ore. The young man whom local Native Americans called "Boy-That-Earth-Talked-To" made a go of both lead and copper mining. To finance his westward journey, he sold mines and surface land in the amount of $1,900.

But the instincts that had worked so well in Missouri seemed to desert Hearst in California. He was around thirty when he went west in 1850 (he wasn't sure whether he'd been born in 1820 or 1821). After arriving, he worked the California gold fields for a decade, but not until he crossed over to Utah Territory in March of 1860 did the earth find its voice again. He was on hand for what he called the "beginning of the Washoe excitement," and over the next few years you could see him just about everywhere you turned: buying interests in mines, notably part-ownership of the Ophir, for which he paid $2,500; hauling ore to San Francisco; investing in a mill; and hiring a gunslinger to run off a trespasser on the Hearst claims. To go with his gift for reading the land, he mastered the business side of mining: procuring supplies, building and operating mills, transporting bullion, reorganizing as a stock company, attracting other investors, and keeping his workers happy.

Hearst cut a fine figure in young Virginia City: a tall, handsome, very eligible bachelor. When word came that his mother was ailing, he returned to Missouri, where he married a local girl, Phoebe Elizabeth Apperson, on June 14, 1862. As they journeyed west together by boat, train, and buggy, Phoebe was already pregnant with their only child, the future newspaper tycoon William Randolph Hearst.

The Hearsts took up residence in San Francisco; at least Phoebe did. George spent much of his time in and around Virginia City, where he managed his claims and hired himself out as a mineral guru, widely consulted for his shrewd assessments of mining prospects. A fellow entrepreneur, the melodiously named Asbury Harpending, summed up that reputation:

> George Hearst was probably the greatest natural miner who ever had a chance to bring his talents into play on a large scale. He was not a geologist, had no special education to start with, was not overburdened with book learning, but he had a congenital instinct for mining, just as some other people have for mathematics, music or chess. He was not a man of showy parts, liked the company of a lot of cronies, to whom he was kind and serviceable—when he wasn't broke himself—was much inclined to take the world easy, but if anyone mentioned mines in his presence, it had the same effect of saying "Rats!" to a terrier. Hearst became alert and on dress parade in a moment.

Or, as his wife succinctly put it, "You know how fond he is of rocks."

Hearst was in little danger of being broke after 1865, when he was considered one of the Comstock's first millionaires. The year before, he'd been elected to the California state assembly, where he served a single term. He suffered a financial reverse in 1866, when a postwar slump afflicted the economy nationwide and his Ophir mine went into borrasca (low productivity or bad luck, the opposite of bonanza), but he'd already branched out by investing in real estate, which helped rescue him. In 1867, he pulled out of the Comstock to start amassing vast land holdings along the central California coast (home of the future San Simeon ranch and Hearst Castle), as well as sizable tracts in Texas and Mexico.

Hearst might have forsaken the Comstock, but he was hardly through with mining. It seemed that wherever he went now, the earth wouldn't shut up. His geological knowhow rewarded him first in Utah, where he "watched for three weeks while a prospector dug away at a hole three feet deep and six feet long in the Salt Lake desert." After going in with a partner to buy the hole for $33,000, Hearst had the pleasure of watching it blossom into a fabulously productive silver mine, from which the pair made $14 million. In 1877 he and the same partner went shopping in the Black Hills, where they bought a one-third interest in the Homestake, soon to be the world's richest gold mine. In 1881 came the Anaconda in Montana, which Hearst invested in for its silver potential. It had some of that and gold, too, but mostly the Anaconda gave up copper, the biggest bonanza of that metal ever recorded.

But Hearst could even make something of earthly silence, as when he turned thumbs-down on the much-hyped Emma silver mine in Utah. English speculators asked Hearst if they should heed cheerleading by Bill Stewart (the former kingpin of Comstock mining attorneys, now a U.S. senator from the new state of Nevada) and buy Emma stock. Hearst advised against it, comparing the deposit to "a turnip turned upside down," that is, top-heavy with ore that would soon be exhausted. The speculators bought anyway, much to their regret (for a full account of this shameful episode, see Chapter 8). Throughout these blazes of success, Hearst prided himself on what we would now call his "hands-on" approach to mining; "I never sold any stock in any mine that was not in operation," he boasted.

The Hearsts' was one of those mining marriages that seem to thrive on lengthy separations. In 1873, for example, Phoebe Hearst took young Willie, then ten, on an eighteen-month tour of Europe, during which the boy developed the lust for bric-a-brac that ultimately satisfied itself in the Hearst Castle, and which Orson Welles was to make so much of in his film *Citizen Kane*.

As a wealthy Democrat, George Hearst was amenable to appeals from his fellow party members. In 1880 he bought a newspaper, the *Examiner*, to give the Democrats a San Francisco organ: it was the start of the family's publishing empire. Two years later, Hearst ran for governor. The *Alta California* sneered that his only qualification for the job was "a plethoric purse," and another paper judged him no more qualified than "a squealing pig," but similar potshots were taken at other mining kings without denting their hide. Rather, Hearst lost his party's nomination because of his shortcomings as a backroom negotiator. The nod went to George Stoneman, a former Union cavalry general, who was elected. Although peeved, Hearst had liked his first taste of politics. He set his sights on the U.S. Senate, and when one of California's senators died in 1886, Governor Stoneman appointed Hearst to fill out the term. The following year he was elected in his own right, joining Senator Leland Stanford of the Central Pacific Railroad fortune in the California delegation. In the 1860s, Nevada's Stewart had been considered the wealthiest senator; returned to office in 1887, he was now a pipsqueak compared to his two filthy rich colleagues from the colossus to the west.

After returning from Europe with his mother, Willie Hearst had been packed off to a New England boarding school and then to Harvard (although he dropped out before graduating). To his father's disappointment, the young man hadn't the slightest interest in mining. But he found newsprint bewitching and asked to be put in charge of the *Examiner*. George was already a quarter-million in the red on his investment, but all he had to lose was more money. He said yes, and Willie took over as editor in chief at the age of twenty-four. It cost George $600,000 or $700,000 more in cash advances, but in 1890 the *Examiner* turned a profit. Just ahead lay Willie's acquisition of a New York outlet, the circulation wars between Hearst and his rival Joseph Pulitzer, and yellow journalism.

In Washington, George Hearst led off what became a parade of Comstock alumni who bought their way into the Senate only to distinguish themselves as drones. Always up for a poker game or a night on the town, he was known for catnapping on the job. "Senator George Hearst," cracked a reporter for the *New York Public Service*, "borrows half the day to finish the night's sleep." Still, he may have been sporadically effective in a low-key way. A California Congressman said of him, "I could name a score of his colleagues who have told me that no Senator could, by simply saying, 'This bill is right, I want it passed,' get as many votes for a measure as Senator George Hearst." This tribute came after Hearst's death midway through his term, from cancer, in 1891. He left an estate valued at $20 million.

In an unpublished autobiography, Hearst had this to say about the sociology of the frontier West: "The first five years in California a woman was a curiosity, and they could coin money keeping little eating houses there; for we had to pay a dollar for any kind of meal. There was no kind of little place that could not take in a couple of hundred dollars a day."

A few years later, in neighboring Nevada, a "curiosity" named Eilly Orrum was running such a "little place." Born in Scotland in 1826, she had emigrated to the States after converting to Mormonism. She had an occult streak, and dreams and portents led her to predict a rosy future for herself, which she tried to nurse along by frequent changes of husband. She came to Washoe country early enough to have known the Grosh brothers, and she liked it there: after her second husband left her to obey a general summons to defend the Mormon faith in Salt Lake City, she obtained a divorce on the grounds of desertion and opened a boarding house in Gold Hill.

Eilly befriended Snowshoe Thompson, a Norwegian immigrant who became a local legend for his feats of carrying the mail back and forth over the Sierra, even through winter snowdrifts (he actually did this not on snowshoes but on skis, for which English had no word as yet). In 1858 Eilly asked her buddy to pick up a peep-stone for her the next time he was in Sacramento, that is, "a ball of glass shaped like an egg" into which she could gaze and see the future. "What I now want a good peep-stone for is to find a mine that I have seen through my old one," she explained. "It is the richest mine in the world. It is at no great distance from here, but I can't exactly make out its surroundings." In an interview with De Quille, Thompson recalled that he'd looked all over, but there were no peep-stones to be had in Sacramento, where shopkeepers laughed at the very idea. A year later, however, some Comstock miners swore that the "hole" that Pancake Comstock had horned in on—that is, the beginnings of Hearst's Ophir—was the very mine Eilly had seen dimly in her old peep-stone, and Snowshoe "always asserted, and doubtless firmly believed, that to [her] alone was due the credit of the discovery of the Comstock lode."

In any case, Eilly stumbled into the mine-owning class when a customer who couldn't pay his bill in cash handed over ten-feet worth of a claim instead. It happened to adjoin the holdings of a teamster named Lemuel Sanford "Sandy" Bowers. She and Bowers married, their claims merged, and the resulting mine went into bonanza, producing ore worth $26,000 in September of 1860 alone. Its riches lay close to the surface and could be chipped out without special equipment, but Sandy knew little more about mining than Eilly, and they hired a superintendent to direct the operations. The money kept accumulating, in such amounts that the couple couldn't resist flaunting it. Not only would they build a mansion along the road to Reno, on Washoe Valley land left over from one of Eilly's previous marriages; they would sail to Europe and furnish the place from abroad as it was going up. And while they were at it, they would see the queen of England, if you please.

They made the crossing, but the audience with the queen didn't materialize. Eilly's two divorces would have posed an insurmountable barrier even if Prince Albert hadn't died while the Bowerses were in England, leaving the regal mourner indisposed to receive visitors. In Paris, however, the couple were "the prize Christmas shoppers of 1861"—furniture, gowns, jewels, painting, sculptures, knickknacks, and on and on. They ran across a silversmith who made them an alluring proposition: he would convert bullion from their own mine into a full table service. All they need do was choose a design and ship him the silver, and he would take care of the rest. Having set the deal in motion with a letter home, the Bowerses went on their flamboyant way. After a year or so abroad, they sailed back to the States laden with items from one of the biggest spend-ing sprees the Continent had ever seen. They'd also acquired a child, a girl named Persia, whom they adopted after her mother died on the voyage and was buried at sea.

The house into which they crammed their loot is now the center-piece of a county park. Built in a blend of Georgian and Italian styles at an estimated cost of $250,000, it has a fortresslike impregnability—the outer walls are made of granite three feet thick—and an interior rife with luxurious touches, such as mantelpieces of Carrera marble and drapes so long that they "puddle" at the bottom. But nothing could save the Bowerses from their own inexperience. Sandy spent and gave away money without bothering to consult his bank bal-ance, nor did he rein in his wife. The couple's naiveté is on display in the mansion's dining room; on the table lie several examples of the French "silverware" they commissioned. Alas, they're fakeware, with only a plating of silver; the rest of their silver was made away with by that Parisian huckster. Meanwhile, the Bowers mine wasn't producing the way it used to, and Sandy was coughing a lot, espe-cially after surfacing from trips down into the mine. He died of what was said to be a lung complaint (probably tuberculosis) on April 21, 1868.

After the funeral, the widow was unruffled when the superinten-dent told her the hard truth about the mine: "We've lost the vein." "Then we'll find it again, and take out ten times as much," she airily replied. Sandy had left her an estate valued at not quite $90,000, but it was encumbered by mortgages and promissory notes. Before she knew it, the Bank of California had seized the mine. She hoped to hang on to the mansion by turning it into a resort, but her mortgage-holders vetoed the idea and demanded that the house and its contents be raffled off. An unsold ticket won the big prize, vindicating Eilly's belief that she had a pipeline to the supernatural: the house remained hers, and she carried out her plan to convert the property into a pleasure ground.

The Virginia City–born lawyer Grant H. Smith waxed nostalgic about visiting the resort as a child: "What boy or girl ever forgot the first picnic at Bowers' Mansion in Washoe Valley, where for the first time in their lives they saw clear running brooks, great pine trees, wide meadows spangled with flowers, and, beyond the meadows, the shimmering expanse of Washoe Lake? It was a trip to Paradise." Paradise, however, wasn't paying Eilly enough to live on. Adding to her woes, Persia died in 1874.

Eilly had the satisfaction of correctly predicting that the Comstock's future lay at the north end of the Lode, and the Virginia City *Territorial Enterprise* credited her with "second sight," although adding snidely, "whatever that may be." But she suffered the frustration of having no capital to invest in the bonanzas she was visualizing. People called her The Washoe Seeress, and an 1877 ad in the *Territorial Enterprise* touted her powers in refined terms: "She may be consulted in regards to events only the shadows of which have yet been projected into the planes of our lives. She sees and feels the presence of those shadows and in her mind they take apprehensible shape." But she might have done better for herself with a zingier message (a rival fortune-teller billed herself as "prepared to tell the PAST, PRESENT, AND FUTURE," which sounds more like it).

She left a mixed record as a prognosticator. She came through for a Mr. G. L. Whitney, who reported having lost a valuable watch chain. Eilly advised him to sift through the rubbish in his rooms, and damned if the chain wasn't there! On the other hand, journalist John Taylor Waldorf never forgot having to dig up the cellar under his family's house as a boy after Eilly declared that treasure was buried there (it wasn't). More to the point, Eilly made little money as a seeress. By contrast, relative Comstock newcomers such as William Sharon of the Bank of California and James Flood, a stalwart of the enormous silver deposit known as the Big Bonanza, were now wallowing in lucre. By using it to build palatial houses in San Francisco, they dwarfed and diverted attention from Eilly's decaying mansion in the Nevada hinterlands.

In 1876, she lost that, too, when the mortgage-holders forced her to vacate the big house for a cottage on the grounds. Not long afterward, she moved to San Francisco. There she maintained an interest in the Comstock by championing the cause of Sarah Althea Hill, who claimed to have secretly married Sharon before his death, and thus to be an heir to his stupendous fortune (we'll hear more about this tug-of-war later). Eilly also went on playing seeress: the mansion has on display a photo of her in old age, standing outside a shack built for her to tell fortunes in at the 1894 San Francisco Midwinter Exposition. But she was hard of hearing now (as an acquaintance put it, she hadn't been able to "distinguish the jingle of a quarter from the ringing of a church bell for the last thirty years"), much to the detriment of her interactions with clients. Her nephew sent a monthly stipend for her support. In 1901 she entered the Home of the King's Daughters, a charitable institution. She died there in 1903, at age 77. (A life of such dramatic highs and lows begs to be fictionalized, and the American writer Vardis Fisher took up the challenge in a 1941 novel about Eilly called *City of Illusion*.)

The Bowerses and George Hearst are case studies in how to succeed (or fail) in Comstock country. All three made their money early, the Bowerses by lucking into claims and consolidating them through marriage, Hearst by successfully applying his Midwestern mining smarts to new surroundings, and then picking up further skills on the fly. The Bowerses, intoxicated by their sudden wealth, squandered it like grasshoppers. Hearst postponed the heavy personal spending until after he'd diversified into real estate and mining operations outside Nevada, and at no time was he a pigeon for con men.

But he and the Bowerses also stand as markers in the Comstock's evolution: they were virtually the last soloists to make a fortune there. (Although dozens—perhaps hundreds—of small-time operators continued to putter around in peripheral Comstock mines, few of them even earned back their expenses. Their best chance of making money was by selling out to some guileless outsider with a silvery gleam in his eye.) After the early 1860s, all new bonanzas occurred far beneath the surface, where it took a consortium of partners, backed by a host of stock-owning investors, to deploy the manpower and heavy machinery and safety devices required to extract ore profitably. It wasn't just the first discoverers—the Groshes, Pancake, Old Virginia, and their ilk—who became yesterday's men on the Comstock. The second wave of entrepreneurs lost out, too, unless they learned how to team up with others like themselves.

Hearst adjusted quickly to the new corporate mentality. By the time he walked away from his Black Hills mining company in 1879, it was "a staggeringly complex enterprise, consisting of ten major mines and several smaller ones . . . ; six mills, comprising a total of 540 stamps, as well as a major interest in the 100-stamp mill of the DeSmet mine; offices, stables, blacksmith shops, carpenter's shops, forges, and one tramway; and more than 500 employees, 257 of them in the mines alone."

The Bowerses, unable to hold their own against a slippery silversmith, would have been utterly lost in such a world.

❧ THREE ❧

The Nature of the Beast

We now know that the Comstock Lode was formed when fluids heated by volcanic forces within the earth thrust minerals into fissures created by faulting, and that the Lode stretched for about two miles, from the head of Gold Canyon to the head of Six-Mile Canyon, through the east side of Mt. Davidson and beneath the towns of Gold Hill and Virginia City. But the first-generation miners were hazy about all this, and as each owner worked his claim separately, a splintered theory took hold: the Lode was a sheaf of parallel quartz veins angling to the west (as did the Ophir and other early claims for the first few hundred feet down). Both these notions were later overturned: at a depth of about five hundred feet, the multiple veins merged into a single strand or ledge, which dipped eastward. This truth was not established, however, until a blizzard of litigation had tied up the courts, enriched local lawyers (especially the hard-charging William Stewart), and eaten up a sizable chunk of Comstock profits.

As we've seen, the early 1860s were a period of shakeups in Comstock country. Some miners, knocked off balance by the Paiute War and the realization that the Comstock was best-suited for big boys playing on organized teams, followed rumors of new gold strikes back to California or elsewhere in Utah Territory. By the time Nevada became a territory unto itself in 1861, the Comstock's remaining white male population had settled into three main classes: a small group of capitalist owners, a large pool of workingmen, and a growing number of suppliers.

A few of the owners were already making fortunes, and the suppliers prospered as the region began to grow again. But even the laborers had hopes of striking it rich by indirect means: buying and selling mining stocks. In so doing, they emulated small-time players in San Francisco, where the dearth of investment opportunities (few manufacturing firms, no railroads till later, etc.) made mining the chief outlet for Westerners' speculative urges.

Investing became easier for everyone after owners changed the way mines were capitalized. As we saw in the case of the Bowerses, at first ownership of Comstock claims was reckoned in "feet" of ore-bearing rock, and to buy and sell interests in a mine you had to go through a cumbersome series of real estate conveyances. But as entrepreneurs mastered the principles of modern finance, they began to form corporations, which issued certificates representing not physical feet but abstract slices of ownership. These could be broken down into smaller amounts and traded far more easily than the feet-shares (and at a distance, too, which is how the San Francisco mining exchange came into being, on September 1, 1862), and especially when a new stock was issued, it might take very little capital to join the ownership class. At the end of the decade, the *Mining Review* catalogued the wide range of stockholders in the mines: "the millionaire and the mendicant, the modest matron and the brazen courtesan, the prudent man of business and the gambler, the maidservant and her mistress, the banker and his customer."

Mining companies liked this proliferation of owners because it fit nicely with certain provisions of California and Nevada law: corporate officers were allowed to levy assessments on their shareholders for unexpected expenses, much as a modern condo board does when, say, a roof develops a sudden leak and there's not enough money in reserves to pay for a new one. Most Comstock investors, especially the nonresident ones, were too overcome by speculative heat—and too ignorant of how silver mining worked—to question assessments, and abuse of the mechanism became rampant. Two well-known Comstock mines, the Yellow Jacket and the Imperial Empire, closed their books for the last time having levied more in assessments than they paid out in dividends. Only six mines—Consolidated Virginia, California, Belcher, Crown Point, Gould & Curry, and Kentuck—could boast of having done it the other way 'round, delivering more value in dividends than they took in as assessments. Several mines never paid any dividends at all.

Even when assessments were wholly legitimate, they could hurt. Repeatedly in his journals, Alfred Doten depicts himself as scrambling to pay an assessment due on mining shares he owns. He rarely moaned about it, however, nor did most other investors. A good indication of how consuming Comstock fever was can be found in an observation by Comstock historian Charles Shinn: "For the purposes of speculation, the mines that did not pay any dividends were often exactly as good as those that did pay."

A different ploy, one that bothered Mark Twain, was also used from time to time. Rather than be stingy with dividends, mine owners would "cook" them. Never mind that the mine might be in borrasca: declaring a dividend, whether justified or not, boosted the prospects for that stock, which speculators then bought at inflated prices. In this way, the owners could sell out without having to worry about paying the ersatz dividend. The hapless shareholders were left to swallow the losses when the stock fell back to its normal price or lower, sometimes all the way to worthlessness.

As a beginning reporter in Comstock country, Twain made this sleight of hand a premise for one of his broadest satires, "Massacre at Dutch Nick's," a piece in the *Territorial Enterprise* about a Nevadan named Hopkins who ran amok with an axe, killing his wife and six of his children. What drove Hopkins 'round the bend was that he'd been "a heavy owner in the best mines of Virginia City and Gold Hill, but when the San Francisco papers exposed the game of cooking dividends . . . he grew afraid." Taking the papers' advice, he invested in a supposedly safe water company, but its owners, too, were dividend-chefs; Hopkins lost everything and went berserk.

This was a journalistic hoax, as one detail among many should have alerted readers: Hopkins had taken a four-mile ride on horseback with his throat slit from ear to ear before straggling into Carson City, spilling his tale of woe, and expiring. Nonetheless, the article was picked up and reprinted as the truth. According to Dan De Quille, "When the California papers . . . found they had been sold [a bill of goods], there was a howl from Siskiyou to San Diego." Actual cases of dividend-cooking may have been so much on editors' minds that they'd overlooked the tale's whoppers to focus on its warning to would-be investors in mines.

Another kind of howling took place in the courts, where the dominant figure was William Morris Stewart, the lawyer who had warned a rash young partner not to join the amateurs saddling up to go fight Native Americans at Pyramid Lake. Had Henry Meredith heeded Stewart's advice, he would have lived and likely made a bundle as a Comstock lawyer. But then it was a good idea to listen to Stewart on almost any subject other than investing your own money, as shown by the ideal man to bring him front and center, Mark Twain. The word "shown" can be taken literally: from time to time, Twain embellished the prose of *Roughing It* with visual effects. One of these is a sketch of Stewart (possibly by Twain himself, no slouch as an artist) that goes with a wistful anecdote.

As young Sam Clemens alighted in Virginia City in the summer of 1861, Stewart already occupied center stage of the Comstock litigation pageant, where he was busy piling up a small fortune by representing well-heeled California owners and investors. Not too busy, though, to offer to do the newcomer a favor once he'd gone to work for the best local paper, the *Territorial Enterprise*. This was during the old feet-measuring era of mine ownership, and as Twain tells it, Stewart promised to give him twenty feet worth of a promising mine; all he had to do was stop by the lawyer's office and pick up the certificates.

Stewart's offer was not a spontaneous outpouring of generosity but, as Twain understood, a quid with an attached quo: "New claims were taken up daily, and it was the friendly custom to run straight to the newspaper offices, give the reporter forty or fifty 'feet,' and get [him] to go and examine the mine and publish a notice of it. They did not care a fig what you said about the property [just] so you said something." But Twain also must have known that the more bullish a reporter's description of the mine, the higher the price those free feet could then command on the market. His colleague De Quille faced the journalist's combination of inside knowledge and weak bargaining position more squarely, complaining in a letter to his sister that:

> Our millionaires, shrewd as they are in business, are no writers. I could say what they were trying to say, therefore I stand in the light of their champion—but they deliver over their dollars with a poor grace, and sometimes I have half a notion to show them the terrible damage I could do them in a single paragraph. But too many of my old friends would be hurt. Those who are trying to put stocks down would give thousands to know what I could tell them in three lines, yet they have never thought of it. I could knock the California stock down $100 per share to-morrow by asking a single question.

De Quille, however, was merely letting off steam. Almost always, he and his fellow reporters found something nice to say about a new mine. If the ore didn't seem rich, you could praise the works, perhaps singling out the tunnel, Twain joked, as "one of the most infatuating tunnels in the land." Most likely, then, the twenty feet Stewart dangled in front of Twain belonged to a mine of which the lawyer was part-owner, and they were offered with the winking expectation that the reporter would at least mention the mine, and perhaps rave about it, in the *Enterprise*.

The stock "was worth five or ten dollars a foot," Twain continues.

I asked him to make the offer good for next day, as I was just going to dinner. He said he would not be in town; so I risked it and took my dinner instead of the stock. Within the week the price went up to seventy dollars and afterward to a hundred and fifty, but nothing could make that man yield. I suppose he sold that stock of mine and placed the guilty proceeds in his own pocket. [My revenge will be found in the accompanying portrait.]

That bracketed remark, which is Twain's, refers to the drawing, which depicts Stewart wearing a black hat and eyepatch. Twain was teasing Stewart, but the piratical image came to be prophetic: the older man's reneging was only a rehearsal for mine-related malfeasance to come.

A few years later, Stewart was an influential U.S. senator and a framer of the Fifteenth Amendment to the Constitution, which guaranteed former slaves the right to vote. He also drafted a statute that has lasted nearly a century and a half: the Mining Law of 1872, which governs hard-rock mining on federal land. Later on, we will see that he also had an overmastering flaw, an avidity for easy money that led him to take part in two whopping mining frauds: in the freewheeling climate of Gilded Age America, Stewart wheeled as freely as anyone. For now, though, let's look at how he not only survived but flourished in a dysfunctional legal system.

He was born on a farm in western New York State in 1825, the first of seven children. He grew into a strapping young man, intensely ambitious, eager to strike out on his own. "Big Bill" spent a year at Yale, but the sensational news of gold discoveries in the Sierra Nevada foothills made book-learning seem insipid. He arrived in San Francisco in 1850, prospected in eastern California with little success, and read law. His tutor was an expert in mining law, which Stewart duly mastered.

But whatever kind of case he took, Stewart the advocate was a try-anything bulldog, boundless in energy and ruthless in tactics, as suited the not-so-lofty dignity of early Western law practice. He once tried a case in aptly named Rough and Ready, where court convened in the backroom of a tavern, the drinking was gavel-to-gavel, and the tab was treated "as costs . . . to be paid by the losing party."

The bribing of juries was widespread, but even uncorrupted ones could perform poorly in the hinterlands, where eligible jurymen were few to begin with and everybody knew everybody else's business. The habit of weeding out anyone conversant with the facts or parties to a case, Twain observed, put "a ban upon intelligence and honesty, and a premium upon ignorance, stupidity and perjury." But Stewart wasn't complaining, and a California murder case illustrates his approach to rustic juries: eschew subtlety and erudition, pour on the crude rhetoric of stage melodrama.

His client was charged with stabbing a man to death at the end of a quarrel. There was an eyewitness, a man named White, whose testimony in an earlier murder case had sent a popular local figure to the gallows. Stewart had the county surveyor map the ground where the new killing had occurred. At the trial, Stewart impugned White by asking, "Have you ever had any occupation except that of swearing away the lives of men?" Rather than simply warn Stewart and instruct the jury to disregard this prejudicial sally, the judge got up and fetched White's testimony in the earlier case, prompting Stewart to bang his fist on a table and say, "Put away that bloody record!" White went on to describe what he'd seen, but his narrative was at odds with the mapped crime scene, as Stewart had foreseen, "because no man under these circumstances could possibly remember the details of the locality." In his closing argument, Stewart repeated his slur about White's propensity to swear away other men's lives, and the jury took it to heart. No sooner had his client been acquitted than Stewart urged him to flee "before the jurymen get out and mingle among their friends and find out what they have done."

Stewart married Annie Foote, the daughter of a law partner, in 1855. (The fact that this partner, Henry S. Foote, had been a U.S. senator from Mississippi may have whetted the son-in-law's appetite for national politics.) Five years later, the Comstock Lode beckoned the young lawyer with a track record in mining law, and Stewart and his family moved to Virginia City.

He found more than enough room to stretch his talents there, for law as practiced in Comstock country was fraught with uncertainties: claims had proliferated, their filing and recording was haphazard, and boundaries on the surface often bore little relationship to the configuration of deposits below. A mine-owner expected to be able to follow any ore he found in his quartz claim wherever it went; the almost-universal boilerplate used in claims put dibs on not only the main vein but also on all its "dips, spurs, angles, and variations." The problem, as J. Ross Browne saw it, was that "everybody's spurs were running into everybody else's angles." Then, too, as ownership of mines changed from by-the-foot to by-the-share, the increase in the number of stock owners gave rise to a new sport: bringing cases against rival companies for such misdeeds as encroaching on a claim. There was an explosion of lawsuits, some of which were legitimate, some of which should have been resolved in good-faith negotiations, and some of which were ginned up to coax settlements out of owners eager to get on with the work of mining. At the height of the disputatiousness, "nine companies had 359 cases on their hands, nearly half of which they brought themselves against adjoining claims. The court calendars were clogged with cases," and lawyers had as much business as they could possibly want.

Beneath all the jockeying and bickering, however, a crucial question kept arising: was the Comstock's treasure trove of (primarily) silver-bearing ore split into separate veins or lumped in a single, complex mass? The issue pitted a small number of entrenched owners against more numerous latecomers, who yearned to strike their own paydirt. Stewart consistently argued that newly discovered deposits were branches of the one-and-only mass—in other words, that the latecomers were horning in on bespoke ore. This made him invaluable to the California interests who had bought out most of the original claimants. Other lawyers, however, were happy to represent the multiple-ledge interests, who clung to their dream of a democratic, California-style paradise in which every prospector had the potential to strike it rich. Virginia City became not only a Mecca for lawyers, but also the locus for an early outbreak of the American aversion thereto, as epitomized in an observation by Browne: "Two evils therefore beset the Washoeites—many ledges and many lawyers."

The legal tangles were compounded by political confusion. Anti-Mormon animus had joined with western Utah Territory's remoteness from Salt Lake City to produce an independence movement. Moreover, at the time many aspects of national law were almost as ill-defined as the territorial version. Consider what happened in 1861, when President Buchanan replaced John Cradlebaugh with Robert P. Flenniken as federal judge for the district embracing the Comstock—or so Buchanan thought. Cradlebaugh refused to step down, on the grounds that the president lacked authority to remove him. When Flenniken sought to exercise his new powers in court, litigants faced a quandary rather like the papal schism of the Middle Ages: two sources of authority, each claiming sole legitimacy. At one point, Stewart was litigating a case before Judge Flenniken while the attorney for the other side, David Terry (a hothead who will figure in scandals to come), was trying the same matter before Judge Cradlebaugh. The impasse came to an end when the Utah Territorial Supreme Court ruled that Cradlebaugh was entitled to keep his post and Flenniken withdrew. The more confusing the legal situation, however, the more an advocate as smart and forceful as Bill Stewart could bend the law to suit his clients' needs.

Congress made Nevada a separate territory in 1861, but the change did little to improve the reliability of Comstock justice. Consider a suit brought against Stewart's client the Yellow Jacket Company for allegedly shifting its property line three hundred feet to trespass on another claim. Amid an almost endless parade of testimony (twenty-eight witnesses took the stand for the complaining mine owners and fifty-one for Stewart's client), a witness swore he'd repeatedly seen and read a Yellow Jacket claim notice posted on the disputed ground. This was double perjury: not only had the witness done no such thing, but, being illiterate, he couldn't have, as opposing counsel proved in simple but dramatic fashion, by asking the witness to read that same notice aloud in court. Not to worry, though. Bill Stewart had things under control: swayed by bribes, the jury brought in a verdict for Yellow Jacket.

Another of Stewart's Comstock cases shows civil law giving way to the law of the jungle, more than once. Stewart represented the Sierra Nevada Mining Company, which sued to eject the American Mining Company from a contested claim. The Sierra Nevada's president, George D. Whitney, who worked out of company headquarters in San Francisco, seemed gung-ho until late February of 1863, when it came time to advance Stewart funds for preparing the case. After dunning Whitney to no avail, Stewart thought he smelled treachery. Determined to proceed on his own, he borrowed $20,000 from a moneylender to assemble witnesses and conduct the necessary survey. By the time the trial got underway, Stewart's suspicion had ripened to a certainty: Whitney had taken a bribe, sold his interest in the Sierra Nevada, and gone over to the enemy. In his cross-examination, Stewart reduced Whitney to a sputtering wretch by impeaching his testimony with statements he'd previously made under oath. Stewart summed up by charging that Whitney "was false to his duty, false to his friends, false to his honor." The jury was wowed—all but a lone holdout, whose palm had been greased. But when the holdout's fellow jurors threatened to string him up if he didn't vote their way, a unanimous verdict was returned for Stewart's client.

At times Stewart's tactics resembled the taunts of a schoolyard bully who notices a weakness in another kid and won't stop probing it. In *Yellow Jacket Company v. the Union Mining Company*, he won a verdict for his client, the Yellow Jacket, by deriding the opposing counsel, Frank Hereford, for his inexperience with Nevada juries.

> [Stewart] compared Hereford accordingly, with absurd gravity and minuteness of detail, to a young broncho horse, untrained and fresh from the plains, brought up into the cold, thin air of the mountain city, and his arguments were likened to the first efforts of the pony who pants and gasps in the new atmosphere. When the new-comer became acclimated and had recovered his wind, so to speak, he might be of some service, but till then Stewart hinted provokingly that he was unfit for rivalry with a trained old war-horse like himself.

Hereford tried to retort, but the tickled jury stuck with Stewart, whose not-so-subliminal message was that they, too, knew better than this greenhorn. Most lawyers would have found it maddening to have to navigate their way through a system in which taunts and raillery trumped the letter of the law, and in which witnesses, juries, and judges could be bought but wouldn't *stay* bought (what the territory needed, Browne quipped, was "faithfully dishonest" judges). Stewart thrived on it.

Even on the rare occasion when he met his match, he could turn it to his advantage. According to an often-told story, in 1862 a lawyer named A.W. "Sandy" Baldwin came to town, found himself pitted against Stewart in a case, and got Stewart's goat by objecting successfully to several of his courtroom maneuvers. Losing his temper, Stewart barked, "You little shrimp, if you interrupt me again I'll eat you." Baldwin shot back, "If you do you'll have more brains in your belly than you ever had in your head." Stewart's response was to bring Baldwin into his firm.

To his credit, Stewart could step back and dispassionately observe the waste caused by this briar patch of lawsuits, and for a while he thought he saw a way out. He tried to enlist the Chollar and his other big clients in a deal by which they would put aside their differences, sell out their holdings, and buy up a bunch of claims located east of the main Comstock mining district, where to Stewart's mind the next big ore deposits lay. He himself would drop his law practice to play a leading role in the new venture. It was a prescient idea (Stewart was right about where future bonanzas were to be found) but the Chollar trustees turned him down, and the flood of litigation rolled on.

The unpredictability of judicial behavior, the corruptibility of witnesses, the erratic behavior of juries, and the belligerence of lawyers elicited a widespread disrespect for law and order, which spilled over into the mines themselves. The most dangerous moments came when miners employed by one company swung their picks and broke through a rock wall to find themselves face to face with another outfit's workers. If everybody was lucky, only a fistfight ensued. Eliot Lord describes a protracted battle that took a turn for the worse:

Yellow Jacket miners cut a drift into the Gentry Company's shaft (April 9, 1864), built a fire in it and smoked out the rival party. Resolved not to be ousted, the expelled miners rolled down rocks and dirt into their shaft until it was filled above the opening made by the hostile drift and began work a second time. The Yellow Jacket Company followed up their attack, opened the shaft again (April 22, 1864) and built another fire. Their rivals resolved to fight fire with fire, and threw down quantities of inflammable rubbish which soon sent up a dense black smoke. The Gentry shaft was closed at the surface and the smoke and vapors found their only vent through the Yellow Jacket drift, driving out the miners. The war was kept up for days "with all sorts of stinking smudges." An incautious Gentry miner was once nearly smothered, and the wind blew the strong odors to the neighboring houses with disgusting effect.

In such a climate, Stewart's willingness to go to any length for a client was to be expected, even admired. His stubbornness and resourcefulness peaked in the drawn-out contest between the Chollar and Potosi Mining Companies, which lasted three-and-a-half years and ran up legal bills of $1.3 million. In the first phase, starting in December 1861, the Chollar sued the Potosi to recover possession of a claim described in the usual fashion as encompassing all "dips, angles, spurs, and variations," which in this case allegedly included a remote underground deposit being mined by the Potosi. The perennial issue was joined: was the Comstock one united ledge or several parallel ones? Stewart pressed the single-ledge theory, which prevailed in a decision handed down on October 20, 1862. The dispute broke out again, however, when the Potosi sank a new shaft far outside the Chollar's surface boundaries and hit rich ore. The Chollar sued to have the single-ledge precedent applied to the new incursion, and the Potosi countersued. Judge Gordon N. Mott was scheduled to preside, but after being accused of favoring the Chollar (i.e., Stewart's) cause, he resigned. His replacement on the bench was John Wesley North, a recent arrival from Minnesota, whom Stewart welcomed as the "most honest, upright, and incorruptible judge that ever was." The two worked side by side in an 1863 convention called to advance Nevada's progress toward statehood, and the ambitious North had reason to believe he would be elected as the new state's first governor.

But like almost everybody else in the region, North dabbled in mining. To finance a quartz mill he was building, he foolishly accepted a loan from a Potosi owner while knowing that the Chollar–Potosi case was likely to come before him. When North ruled against the single-ledge theory in another matter (an injunction proceeding involving the Burning Moscow Company and the Ophir, which was Stewart's client), Stewart turned against him. To put pressure on the judge, Stewart ignored the mill loan for the time being and leveled a shakier charge: that North had taken a bribe from Burning Moscow. North threatened Stewart with a lawsuit for defamation, and the lawyer backed down. The following notice appeared in the *Territorial Enterprise* for December 22, 1863.

> Hon. J.W. North—Dear Sir: Proceeding upon facts and statements which appeared to warrant me in so doing, I have recently made public charges reflecting upon your character as Judge and an honest man. With your assistance I have investigated those charges and I pronounce them unsustained, and take great pleasure in so stating. In my judgment there can be no just occasion for the indulgence of any suspicion of your judicial integrity or private character. Yours very truly, William M. Stewart

That seemed to be all-inclusive, but if North thought he'd muzzled Stewart, he underestimated the lawyer. A few days later, North restated his opposition to the single-ledge theory in another Ophir–

Burning Moscow ruling: although down lower the geology might be different, North discerned separate ledges at the depth where the two companies were then working. Stewart made up his mind: North had to go. First, Stewart campaigned to thwart the judge's gubernatorial ambition; with the backing of big mining, Stewart succeeded: the nomination went to someone else. Then, notwithstanding his retraction, Stewart began maligning North, this time citing the loan he'd accepted from that Potosi fellow.

North didn't lack for supporters. Some newspapers praised him as a populist who deserved credit for jousting with Stewart, the champion of extraterritorial mining monopolists, and the dispute got caught up in the campaign to adopt a constitution preparatory to Nevada's becoming a state. At least one commentator scouted out exactly what Stewart was up to: "No other reason could induce the Stewart crowd to labor for the Constitution save that by its adoption, they will remove Judge North and have a District and State Judiciary of their own making." Undaunted, Stewart challenged North to a debate in Virginia City on January 16, 1864. Stewart and his partner Sandy (the former "little shrimp") Baldwin operated as a tag-team, with Baldwin rehashing the bribery charge and Stewart accusing the judge of being soft on Negroes, whereas he, Stewart, was "one of those who believe that this country was made for white men. . . ."

In reply, North reminded the audience of Stewart's published avowal of North's integrity, and ignored the appeal to racial bigotry. Later North claimed to have felt swells of anti-Stewart sentiment rippling through the house, and for once his instinct served him well. Both the constitution and the ticket backed by Stewart went down to defeat in the January 1864 election. (The chief objection to the constitution was that it would have taxed the estimated value of mining claims whether developed or not, rather than, as everyone associated with the industry preferred, the net proceeds from working mines. Alf Doten expressed the prevailing sentiment this way: "The goose that lays the golden eggs should not be impeded in her praiseworthy occupation, but the eggs, after they are laid, might be taken with impunity.")

Afterward, the *Gold Hill Daily News* couldn't resist publishing a dig at Stewart: "The A No.1, full-rigged ship 'Constitution,' Bill Stewart, Captain, sailed this morning." Trouble was, the paper went on, the ship had sailed for the Salt River, where lost causes go. When Stewart's attempt to have North reassigned to another judicial district failed to pass the territorial legislature, North wrote his father-in-law a crowing letter: "This was my triumph before the Territory, and I am once more at rest. My enemy has to come before me to attend to business and he is meek as a whipped cur."

But the whipped cur still had sharp teeth. A new case involving the Chollar Company came before North, and again he ruled against the single-ledgers. Chollar appealed the decision to the Territorial Supreme Court, which consisted of all three territorial judges sitting together, including North himself, who would thus be ruling on an appeal from his own decision. A second judge had already sided with the single-ledgers in an unrelated case, so this left the deciding vote to be cast by the third, a recent appointee named Powhatan B. Locke, whom Stewart rated as "probably the most ignorant man who ever acted in any judicial capacity in any part of the world." In his off hours, Locke was a good-time Charlie, and lawyers for both sides arranged festive evenings to curry favor with him. To maintain the appearance of impartiality while being driven back from one such bash, Locke divided his time between a Chollar carriage and one owned by the opponents, all the while "drinking, quarreling with the teamsters on the road, and hugging his companions."

No amount of hugs, though, could spare Locke from having to make a decision, which was bound to displease one party or the other. Or was it? In a preliminary ruling, North reiterated his support of the multiple-ledge theory; Locke concurred but filed an addendum stating that by doing so he didn't mean to decide the case on the merits; that had to await a full trial of the issues. This was a bit of good news for Chollar partisans (and their mouthpiece, Stewart), until pressure from the other side prompted Locke to withdraw his addendum and pronounce it "null and void."

Locke's waffling gave Stewart a capital opportunity, and he was not slow to act on it. Shrewdly, the lawyer blew up the cancelled addendum into a symptom of a corrupt judiciary. Meanwhile, the U.S. Congress refused to accept Nevadans' rejection of the 1863 constitution as the final word on statehood. As a territory, Nevada was helping shore up the Union's finances; as a state, it would give the Republican administration additional votes for reelection and then passage of the Reconstruction amendments already being contemplated. A new Nevada constitution was drawn up—with no taxation of undeveloped mines—and submitted along with it was a measure to dismiss all three federal judges and appoint new ones. This was Stewart's handiwork, and in the context of Locke's vacillations it went over well. In a remarkable turnaround, Stewart went from being an enemy of the people for his association with wealthy Californians to being a popular tribune for his insistence on impartial justice. He trotted out the old charges about North's dishonesty, and some newspapers turned against the judge. One of these was the *Territorial Enterprise*, which published a petition, supposedly signed by 3,000 Nevadans, calling for all three judges to resign.

The *Virginia Daily Union* editorialized that the petition might as well have sported the initials W.M.S. "written at the bottom of each article," but North was beginning to wilt under the pressure, which included the failure of his quartz mill, the venture that had gotten him in trouble to start with. One morning he fainted at the breakfast table, and there were rumors that he might resign in advance of the vote on the new constitution. On August 22, he did so in a telegram to President Lincoln, which cited "severe & protracted illness." The resignation was not to take effect until a successor had been appointed, and this concern for an orderly transition caused North to suffer one last indignity. He'd delegated a case involving the single-ledge dispute to a referee, who filed a report saying that the Comstock was, indeed, a single ledge. North had no choice but to certify the vindication of his worst enemy's pet theory.

One of the remaining two judges resigned immediately, but the other, the feckless Powhatan B. Locke, held out until one night when Stewart called a meeting of the Comstock bar. He sent a couple of lawyers to fetch Locke, by force if necessary. When Locke walked in, Stewart ordered him to resign, and he buckled. The resignation, Stewart recalled, "was read aloud, to be sure that it was all right, signed and mailed; after which the whole meeting became hilarious, and Judge Locke imbibed so freely that he became more stupid than usual."

Stewart and his cronies pushed their own candidates to replace the banished judges. President Lincoln wouldn't go that far, but voters approved the new constitution by a wide margin. In what was said to be the longest telegram ever sent, the whole document was transmitted to Washington, at a cost of $3,416.77, and Nevada entered the Union on October 31, 1864. This was irregular; in an exception to the rule that to be eligible for statehood a territory should have a population of 60,000, Nevada had leapfrogged ahead of Nebraska (made a state in 1867), Colorado (1876), and its parent, Utah (not until 1896). But statehood did bring with it a cleansing sense of civic pride. The new Nevada judiciary proved to be honest and impartial, and miners stopped duking it out when they broke through into each other's shafts.

In 1865, a German expert, Baron Ferdinand von Richthofen, filed a report that drew upon the best available geological evidence to confirm the single-ledge theory once and for all. The baron also laid out the process by which hot water, steam, and gases had welled up under the future site of Virginia City, decomposing the surrounding rock and filling the gaps with mineral-rich quartz. His theories won acceptance, not least because hot water was still percolating through the tunnels, accounting for the hazards of heat stroke and scalding braved by Comstock miners.

At this point, there wasn't much left for Stewart to do in Virginia City. He'd outfoxed his foremost enemy, his view of the Comstock's geology had prevailed, his stock with the populace was high, his guerrilla-warfare style of trying cases was becoming passé, and his druthers for the Comstock economy were taking hold: the Bank of California had opened its Virginia City branch that summer, and its swaggering presence helped ensure that from then on the Lode would be the possession of a few well-financed companies. The field narrowed further when the Chollar and the Potosi owners finally came to their senses and did what they should have done at the outset. After having poured an estimated $9 million (or one fifth of the value produced by all Comstock mines up to that point) into their version of *Jarndyce v. Jarndyce*, they quit squabbling and merged as the Chollar–Potosi Mining Company on April 22, 1865. Stewart wasn't there to witness this anticlimax; having been elected one of Nevada's first two U.S. senators on December 15, 1864, he'd already relocated to Washington, D.C.

North still had some fight in him, however. He sued Stewart for slander. But when North forswore damages and demanded only that his name be cleared, the case was assigned to a panel of three referees. On September 16, 1865, they mostly sided with North, calling "wrong and unjustifiable" Stewart's revival of charges he'd ostensibly taken back in his published apology; but they also criticized the judge for compromising his position and "lower[ing] his dignity as a man" by accepting that loan for his quartz mill. By now, of course, Stewart was in far-off Washington, and North, too, had left the state. This gave Stewart's supporters a clear field in which to wave around those portions of the report favoring their man. As happened so often in his long career, the Stewart camp managed to twist facts to advance his interests.

By his own reckoning, Stewart's share of the Comstock legal loot was $500,000. This was quite a nest-egg, but Stewart craved more. He would have settled for the kind of luck that befell two other Comstock lawyers when they represented the owner of an obscure mine called Central No. 2. The owner couldn't pay their fee (a relatively modest $1,200), and the lawyers sued him. He didn't contest the action, and they found themselves owning the mine, which they held on to for a decade before exchanging it for shares in other Comstock properties. Later the lawyers sold this stock, too, sank the proceeds in San Francisco real estate, and ended up worth about $4 million apiece. That was the ballpark Stewart wanted to be in, and if he couldn't enter it honestly, he was willing to cheat his way there. As we will examine in depth later, after going into politics he remained active in mining as a capitalist, a role he played in the two ventures that were to sully his reputation, the Emma Mine in Utah and the Panamint Boom in California.

One last lawsuit deserves to be mentioned: in some ways, the most outlandish of them all. (It was pending at the time of Stewart's departure for Washington, but he wasn't involved in it.) An entity calling itself the Grosh Gold and Silver Mining Company sued the Ophir and the Gould & Curry on the dual theory that (1) in 1857 the Grosh brothers had located claims now encompassed by those mines and (2) the new "Grosh" firm had acquired the rights from the brothers' heirs, all the way down to the 3,700-foot level, of whose existence the Groshes themselves had never dreamed. This was bunkum on both counts, and the *Sacramento Union* treated it as such:

> The Ophir on the Comstock
> Was rich as bread and honey,
> The Gould & Curry further south
> Was raking out the money.
>
> The Savage and the others
> Had machinery all complete.

When in came the Groshes
And nipped all our feet.

But the hoax roped in some prominent San Franciscans, who agreed to serve on the new company's board of directors, and the Ophir and Gould & Curry had to line up witnesses and mount a defense before they could get the suit dismissed in 1865. At least, however, the court made the liars pay back the defendants' costs.

With the Grosh fiasco, the Comstock litigation rush came to an ignominious end. One commentator cautions against making too much of the subject, pointing out that courtroom battles fought in the Anaconda copper region of Montana some years later make "Comstock methods look like the work of amateurs." Be that as it may, I've dwelt on these lawsuits not only because they provide a sobering glimpse into frontier justice, but also for the Stewart connection. He took part in most of the major cases, and the no-holds-barred approach to law and policy that he developed in Comstock country stayed with him after he became a powerful national lawmaker. Groucho Marx once quipped that "military justice is to justice what military music is to music." Comstock justice was equally impaired. Its sour notes reverberated throughout the West and beyond for decades to come, and Bill Stewart had been the bandleader.

❧ FOUR ❧

Working Low, Living High

T he body of a man falling a distance of one thousand feet or more emits toward the latter part of its course a humming sound, somewhat similar to that heard from a passing cannon-ball of large size." This unnerving statement (note the assumption that readers will be familiar with a cannonball's hum!) appears in Dan De Quille's *The Big Bonanza*, an account of the Comstock from its start to the mid-1870s, penned by a newspaperman who was on hand for it all. In the late 1860s, working a thousand feet underground was par for Comstock miners, and the helpful De Quille equated a fall of that magnitude to plummeting from the summit of Mt. Davidson all the way to the streets of Virginia City.

These grim details call to mind a larger truth about Comstock mining. Thanks to Deidesheimer's stabilizing cubes, cave-ins were less common than in other districts. Rather, most Comstock deaths and injuries had to do with getting in or out of mines, or, in case of fire, not being able to get out at all. Owing to the great distance from the surface, the dim lighting, and the difficulty of maintaining communication through labyrinthine tunnels and drifts, miners were in danger of falling into chutes, being crushed or maimed by mishandled equipment, or simply getting stranded down below to burn to death or suffocate.

Peril seemed to lurk around the mine shafts in particular, with their ladders and elevator cages. On September 1, 1865, for example, Alfred Doten reported in his journal that a "green hand" named James Davis was descending a ladder in the old North Potosi shaft, when he "got dizzy or nervous or made [a] misstep." Davis fell eighty feet, hitting other men on the ladder; they held on, but he was "picked up dead." In 1868, three men were on their way up in the Yellow Jacket when the cage struck a timber lodged in the shaft; the cable broke, and they fell two hundred sixty feet to their deaths. In 1880, eight men were waiting for a lift in a shaft of the New Yellow Jacket when a cage going up an adjacent shaft hit an obstruction (careless packing may have left a tool sticking out of the cage). The cage tipped, and its contents rained down on the men below, killing five and injuring the other three.

The shafts themselves could pull a careless man to his doom. Imagine a worker somewhere in a mine's bowels, pushing a car full of ore toward a shaft with an open gate, which leads him to expect a cage waiting, although in fact it's not there. The car goes hurtling into space, and the miner's momentum carries him after it. Down he goes, "dashed from side to side against the timbers and planking . . . till the bottom is reached, hundreds of feet below." Few bodies falling that far landed intact; colleagues would gather up the severed parts and place them in candle boxes to be carried to the surface. (Filled with dirt, candle boxes had another use in the mines: as receptacles for human excrement.)

The communications problem can be illustrated by an 1874 incident involving four miners dispatched to the 1,700-foot level of the Ophir, with orders to insert dynamite charges into a formation they intend to blast apart. When all is ready, one of them pulls a rope to ring a bell on the surface, signaling the operator to lower the cage they will ride up to safety. The cage descends. The men light the fuses, enter the cage, and pull the rope again. This time nothing happens. Another yank on the rope. Still nothing. In desperation, one man jumps out of the cage and runs back to see about defusing the charges. He manages to smother two flames, but two other fuses have already burned their way into drill-holes, out of reach. He dashes back to the cage, screaming at his colleagues to save themselves by scrambling up the elevator's cable and the shaft's timbers. Three of them climb high enough "to flatten their bodies against the walls and screw themselves among the lower timbers of the shaft, and [escape] unhurt." The fourth, however, doesn't get that far. When the explosion comes, a rock strikes him above the right eye, boring into his skull.

Operating the cage demanded one's full attention; during this writer's tour of the Chollar mine in the summer of 2007, the owner, himself a former operator, said that "nobody was supposed to talk to the hoist man." But the Ophir's operator, it turned out, had a good excuse for not raising the cage that day. The bell-rope had snagged on a timber, and the bell didn't ring a second time. Somehow the wounded man lived despite having a hole in his skull; even more amazingly, he "complained but little about his injury."

That fellow's stoicism may have been extreme, but Comstock miners were generally fatalistic about accidents. Risk came with the territory; you prided yourself on doing your job in spite of them; and for all the lawyers slithering around, the idea of suing owners for failing to provide a safe workplace seems to have occurred to no one. The miners rightly thought of themselves as a rare breed: rugged, hard-drinking, and given to playing pranks on the surface that matched their heroic deeds underground. Not just anybody could thrive in the bipolar Comstock atmosphere of deep mining and high-altitude R&R.

The miners may have been willing to tough it out, but the owners realized that deaths and injuries had a demoralizing effect, and that stoppages for cleanups and funerals cost time and money, especially with water always ready to rush in and flood idle passageways. Engineers developed catches to prevent elevator cages from going into free-fall when a cable broke, and new cars came with a similar safety feature. The cages also added roofs to protect their riders from falling tools and debris.

According to statistics compiled by Eliot Lord, the total number of Comstock mining fatalities between 1863 and 1880 was two hundred ninety-five, along with six hundred six injuries; and we know that on average 1,500 men worked in the mines during the busy years 1866 to 1868. For its time, this wasn't a scandalous safety record, and miners working on the Comstock did have one advantage: the mining kicked up little of the dust that took a cumulative toll on workers' lungs in other districts. So if a Comstock miner made it to retirement without suffering a fatal accident or serious injury, he could probably look forward to a healthy old age.

The most striking work condition in Comstock mines was more of a handicap than a killer: the debilitating heat, a lingering effect of the volcanic forces that had molded Comstock ore. As miners pursued veins deeper into the earth, bigger blowers pumped compressed air down through the shafts and tunnels, providing ventilation and a modicum of cooling. But the heat more than kept pace, rising to one hundred thirty degrees Fahrenheit and above, and miners coped as best they could. They stripped down to nothing but breechcloths and shoes, a sight that elicited a hymn of praise from De Quille: "All are naked to the waist, and many from the middle of their thighs to their feet. Superb muscular forms are seen on all sides and in all attitudes, gleaming white as marble in the light of the many candles. We everywhere see men who would delight the eye of the sculptor." These sons of Hercules drank ice water by the gallon; in the summer of 1878, one mine sent down ninety-five pounds of ice per day for each man working. Supervisors cut work periods back to half an hour, then to fifteen minutes, after which the men were free to stagger to the nearest ventilation shaft for an air-gulping break. The rule of thumb was that it took four of them at the lower depths to do the work of one near the surface.

Yet the miners were ordered deeper still, the heat did not relent, and hot water posed a hazard all its own. "In July 1877," a historian wrote, "miners sinking a shaft in the Savage encountered water so hot (157 degrees) that they worked in clouds of stifling vapor, their pick-handles so hot they were obliged to use gloves; cloths repeatedly dipped in ice water were wrapped about the drills." One day, at the 2,000-foot level of the Imperial, miners encountered jets of scalding vapor shooting out from the walls of the drift they were excavating; in order to continue, they had to seal off the walls behind a double layer of planks and stuff the seams with tow.

In her *Ten Years in Nevada*, Mary McNair Mathews reprints a harrowing newspaper account, circa 1878, of a miner trapped by a sideways geyser. When his drill broke through a rock wall in the Julia mine, hot water and steam spewed into the drift and kept pouring out, cutting him off from escape. "He was held a close prisoner, as he could not pass out through the jets of boiling water; and even in his prison he was in danger of being suffocated and cooked by the steam and heat." He bought himself some time by opening the drill's exhaust-valve, which gave him fresh air and cooled him down a bit until a mate dressed in gum-rubber boots and coat could rush in carrying more of the same: "Shielded by their heavy gum clothing, the pair rushed forth and waded out along the drift."

In 1880, water flooding the 3,000-foot level of the New Yellow Jacket sent a thermometer up to one hundred seventy degrees, the highest on record. Heat of such magnitudes can cause stomach cramps, which were treated by hauling victims to the surface and massaging them. If you rose too quickly, though, you might faint, a hazard to which visitors to mines were also susceptible and against which they were repeatedly warned.

The Comstock workforce was not only hardy but skilled. Take, for example, the men we probably think of as quintessential miners: the excavators, swinging picks to punch their way deeper into the earth. In fact, picks were considered old-fashioned in the world of industrial mining. The modern way to proceed was by drilling holes, filling them with explosives, and blasting a rockface into fragments, all of which called for teamwork. One miner would hold a drill bit while another struck its head with a sledgehammer. After the bit went a ways in, the first man would replace it with a longer bit, and the pounding would resume until the hole was about three feet deep. Once the team had drilled several strategically placed holes, they would introduce black powder and fuses, light the fuses, and retreat to a safe spot. (Other, lesser mortals would gather up the rocks loosened by the blast, pack them into cars, and haul these away.) Their job became easier in 1868, when dynamite replaced blasting powder, and again in 1874, when steam-powered drills came into common use.

Milling, too, was complicated, arduous work. Mark Twain toiled in a mill that crushed and amalgamated ore in one continuous operation, and in *Roughing It* he gives a vivid sense of how the combined process worked while also making the case that the mill hands earned every cent of their pay. (Note that the ore passing through this mill was an exception to the rule that Comstock silver didn't keep company with base metals.)

> We had to turn out at six in the morning, and keep at it till dark. The mill was a six-stamp affair, driven by steam. Six tall, upright rods of iron, as large as a man's ankle, and heavily shod with a mass of iron and steel at their lower ends, were framed together like a gate, and these rose and fell, one after the other, in a ponderous dance, in an iron box called a "battery." Each of these rods or stamps weighed six hundred pounds. One of us stood by the battery all day long, breaking up masses of silver-bearing rock with a sledge and shoveling it into the

battery. The ceaseless dance of the stamps pulverized the rock to powder, and a stream of water that trickled into the battery turned it to a creamy paste. The minutest particles were driven through a fine wire screen which fitted close around the battery, and were washed into great tubs warmed by super-heated steam—amalgamating pans, they are called. The mass of pulp in the pans was kept constantly stirred up by revolving "mullers." A quantity of quicksilver was kept always in the battery, and this seized some of the liberated gold and silver particles and held on to them; quicksilver was shaken in a fine shower into the pans, also, about every half hour, through a buckskin sack. Quantities of coarse salt and sulphate of copper were added, from time to time to assist the amalgamation by destroying base metals which coated the gold and silver and would not let it unite with the quicksilver. All these tiresome things we had to attend to constantly. . . . There is nothing so aggravating as silver milling.

The men may have forgone lawsuits, but they were well aware of the abnormally harsh conditions they were subjected to, and in 1863 they tried to organize a union. They failed that time, but the following year owners made noises about reducing wages from the traditional $4 for an eight-hour day to $3.50. The proposal incited miners and mill hands to march from Gold Hill to Virginia City, where they assembled in front of the International Hotel. A speaker with little sense of his audience regaled it with diction the likes of which few other American working stiffs have been subjected to: "By the law of ancient Rome a convicted traitor was hurled from the Tarpeian rock. Let the man who in this crisis advocates a reduction of miners' wages be girdled with burning faggots and receive the fate of the Roman felon." The owners relented (just saying no to that girdle of burning faggots), and to cement their triumph the miners met again five days later, on August 6, 1864, to form the Miners' League of Storey County. One of the bylaws required each member to swear "never to work in the county of Storey for less than $4 per day."

A month later, the new union tried to flex its muscle by demanding that owners hire its members exclusively, that is, accept a closed shop. The *Gold Hill Daily News* endorsed the idea, editorializing that "if labor isn't king here, we really do not know who is." But mine owners squawked, and the paper had to backpedal: "We remarked day before yesterday . . . that Labor is King in Washoe. We used a figurative expression, and will here amend it. Labor is king provided the king behaves himself and does not trespass upon other vested rights." At the request of local officials, the territorial governor called in federal troops to intimidate the League, and the owners got tough, first canning the League's officers, then working their way down through the rank and file. In this way, the union achieved the opposite of what it wanted: not belonging to it became an unspoken condition of employment. Wages dropped to $3.50 a day at leading mines, reflecting stagnant conditions all along the Comstock, and the Miners League had little choice but to disband.

Within a couple of years, however, new unions had sprung up in Virginia City and Gold Hill. In the interim, organizers had gone into politics, getting their sympathizers elected to county and city offices and thus denying owners those officials' support in the event of labor disputes. As the economy improved, the daily rate climbed back up to the $4 level, where it remained sacrosanct ever after. To the journal-keeping Doten, however, the unions' insistence on the full amount for everyone was too rigid. On August 5, 1867, union members marched to the Savage mine to protest the $3.50 rate being paid certain menial workers: "car men, wheelbarrow men, pick & drill carriers, water carriers, shovellers, etc." The upshot was that eight men holding those jobs were let go and "first-class" miners were hired to take their places at the full $4 rate. "It would seem to work a little injustice on those 8 discharged," Doten commented, "they being unfit for 1st class miners, & only fit for the positions they held." The $4 rate was higher than the American norm for the industry (and over in England miners were being paid the equivalent of $5 *a week*). Many mines stayed open 'round the clock, with the workday divided into three eight-hour shifts. Miners could pad their paychecks by working a seven-day week, and their collective spending power (or, more likely that of their wives and children, because the men themselves were underground so much) added to the overall prosperity.

Not surprisingly, the new unions subscribed to the racial prejudices of the day: they pressured mining companies not to employ Chinese, or "coolies," as they were called. In 1869, the unions tried to extend the ban to the Chinese crews grading the roadbed for the Virginia & Truckee Railroad, a project of the Bank of California. The unrest climaxed on September 29, when three hundred fifty union men marched on the Chinese workers' camp. The county sheriff read (literally) the riot act, but the marchers refused to leave until their spokesman had finished denouncing the railroad's hiring practices. The Chinese fled but returned a few days later, after the railroad's boss, William Sharon, assured the unions that putting the Chinese back to work was a matter of expediency, limited to the time it took to finish the grading work. He also emphasized the paltry wages the Chinese were receiving: "Some recklessly assert that white men could have been got to work as cheap, but every man of you know better than that." "When [the roadbed] is completed," he continued, "the Chinese are no longer wanted and can go." But Sharon had to sign a pledge not to employ any Chinese within the limits of Virginia City or Gold Hill before he was let off the hook.

There were limits to the revived union's power, however, most notably the tenuousness of miners' jobs. Not even veterans were guaranteed a place during periods of borrasca, and there was nothing to protect them against innovation. If you were laid off or replaced by a machine, there was little you could do but wait and hope to be needed again.

Chinese couldn't go down into the mines, but Irishmen, another group disfavored in nineteenth-century America, could. The anti-Irish prejudice infecting certain Eastern cities didn't spread to Virginia City, and indeed Irishmen were the most numerous ethnic group working in the mines. There were also Cornishmen, as well as enough Germans to support three short-lived German-language newspapers. In that pre-melting pot era, the various groups formed lodges and societies for mutual support and wore their national costumes on patriotic and feast days. "During the bonanza period," wrote a historian, "it was unusual for a week to pass without a parade, ball, picnic, or other social event sponsored by one of the many Comstock societies of foreign-born." Along with the Chinese, Mexicans, blacks, and Native Americans occupied the lowest social rungs, but the discrimination against them seems to have been less noxious than in most other American towns: by 1880, children from the latter three groups were being educated with whites in the Virginia City public schools.

Men consistently outnumbered women during the Comstock's heyday. At first, the proportion was lopsided, ninety-five percent to five percent in the 1860 census; but by 1910, the male lead had dwindled to fifty-eight to forty-two. The most common occupation for women was keeping house, but in the early years many of them had run boardinghouses for paying customers. In the middle period, prostitutes gravitated to the mining district, forming the largest group of Virginia City's wage-earning women according to the 1870 census. Yet the numerical count of prostitutes—one hundred sixty that year—does not seem outlandish among a total female population of more than 2,200; and the census results are complicated by the fact that many respectable women earned money in several different ways and would have been hard-pressed to claim any one of these as their mainstay on the government's form. At any rate, a decade later, prostitution had dropped to third place among wage-earning occupations for women, behind servant-work and sewing. The rowdy young mining town was evolving into a community of families.

Before the rough-and-tumble era faded out, however, it awarded posthumous fame to Julia Bullette, who stands out among Comstock prostitutes because of her penny-dreadful death. A self-employed entrepreneur, she rented a room on D Street in which she both lived and turned tricks. On January 19, 1867, she tried to enter Piper's Opera House to see a play called *The Robbers*. She was denied entry at the front door because of her occupation, and she refused to be seated in a special section for her kind. So back home she went, where in any case she had a midnight rendezvous to keep. In the morning, her Chinese servant found her body: she'd been strangled and beaten to death.

All this would be just another sordid story except for the emotional response it triggered. The *Territorial Enterprise* sentimentalized Bullette as a member of "that class denominated 'fair but frail,' yet being of a very kind hearted, liberal, benevolent, and charitable disposition. Few of her class had more true friends." Mourners recalled her nursing of sick and injured miners and her donations to the Virginia City fire company. The firemen marched in her funeral procession, their band played, and "16 carriages loaded with friends and sisterhood of the deceased went out with her." A few months later, one Jean Millian was arrested for the murder: he'd been caught trying to sell Bullette's diamond pin to a jeweler who knew her, and a search of his room had turned up more of her belongings in his trunk. When he was convicted (on this circumstantial evidence alone) and sentenced to death by hanging, the firehouses rang their bells. Doten, who had known Bullette, remarked in his journal, "This is the first instance I ever knew, of public rejoicing over such a verdict, where a man's life is at stake." The hanging, which took place on April 24, 1868, was witnessed by a throng estimated at 5,000, roughly a quarter of the local population.

Bullette doesn't appear to have been appreciably more generous with her labor or money than other Comstock women, but her death brought people together in acknowledgment of a fact of life they typically ignored. By making such a to-do over her, Comstockers were briefly lifting the veil of respectability, suspending the Victorian-era rule that prostitutes could be tolerated but not noticed, admitting that in an outpost starved for female companionship they might perform a valuable service. Writers more intent on selling books than telling the truth inflated Bullette's status until she was the town's madam-in-chief, served by a French maid, as well as an angel of good works. (See, for example, the fanciful chapter on Bullette in Lucius Beebe and Charles Clegg's *Legends of the Comstock Lode.*) The upshot is that Julia Bullette ranks with Eilly Bowers and Bonanza King John Mackay's wife, Marie, in the small company of Comstock women who are remembered by name.

How much the children of Virginia City knew about its whores and bawdyhouses is hard to say, although the opening of the Fourth Ward School in 1877 caused tension because it stood near a red-light district. At any rate, the kids had plenty of other diversions at their disposal, including Mt. Davidson to explore, steep hillsides to sled on, pools of waste water from the mines to swim in, and a task to perform for their families: gathering scrap wood from mine dumps to help satisfy every household's craving for wood to burn in stoves and fireplaces. In *A Kid on the Comstock*, journalist John Taylor Waldorf recalled that discarded lumber came mixed with other waste in cars lifted out of mines and trundled over to the dump, where they were upended into a pit. To get the jump on fellow scavengers, a boy or girl might have to go down in the pit early and be ready to dodge rocks and other falling debris.

The emphasis Virginia Citians placed on educating their kids is evident in the above-mentioned Fourth Ward School, the most impressive building to have survived from the old days and now a museum. Able to accommodate 1,000 students, it featured blackboards, pot-bellied stoves in the middle of classrooms, and desktops with built-in inkwells. A century later, it gave rise to a delightful historic-preservation decision. As Nevada historian Ronald M. James explains it, in 1986 he and his father-in-law, Don Dakins, were working on restoring the school, which had stood empty for some fifty years. The wooden outsides of the staircase to the second floor were marred by black streaks, which James considered unsightly and wanted to remove. But as Dakins examined the marks, he figured out what had caused them: shoes worn by pupils sliding down the banister and using their feet as brakes. "Look here, where they approached the knob at the end of the stair rail," he pointed out. "The marks get bigger and bigger." Rather than rub out this evidence of kids being kids, the two men left it alone, and it has become a crowd-pleaser on tours of the restored school.

Youthfulness seems to have been a permanent Comstock trait. Smith remembered many of the adults he grew up among as being kidlike, with everyone harboring the same ambition: to invest in mining stocks and make a killing. "Life was . . . a great adventure," he wrote, and Comstockers "gave the impression of never reaching settled middle age." Another commentator who'd spent time in Virginia City stressed that the prevalent civic emotion was not "a mere sordid lust for gold" but "a big-hearted, generous desire for achievement, to acquire the means of doing greater things." Even Mary McNair Mathews, who had to deal with a soap-opera widow's quota of tribulations during her stay there, declared that "few people ever enjoyed life more than we did."

While miners and management had been sorting out pay and other issues, the town was changing fast. In 1863, J. Ross Browne, the traveler who'd compared the infant settlement to the anthills of Africa, paid a return visit. What he saw surprised him:

The business part of the town has been built up with astonishing rapidity. In the spring of 1860 there was nothing of it save a few frame shanties and canvas tents, and one or two rough stone cabins. It now presents some of the distinguishing features of a metropolitan city. Large and substantial brick houses, three or four stories high, with ornamental fronts, have filled up most of the gaps, and many more are still in progress of erection.

Browne found fault just the same: the architectural hodgepodge struck him as "grotesque." But he failed to mention that Virginia City's residents hailed from all over the United States, as well as Europe and Asia, and that after mushrooming wildly the town had sorted itself out into four sectors: shops, banks, groceries, and other businesses on C Street; the red-light district on D (where Bullette lived); Chinese gambling and opium dens below that; and rising above C Street (as far away from the whores and users as possible) the middle-class residential district. When you factor in those grandiose mills and their outbuildings spread out like fortresses across the industrial zone farther down on Mt. Davidson, to bemoan the absence of a uniform style seems persnickety.

Rooming houses, which could be found in every sector, were popular with unmarried miners. The plainer houses were strictly utilitarian: "scores of angular, barracks-like boxes, two or three stories high, with lines of cubicles opening off narrow hallways." Room and board in such a place went for between $40 and $60 a month. Better-heeled transients could stay in a swankier lodging house or a hotel, with the five-story International providing the maximum in comfort. Hotels also housed more-or-less permanent residents, the so-called "Washoe widowers," whose families stayed "below" (in San Francisco, that is) while the pater tended to mining business in Virginia City. In addition, there were absentee owners, such as two of the four Bonanza Kings, James C. Flood and William S. O'Brien, who showed up in Virginia City only rarely but made their presence felt from afar by buying and selling stock on the San Francisco exchange. (We'll get to know all four Kings better in Chapter 6.)

Those who did pay visits could shorten their travel time by using the Geiger Grade, a toll road north to the village that became Reno, then by crossing the Sierra Nevada through Donner Pass. The Grade inspired one of the few tributes to Comstock scenery ever recorded, even if the admiration was confined to a particular time of day:

When [a traveler] started out at nightfall in the coach from Virginia City to Reno over the Grade, he had before him a drive which could not be surpassed anywhere. The moon soon flooded the mountains with its gentle light and softened and concealed the barrenness of their aspect, while the gigantic boulders cast afar deep mysterious shadows. The dull-colored, dusty sage brush idealized by the mellow rays of the moon, took on shapes of fantastic beauty and in the freshness of the evening, after the scorching heat of the day, exhaled a pungent, aromatic fragrance.

The writer summed up the experience as "a sort of Washoe midsummer night's dream."

Others had a more kinetic time of it on the Grade. With its surface regularly watered to keep the dust down, it encouraged drivers to flaunt their skills. After taking the route in 1865, Schuyler Colfax, speaker of the House of Representatives, said that it took more talent to drive a stage over the Sierra than to serve in Congress.

There were times, however, when even the most skilled driver had to defer to the weather. Virginia City's chief drawback (one J. Ross Browne said nothing about) was its remoteness, which could be accentuated by winter storms. In early 1867, blizzards socked the Comstock in for two weeks; when the roads and trails finally opened up again, a record one and a half tons of backed-up mail had to be lugged over the Sierra. Yet the region hadn't been utterly cut off from the outer world. A telegraph line strung on poles had connected Virginia City to Sacramento in the spring of 1861, and since the completion of the transcontinental telegraph system later the same year, wire services were bringing national and world news to the Comstock's four newspapers: in Virginia City, the *Territorial Enterprise*, *Virginia Daily Union*, and *Virginia Evening Bulletin*, and up the road, the *Gold Hill Daily News*.

Although occasionally suffering from its forlorn location, Virginia City also gained from being where it was. Whereas the distribution of gold in the California Mother Lode had seeded a two-hundred-mile-long belt in the Sierra foothills with dozens of small mining camps and supply towns, Comstock silver and gold were concentrated in and around Mt. Davidson. Accordingly, Virginia City and its suburb, Gold Hill, became the unrivaled hub of Comstock industry and prosperity. True, the ore barons were quick to pack their Comstock loot off to San Francisco, where they poured it into mansions and urban development. But the miners stayed in place; and their insistence on being well paid kept some of the locally generated wealth from dissipating. They worked hard and played harder, and Virginia City grew into the kind of bustling pleasure town for which Nevada was to become famous. Mark Twain's description of the place in 1863 makes it sound almost Manhattanesque—if, that is, Manhattan sat atop vaults stuffed with silver: "It claimed a population of fifteen thousand to eighteen thousand, and all day long half of this little army swarmed the streets like bees and the other half swarmed among the drifts and tunnels of the 'Comstock,' hundred of feet down in the earth directly under those same streets."

On another occasion, Twain replied indignantly to his mother's suggestion that he was wasting his time in Virginia City:

> you gravely come forward & tell me "if I work hard & attend closely to my business, I may *aspire* to a place on a big San Francisco daily, some day." There's a comment on human vanity for you! Why, blast it, I was under the impression that I could get such a situation as that any time I asked for it. But I don't want it. No paper in the United States can afford to pay me what my place on the "Enterprise" is worth. If I were not naturally a lazy, idle, good for nothing vagabond, I could make it pay me $20,000 a year.

One of the most endearing traits of Western mining communities was their yen for dramatic entertainment: no sooner did settlers feel their tent-camp putting down roots than they thought about building a theater. Virginia City had one up and running as early as September of 1860, and in its heyday the town boasted a number of venues, in which you could take in a gamut of productions: *Hamlet* starring Edwin Booth; a lecture by famed preacher Henry Ward Beecher; a performance by Buffalo Bill Cody's Wild West show; a circus billing itself as "Montgomery Queen's great show, with an African Eland, and Abyssinian Ibex, Cassowaries, and the Only Female Somersault Rider in the World"; and a play with the can't-miss title *Hugo the Hunchback of Florence*. Doten was an inveterate theatergoer, as well as an amateur performer, and his journals are stuffed with mini-reviews of productions he'd seen or in which he'd taken part. "Good play, good Co & good house," he wrote of *Hugo the Hunchback*.

For tourists, however, the greatest show in town was the mines themselves, with their far-flung plants and spanking new gadgetry: Comstockers never tired of showing off and bragging about the spectacle. In the culturally bleak stretch between St. Louis and San Francisco, Virginia City became not just an obligatory stop for traveling lecturers and theatrical companies, but also an attraction the curious simply had to see, as witness the list of dignitaries who traipsed through in the 1860s and 1870s: ex-president Ulysses Grant, inventor Thomas Edison, former Union general William Tecumseh Sherman, suffragist Susan B. Anthony, renowned agnostic Robert Ingersoll, and many more. If they came in from Carson City on the Virginia & Truckee, so much the better: snaking up mountainsides and chugging across the five-hundred-feet-long, eighty-five-feet-high trestle over Crown Point Ravine near Gold Hill, the railroad was an attraction in itself.

A visit to a mine took the form of a ritual. First, you changed into an outfit provided by the mining company: "heavy shoes, cotton shirts and breeches, felt hats, and, for the long, swift ride in the cages, thick woolen coats." The ladies donned "roomy smocks of brown alpaca, woolen skirts, and stout shoes, topped off by shapeless felt hats of the same sort provided for men." After stepping into a cage and being whisked down—in the days before roller coasters, probably the most thrilling ride in the West, if not the whole country—you exited into an underground gallery and opened your eyes wide to take in the extensive workplace, with its chutes and ladders and stacks of timbered cubes, all revealed in the fitful light of hundreds of lanterns and candles. Then you could zero in on the spectacle of scantily clad men swinging picks and wielding drills and pushing ore-cars, and marvel at demonstrations of high-powered pumps, blowers, and elevators in action. Before leaving, you might get to touch a hot spot and would probably be given a piece of ore to hold, perhaps to keep. Afterward, you could ease your re-entry into the upper air by soaking in a tub of cool water. Few emerged from this treatment unfazed. At the end of his two-hour immersion in the Big Bonanza mines in 1879, the famously taciturn Grant exclaimed, "That's as close to hell as I ever want to get!"

If your mine tour had shaken you up beyond the restorative pow-ers of a cool tub, you could settle your nerves with drinks and poker in a saloon or, better yet, the Washoe Club. Next came more drinks and dinner in a restaurant, followed by a show at one of those three theaters. Finally, if you were feeling randy, you might round out a long and stimulating day by sampling the fleshpots below C Street. (Given that Grant was traveling with his family, we can assume he stayed on the high road.)

On one memorable occasion, in 1879, a mine became a party house for Comstock residents: an owner in Gold Hill put one of his company's underground chambers to convivial use by holding a community dance there. About a hundred people were said to have reveled more than 1,000 feet below ground; sounds like great fun, but it seems to have been a one-time-only shindig.

As the region matured, it became both more self-sufficient and in-creasingly able to import what it lacked, expenses be damned. Local foundries were built, reducing the dependence on San Francisco for heavy machinery; the bricks for the houses that impressed Browne were probably made on-site from local clay; and starting in 1863, the streets were lighted by gas from the Virginia Gas Company. The outside world became less a source for necessities than an emporium for luxuries. The railroad, when it came in 1869, regularly delivered what Lord called "a cornucopia of dainties":

> Choice cattle, fatted on the succulent grasses of the Truckee meadows, are slaughtered for their tables. Fresh vegetables from the valley of the Carson are brought daily in their season to the mines. Venison from the sierran foot-hills, plump wild-fowl from the Californian estuaries, and fish, which twenty-four hours before had been swimming in sea or river, can be seen in profusion on the market stands of Virginia City. Strawberries, apricots, pears, peaches, grapes, apples, figs, and all other products of the luxuriant gardens and vineyards which are the boast of the Pacific seaboard cover the counters of the open stalls in luscious heaps.

Furnishings were imported, too, notably mirrors, which became talismanic presences, especially the panoramic ones taking up the wall space behind the bars in saloons. Maneuvering king-size mirrors over mountains and around the bends of winding trails to deliver them unshattered became a kind of sport, with saloonkeepers running an informal competition, egged on by enthusiastic newspaper coverage, to import and install the most elaborate model.

Grant Smith characterized Virginia City as a place both dignified and broadminded. Men and women went about town in strait-laced garb and maintained a high-toned decorum. "The newspapers and the stage were clean to the point of delicacy, out of respect for the ladies," he recalled; "suggestive jokes and even mild profanity were taboo." (In their private clubs and down in the mines, of course, men could talk as freely as they liked.) Adah Menken, a dancer and actor known as the "Great Unadorned," caused a stir in 1864 with her racy interpretation of Byron's *Mazeppa*: she streaked across the stage on horseback while wearing a flesh-colored body stocking. But she got away with it and later spoke of the fine time she'd had in Virginia City.

Drinking was the favorite pastime of the townsfolk, who had evidently become inured to the weakness often felt by those who jumped off a stagecoach from the lowlands and rushed right into a saloon: quaffing a high-altitude slug and having it go right to their head. The saloons divided by price into "bit" joints (twelve and one half cents for a drink or cigar) and "two-bit" (a quarter per drink or smoke). The town's roster of hundred-plus saloons was not out of line with the number of bars per capita in Eastern cities, but there does seem to have been a Lode-wide tendency to get oiled early in the day and stay that way, especially when miners were out of work. In his memoir, *An Editor on the Comstock Lode*, Wells Drury recalled being hired as a reporter for the *Gold Hill Daily News* in 1874 for $7.50 a day, plus a $2.50 daily boozing allowance. "This last, which never proved enough," he explained, "was not so much for the scribe as for the entertainment of the citizenry interviewed (saloons were the inevitable meeting-places) on his rounds as news-gatherer." Temperance groups protested (their pet peeve was that bartenders let miners buy on credit, which the grateful borrowers were sure to square away first thing after cashing their next paycheck) but made little headway. For those whose taste in vice ran to the exotic, opium (introduced to the Comstock by the Chinese) was available for smoking, as well as in the more respectable form of an additive to medicines.

People played cards, roulette, faro, and the like, but these must have seemed rather trifling compared to that townwide game of chance, the mines themselves. Mary McNair Mathews noted that stock-boards, by which passersby could keep track of how leading stocks were doing, "hung in every broker's window, bank window, express office, and many saloons and groceries." An October 12,

1869, entry in Alf Doten's journal gives a sense of the market's fluctuations and one player's attempts to stay on top of them: "Sold out of the Sierra Nevada today for $400—$8 per share—PM it rose to 9½ on the strength of good deposit found—Will try and buy it back." Drury asserted that "all of us dabbled in mining stocks. . . . Everyone, even the lowliest, believed that somehow he would share in the Bonanza—if not now, then presently." Another Comstock newsman, John Taylor Waldorf, recalled how his mine-worker father counted on his Ophir stock to rise enough for the family to be able to go back East, where the parents thought they all belonged. When the bottom fell out of the Ophir, a neighbor kid razzed, "Maybe you're goin' to Gold Hill." In a grander way, the risk-taking spirit infected those at the top, the owners and capitalists, who repeatedly backed up their faith in bonanzas-to-come by financing further discovery and heavier equipment.

One of the best tributes to Virginia City's sophistication and joie de vivre was the behavior of an outsider, the humorist Artemus Ward (1834–1867), a man who'd been just about everywhere and done just about everything. In a mock form letter sent ahead to guide newspaper editors in drumming up business for his lectures, he'd written, "If it's a temprance community, tell 'em I sined the pledge fifteen minits arter Ise born, but on the contery ef your peple take their tods, say Mister Ward is as Jenial a feller as we ever met, full of conwivialtity, & the life an sole of the Soshul Bored."

You can guess which of Ward's personae landed in Virginia City in December of 1863. He immediately hit it off with Sam Clemens, who was already signing "Mark Twain" to his reports and japes for his employer, the *Territorial Enterprise*. Ward found himself so attuned to the local ethos of nonstop carousing and pranks that he extended his tour, rustling up gigs at nearby towns to justify the layover. (As the quote in the previous paragraph shows, in his writings Ward used misspellings to feign a lack of education and to mimic dialect, an indication of the growing national enchantment with the varieties of English as spoken on this side of the Atlantic.

Twain shared that interest, watched the visitor carefully, and, starting a few years later, based his own lecturing career partly on what he'd learned from Ward's performances.) Finally, after eleven bibulous, hilarious days of palling around with Twain and the rest of the boys, Ward managed to tear himself away from Washoe.

Despite all the progress, in the early 1870s Virginia City still lacked one asset of a first-class town: a reliable water supply. Local water was so alkaline as to make some residents sick, and of those who could stomach it, many cut it with whiskey. Regardless of its quality, water was in short supply. After exhausting the local streams, townspeople had combed the surrounding hills looking for depressions in which snowfall could be trapped, dammed up, and, with the spring melt, released as needed. But as Virginia City grew, these sources became inadequate, and the town suffered frequent water shortages. The Sierra Nevada had plenty of wonderful water, quite a ways off (twenty-five miles) but not prohibitively so. The problem was the lay of the land: between the Sierra peaks and the Virginia range stretched the wide Washoe Valley. But what did the Comstock stand for if not overcoming technological challenges? As one of the Bonanza Kings put it, "Everything can be done nowadays; the only question is—will it pay?"

As they had in dealing with the problem of cave-ins inside the mines, Comstockers turned for help to a German-trained engineer, Herman Schussler, then working in San Francisco. Hired by a private firm, the Virginia and Gold Hill Water Company, Schussler came east, examined the situation, and devised an ingenious solution: an inverted siphon, which would exploit a differential in elevation; the intake in the Sierra would be four hundred sixty-five feet higher than the outtake in the Virginia range. Schussler could rely on gravity to send water down through the pipe, and on the water's own accumulating pressure to push it back up. And what a pipe it was! Made of riveted iron, with an interior diameter of twelve inches, capable of withstanding immense vertical pressure—1,720 feet to be exact, almost twice that under which water had ever been piped before—it issued from wooden flumes on its west end and crossed more than seven miles of the Washoe Valley before connecting with wooden flumes to the east. Although as a whole the valley was flat, up close it was riddled with gulches and boulders, and each section of pipe had to be tailored precisely for its unique position on the route and no other.

Building and testing the great conduit must have made men's pulses race. Here is De Quille describing an early glitch:

> At the first filling of the pipe, a stream of water, about the thickness of a common lead-pencil, escaped through the lead packing of a joint, at a point where the pressure was greatest. This struck against the face of a rock and, rebounding, played upon the upper side of the pipe. The water . . . soon bored a hole through the top of the pipe, and from this hole, which shortly became two or three inches in diameter, a jet of water ascended to the height of two hundred feet or more, spreading out in the shape of a fan toward the top.

Lookouts stationed along the pipeline sent up smoke signals to warn their superiors of the break, the break was repaired, and jubilant citizens turned out on the evening of August 1, 1873 to celebrate the delivery of Sierra water to Virginia City. "The crowd were as wild with joy," said the *Territorial Enterprise*, "as were the Israelites when Moses smote the rock." A second pipeline was laid two years later, assuring the town—and the mines—of ample fresh water.

The new waterworks did little good, however, when fire ravaged Virginia City on October 26, 1875. It started at dawn one day in the dry time of year—in De Quille's memorable phrase, "the whole town was as inflammable as scorched flax"—when the Washoe zephyr was blowing. A fight broke out in "Crazy Kate" Shea's board-inghouse on A Street, behind what is now the county courthouse, and one of the belligerents knocked over an oil lamp. The fire leapt to nearby wooden houses, where it found delicious fuel: interior walls lined with cotton covered with wallpaper, and partitions made of muslin. Fire bells rang, the mines' steam whistles blew, and roused sleepers had to rush out in their nightclothes because their houses were "wrapped in fire before they were aware of their dan-ger." The flames rose into a pyramid. The zephyr scooped up burn-ing shingles and other debris, carrying them east to ignite more buildings. Firemen arrived, but the water they sprayed had no ef-fect. The wind blew stronger, slinging "spiral columns of flame" into the air; observers twenty miles away reported having seen the tops of these flares. The fire was out of control, but no one had to say so: it could speak for itself. Like any mining center, Virginia City was a storehouse of explosives, and the fire advertised its prog-ress with

> a constant roar of exploding cartridges, guns, pistols, fire-crackers, bombs, rockets, and all manner of fireworks, sound-ing like the steady discharge of small arms in a great battle. Amid and above all this din were heard the frequent and star-tling discharges of giant-powder, gunpowder, and Hercules powder, as building after building was blown up in various parts of town.

Some of these blow-ups were intentional, ordered in hopes of making fire-breaks. But the fire rushed on, consuming one land-mark after another: the building in which county business was transacted, the home of the Washoe Club, the International Hotel, the Bank of California, the offices of the *Territorial Enterprise*, Pip-er's Opera House, the Virginia & Truckee Railroad depot, along with scores of residences. In little more than three hours, most of downtown Virginia City was reduced to smoldering foundations and scorched chimneys, and the townspeople were making a last stand to save their common livelihood: the mines. The fire had to be kept away from each and every one of them because of two conditions: the mines' interconnectedness and their infrastructure of timbered cubes. There was no telling how far and long a fire might burn once it entered the shafts, nor how many cave-ins it might cause by consuming those supporting timbers. The men of the town formed bucket brigades and threw earth into mine shafts in an effort to plug them up.

The town's hopes came to depend on what happened around St. Mary in the Mountains Catholic Church, the town's largest, which stood in the fire's path down to the mines. Whether the church was sacrificed to the mines is a subject of debate, as is the role of Bonanza King John Mackay in the controversy. There is evidence that St. Mary's was dynamited to serve as a firebreak, and in the most colorful version of the story Mackay snaps back at a pious old Irish lady who begs him not to do this: "Damn the church, we can build another one if we can keep the fire from going down the shafts." What's certain is that the church roof caved in, taking the steeple with it, and the brick walls served as the needed barrier to the fire's advance. Whether or not Mackay had a hand in ruining St. Mary's, he dug deep into his pockets to help pay for its reconstruction. (His wife was known for her charity work in Virginia City, and their son contributed money to the University of Nevada; to this day, the Mackay School of Mines on the Reno campus sets the family apart from the other Bonanza Kings, who gave nothing back to Nevada.)

In the end, only three people are known to have been killed, but hundreds were left homeless, and more than 2,000 buildings, valued at $10 million, were lost. Although two mills had been destroyed, as well as over a million feet of timber, for the most part the mines themselves had been spared. Relief supplies began arriving the following morning, while in San Francisco the news drove the stock exchange into a sharp decline; later in the day, however, revised information calmed fears, and the market rallied. The restoration of

Virginia City began almost immediately, and when a tornado struck a week later, destroying some of the partially rebuilt structures, people just shrugged and started over. "In sixty days after the fire," wrote De Quille, "the principal streets running through the burned districts were again lined with business houses, the majority of which were of a better class than those destroyed. . . ." In an outburst of alliteration, he compared the rebuilt downtown to "a new patch placed on an old pair of pantaloons."

De Quille's chapter on the fire brings his book *The Big Bonanza* to a bravura close, with a final paean to his fellow citizens: "the great work of rebuilding [was] so speedily accomplished that a new town seemed to spring up out of the ground." But speed wasn't the rebirth's only notable characteristic. In putting themselves back together, the residents of Virginia City also showed chutzpah. To house the county government, they commissioned a prestigious San Francisco architectural firm to submit three designs; they went with the most expensive model, which stands to this day as a monument to civic gumption. As for private industry, at the end of the year the Bonanza Kings demonstrated why they were deemed royal. Never mind that the fire had cost their Consolidated Virginia mine $800,000 worth of buildings, timber, and supplies; to the astonishment of shareholders and financial markets alike, the mine declared a dividend.

❦ FIVE ❦

Capitalists Behaving Badly

Nevada reporter and editor Wells Drury made a curious observation about the self-image of miners:

People who live in mining regions have a theory, amounting to a superstition, that money made in mining is cleaner than money made in almost any other way. There may be no valid foundation for such belief, but it is well nigh universal, down among the ravines where the stamp-mills roar, and along the sloping reaches of the placer diggings. The idea seems to prevail that the miner who digs metal out of the ground gets a clear and indefeasible title from the Creator, higher and brighter than any that can be obtained from the result of bargaining and chaffering in markets, big and little, or in matching wits even in the highest forums. The miner feels himself to be in partnership with the Dread Power that threw up the vast mountain ranges and tossed them about so carelessly that sometimes occur prodigious rifts—subterranean chambers, broad and deep—like the ones which eons ago opened along the side of old Mount Davidson on the Comstock Lode and which in the course of the ages, by the process of volatilization, condensation and precipitation, became filled up, and grew into the marvelous body of ore known in history as the Big Bonanza. It is a cardinal belief of the miner that in rescuing the precious metal from rock or gravel he is harming no man, but is actually lending a helping hand to Providence in the work of benefiting all humankind. That is why the miner habitually speaks of the proceeds of his industry as "clean money."

That paragraph made it into print in 1936, several decades ahead of America's great environmental awakening. We now know that, unless done with great care, hard-rock mining can ravage landscapes and pollute streams; but like most of his contemporaries (and predecessors), Drury was either oblivious of those truths or disregarded them in the belief that Nature would bounce back quickly on her own.

In its time, then, the notion that the miner thought of himself as doing God's work may have rung true. Anyone who enjoys a run of luck at the poker table or the slot machines probably feels much the same way: hooked up to some elemental and benevolent force, singled out by Fortune as a "pure" conduit for her favors. But one can't help wondering how long the mine-owners' sense of cleanliness lasted, because after "rescuing the precious metal from rock and gravel" so many of them turned right around and soiled themselves in processing and selling and transporting the stuff. It wasn't mining per se that got so many Comstock nabobs dirty; it was what they did next.

The first wave of miscreants was a group of California financiers led by William Chapman Ralston, head of the Bank of California in everything but title; and William Sharon, his field agent. Although working closely together, they played strikingly different roles. In San Francisco, Ralston came across as a benevolent father figure, boosting the city he loved with free-spending bonhomie, whereas in Virginia City Sharon was a cagey overseer, pugnaciously maximizing profits for distant investors in the bank he served. Each man might have been cast for his part: Ralston with his stocky figure, clergyman's features, and affable ways; Sharon with his beady eyes, bristly moustache, and manipulative bent. Until the chaotic last few months of Ralston's life, just about everybody loved him. Sharon had his partisans, too: in her memoir of life in Virginia City, Mary McNair Mathews claimed that "he had a heart for every poor person who went to him, and I think most of his charities were given in secret." But that was a minority view. The acerbic journalist Ambrose Bierce gave voice to the consensus in his poem "Three Kinds of a Rogue," which accused Sharon of being "ambitious of immortal shame" and ended with this scathing apostrophe:

> Sharon, some years, perchance, remain of life—
> Of vice and greed, vulgarity and strife;
> And then—God speed the day if such His will—
> You'll lie among the dead you helped to kill,
> And be in good society at last,
> Your purse unsilvered and your face unbrassed.

A pithier detractor of Sharon summed him up as a "scrawny little Midas."

Ralston and Sharon teamed up during a time of crisis. Each year from 1861 to 1863 had seen a doubling of the gross Comstock product; but the rate had dropped sharply in 1864, and Nevada entered the Union with its raison d'etre mired in a Lode-wide slump (even so, the mines' total yield for 1864 was a cool $16 million). The easy pickings—ore lodged near the surface—had all been grabbed. There might be more wealth lower down, but testing that proposition would require further sizable investments of labor and capital, and risk-takers were suddenly scarce.

Originally from Ohio, Ralston had moved to San Francisco in 1854 and done well for himself as part-owner of a steamship company. In June of 1864, after several years of investing in the Comstock, followed by service as treasurer of the Ophir and the Gould & Curry mines and hands-on experience as a banker, he founded the Bank of California in San Francisco with an established Sacramento businessman, Darius Ogden Mills. In what became a standard Ralston move, he insisted that Mills take the title of bank president while he, Ralston, stayed in the background, officially the cashier but actually the brains. With startup capital of $2 million, the new enterprise was immediately the biggest bank in the West.

Sharon was another Ohioan with a background in transportation by water: at age seventeen, he'd bought a flatboat. But it was wrecked on the Ohio River, and he lost his investment, the first of several wipeouts in his turbulent early career. He picked himself up, studied law, migrated to San Francisco, and went into real estate, earning a reputation for astute dealing and cutthroat poker-playing. He invested in mining stocks. His most spectacular failure came in 1864, when he poured his entire savings, $150,000, into Comstock certificates and lost it all.

But Ralston saw qualities he liked in the 43-year-old bankrupt, intelligence certainly, and perhaps the ruthlessness that Ralston himself lacked. Sharon's card-playing was also a plus (a contemporary praised him for his "bewildering bluffs and high-class technique"), and on hearing that Sharon usually won, Ralston said, "He sounds like the very man I want." Ralston first signed up Sharon for a one-shot deal: go see what he could salvage from a failed Virginia City bank in which the Bank of California had invested. Not only did Sharon perform this task well; he studied local conditions, decided that the Lode had so much promise that the Bank of California should open a branch in Virginia City, and nominated himself to run it. Ralston persuaded a reluctant board of directors to agree, and the bank's new Virginia City agent immediately made his presence felt there: setting up shop on the second floor of an existing building, hosting after-hours poker games, entering birds in cock-fighting contests, and playing his fiddle. His energy and glad-handing brought in customers, including miners needing to cash their checks. Sharon got the mining companies to stagger their paydays, but even so the check-cashing took a toll on bank employees. A teller explained how he used to handle the transactions: "The hours were long and the work exhausting, practically consuming the entire day and most of the evenings of the week. . . . I paid the checks thus presented, hour after hour, with a brace of half-cocked revolvers under the counter ready for service."

Sharon began lending money to mine owners at two percent per month, a welcome departure from the going rate of three to five percent. Some analysts have seen this as the opening move in a Machiavellian campaign informed by inside knowledge and waged with clockwork timing. In this reading, Sharon and Ralston had reason to suspect that the way to score on the Comstock was to dig deep, judged that owners couldn't scrape up enough capital (from the Bank of California or anywhere else) to sustain such demanding work over the long haul, and intuited that borrowers would default on their loans and the Bank would end up owning and operating most of the valuable mines. Seems unlikely. Cut-rate lending is just the sort of tactic an embryonic bank would adopt to establish itself. The novelty—and here Sharon called upon his gambler's nerve—lay in applying such a risky move to the inherently dicey business of mining. For that matter, it looked like no go at first: when payments fell due and most borrowers couldn't make them, Mills, the bank's president, wanted to close down the Virginia City branch after little more than a year in business.

Mills had reason to be wary. This was 1865, and a nationwide postwar depression was exacerbating the local slump; Virginia City was losing population; and Mills had always viewed mining as too flaky an endeavor for a bank to support. But Ralston not only stressed that historically silver booms lasted longer than gold ones but also pointed out how intertwined San Francisco's economy and the Comstock had come to be: the San Francisco Stock and Exchange Board had been organized primarily to handle mining-stock transactions, and pulling out of Virginia City would look like a vote of no confidence in the industry. Sharon drew upon his knowledge of the Comstock to argue that plenty of shallow-lying ore had been overlooked and could be mined profitably. Furthermore, he said, there was no reason to think the Lode petered out uniformly at five hundred feet, the depth at which most companies had encountered logistical problems and stalled. Then Sharon made an audacious proposal: rather than pull back from Virginia City, the bank should stick around, take over mines from defaulting owners, and produce ore itself. Mills resisted the idea, giving in only after Sharon and Ralston pledged to protect the bank against losses: the takeovers would have their personal guarantees.

To restore confidence, Sharon coaxed an optimistic letter out of the state mineralogist and opened a second bank branch in adjacent Gold Hill. He sent miners down deep into the bank's newly acquired Yellow Jacket mine, where they found profitable ore. Mining stocks began to recover, the population of Virginia City stabilized, and the bank built and moved into its own offices there. Although far removed from the action physically, Ralston tried to keep tabs on Sharon. In a letter that shows the mentor's two faces, Ralston cautioned Sharon to go easy with a mine superintendent named Isaac Requa because "he owns too much 'Chollar' for us to make an enemy of him. Give him sugar and molasses at present, but when our time comes give him vinegar of the sharpest kind. He is our friend, and I think will assist us. But go slow in all your operations and do nothing without consulting me."

Whether foreseen or not, several mines defaulted, and the bank took them over. Meanwhile, Sharon had discovered a way to obtain control of even sound operations, by making small loans to their stockholders. His rival, Adolph Sutro, the businessman-cum-reporter who had stayed on to become a force on the Comstock, explained how this worked: "Everybody speculates, every miner, or chambermaid, or washerwoman, and as soon as they get into one stock they want to speculate in other stock, and they have to pawn it, and the Bank of California, a regular pawn-broker shop, loans money on them. . . . When the election comes off, all this stock stands in the name of the Bank of California."

Sharon began acquiring mills, too, often after having reduced them to idleness by sending ore from bank-owned mines to be milled elsewhere. Soon, however, he was taking the opposite tack: the bank would give credit only to mines willing to feed their ore exclusively to bank-owned mills. Next (and if you want to accuse Sharon of channeling Machiavelli, here is the place to do so) he pondered the fragmented state of Comstock ownership, with dozens of partners in the bank and often hundreds of stockholders in a single mine. Why divide profits up into so many piddling shares? Why not create a separate entity to run the milling business, with a small, select group cutting slices out of that freshly baked pie? Under Sharon's guidance, he and six cronies formed the Union Mill and Mining Company.

A principle of accounting led him to his next idea. Expenses must be paid before profits can be declared, and milling was an expense of the mining business. This meant that the milling group would be getting its cut ahead of the mine's stockholders. As Sharon continued to study the fiscal relationships, he saw the conclusion toward which his scheming had been leading him. Suppose you thought of mines as existing not so much to disgorge silver as to keep mills busy and profitable. By working the mills extra hard and billing the mines accordingly—$12 per crushed ton was the going rate—you could divert revenue to the fortunate few who owned the mill while mine stockholders and even bank investors had to wait their turn. Sharon and his pals, in other words, didn't mind if high milling expenses reduced their profits as mine owners because, as mill owners, they were butting into line and raking it in early.

Finally, Sharon perfected his scheme by resorting to outright fraud: he had his workers throw crud in with true ore. Under the new regime, it didn't much matter *what* your mills crushed, just so they *did* crush. John D. Winters, Yellow Jacket superintendent from 1864 to 1870, later owned up to his part in the cheating: "To feed [Sharon's] mills, I've mixed waste rock with the Yellow Jacket ore, till it would scarcely pay for crushing, when the company might have been paying dividends for years." Sharon's deceptions led to such oddities as a two-week period when the Yellow Jacket's profits were $58,000 *less* than its milling expenses. Somehow between 1863 and 1874, the Yellow Jacket produced silver valued at $13 million but paid out dividends of only $2 million.

After two years, Sharon and his cronies owned most of the major Comstock mines along with seventeen mills, and their machinations had earned them a label borrowed from a famous Manhattan political cabal: the Bank Ring. "Everybody was at its mercy," wrote an early Nevada historian. "People despaired of ever escaping from its relentless grasp." Sharon tightened that grasp by stacking the boards of his companies with cronies, some of whom served as trustees of twenty or more mines, and by providing himself with expert intelligence: he retained a crack engineer to roam through the mines, chip out ore samples for assay, and furnish confidential reports.

Relying on these exclusives, Sharon knew just when to buy or sell a given stock. One of his favorite tactics was to go short: sell shares you don't own but are being paid for at today's market price; you agree to deliver them at a specified later date, gambling that the price will decline between now and then, in which case the difference will go into your pocket. (The buyer makes the opposite bet: that the price will go up in the interim, so that, after taking possession, he can turn around and sell the stock for a profit.) For Sharon, though, selling short wasn't that much of a risk; not only did he know more than anyone else, but he could engage in backstage maneuvering, such as inveigling reporters to praise or badmouth a stock, until it behaved as he wanted it to. He also built upon his success as a miller by branching out into other industries. It wasn't long before he'd strung together one of the first examples of a vertical monopoly, in which a parent firm controls most or all of the stages in manufacture and distribution, from raw materials to end product. Sharon's new acquisitions included timber companies, sawmills, steamship lines, and short-line railroads—all of which did ample business with the Ring's mines—and he set his sights on building a full-scale railroad.

In all, it was an impressive bag of tricks, and few observers were able to take its full measure. One who did, however, was Sutro, who in 1872 poured out most of that bag's contents in damning testimony before a committee of the U.S. House of Representatives:

The great game is this: By having control of a mine, they know exactly what is going on in that mine. If it contains but a little good ore, or low-grade ore, it sells at a low rate. They keep watching it; these superintendents have men in the mine watching; and when a body of ore is struck, they are shut up at once. Nobody is allowed to go in there except the few men who are digging. They put a bulkhead across. They just prospect it sufficiently to find out what it amounts to, and keep the men down there digging away, and treating them in splendid manner (they give them champagne). The moment they find there is ore down there, they telegraph in cipher to San Francisco . . . and buy up the stock. And sometimes the ring goes to work and breaks down [i.e., drives down the price of] the stock before they buy; they start the miners in drifts in the wrong direction, and say there has been a cave[in], for fear anything would leak out about it. They take out poor ore, or bed rock, which necessitates assessments, and thus runs the stock down. Everybody that owns stock is assessed, and they get it all in the end.

That may be a bit overheated, and the pronouns can be confusing (just take most "theys" as simply referring to the bad guys at the

Bank of California). But it gives a sense of the range of deceptions and power plays open to an unscrupulous owner, which the Bank Ring surely was, as well as of how infuriating its misdeeds could be to outsiders.

Back in San Francisco, Ralston had been distancing himself from Sharon's Comstock maneuvers. True, the bank had a dizzying amount of capital tied up in the Silver State (at one point, $3 million out of the $5 million total was out on loan to Comstock mines) and although some new ore deposits had turned up, no full-fledged bonanza had raised its sparkling head. But powered by assessments, revenues were mounting up, and Sharon excelled at gaming the stock market, so why worry? Ralston had better things to think about, especially developing and rigging out the city he loved with a paternal ardor. He helped finance the construction of dry docks and the extension of the city's boundaries by reclaiming land from the bay. One of his dreams was to make up for San Francisco's distance from the rest of the country by making it self-sufficient, and to that end he used Comstock money to found or control companies producing railroad cars, woolens, sugar, watches, furniture, wine, silk, and tobacco. He started a real-estate firm and backed a drama company headed by Shakespearean actors, for whom he built a theater; he gave to and raised funds for charities. With a partner, Asbury Harpending, he invested in the four-hundred-room Grand Hotel at Market and Montgomery Streets.

Across from the Grand, Ralston began building an even more magnificent hotel, the Palace, a seven-story, eight-hundred-room Gargantua encompassing 2.5 acres and ultimately costing $7 million. (The original Palace burned down after the 1906 earthquake; the one now on the same site was built in 1909.) Rather than pile up more statistics, let's zero in on two facets of the hotel's splendor. First, the latest in gadgetry, with which Ralston had a boyish fascination. The plans for the Palace called for:

all sorts of electrical novelties, including clocks; the latest devices for fire protection—a thermostatic bulb in every room and hallway that would indicate in the central office the location of any excessive rise in heat; an annunciator for each floor; a "tube receptacle" for mail leading to a letter box in the main office; an intramural pneumatic dispatch tube for messages and packages, connecting to all floors; 2,042 ventilating tubes running from all rooms to the roof; an electrical indicator registering the watchman's rounds in the main office; and to supplement the seven staircases, five hydraulic elevators.

And, second, consider the dinner service, to the assembling of which he devoted an ungodly amount of attention. Among its trappings were: "9,000 Haviland plates and a corresponding number of matching pieces. The gold service . . . serves 100. Besides Bavarian china, it includes flatware, glassware, and every conceivable accessory from horseradish holders and cigar lighters to stands for quill toothpicks."

Extend that level of detail in every conceivable direction, and you'll have some idea of the sumptuous scale on which Ralston designed and furnished his Palace. The *San Francisco Chronicle* mocked the excesses by claiming that the Palace kept 25,000 bellboys waiting in a basement holding pen. "When a bell is rung by some impatient lodger . . . , a bellboy . . . is put in a pneumatic tube and whisked right to the room designated by the bell-dial." The hotel's chief contribution to the city, however, may have been the fine French cuisine it introduced, the concoctions of a chef lured away from Delmonico's in Manhattan and the foundation on which San Francisco's venerable tradition as an eater's paradise was built. (Sadly, Ralston never got to smack his lips over those vittles; before the hotel could open, he was dead.)

Like the tycoon in the "L'il Abner" comic strip whose slogan was "What's good for General Bullmoose is good for the USA," Ralston talked himself into believing that these lavish projects weren't just schemes to flatter his ego and fatten his purse but also civic boons, and probably some of them were. Yet his patriotism hardly stopped him from seeing to his own luxury. For himself and his family, he bought and expanded an Italianate villa, Belmont, twenty-two miles south of the city, fluffing it up into an ornately landscaped showcase at which he gave Lucullan feasts and organized romping entertainments. To provision it, he bought his own steamer, the *Brisk*. He got himself there, however, by coach-and-four, which he drove like a hippodrome charioteer, often starting out at the same time as the San-Francisco-to-San-Jose train, which he liked to race. Despite making two pit-stops to change horses, he usually won; his ace in the hole was a long stretch of road near the end, specially resurfaced with crushed rock to give his horses better footing. To work off tension—and his multifarious life had plenty of it—he took afternoon swims in the ocean. As San Francisco ripened into Queen of the West, Ralston took on the role of Prince-Consort.

The full-scale railroad that Sharon built, the Virginia & Truckee, still runs for a couple of touristy miles, from Virginia City to Gold Hill and back. These days, riders on the two-car train might pass a flamboyant pedestrian along the right-of-way: a grizzled codger wearing jeans with suspenders over a flannel shirt and leading a mule. *Too perfect*, the passenger might think, a moment before realizing that this is an actor playing a part. Later in the day, Ye Old Miner might be found working C Street, happy to be photographed with his mule, for a "donation." Like the train itself—like virtually everything in Virginia City now—he is a prop in the world of tourism.

Plans are afoot to rebuild the railroad to its full length, duplicating its sinuous path down the mountains to the Carson River and then, after a sharp western turn, to the terminus at Carson City, for a total of twenty-one miles. (That was the original route: an extension to Reno and a number of spurs came later.) Coiled around the mountains like an anaconda, the right of way made "the equivalent of seventeen complete circles" while negotiating the 1,575-foot differential between Virginia City and the Carson Valley. Dan De Quille called it "undoubtedly the crookedest railroad in the United States—probably the crookedest in the world," and the repeated double entendre was surely intentional. The ostensible reason for bringing the nineteenth-century's cardinal technology to Virginia City had been to lower costs to the point where it made sense to go after medium-grade ore, while at the same time reducing the congestion caused by legions of wagons hauling supplies into and ore out of town. Once built, the V&T became the cornerstone of the Bank Ring's empire; its hierarchy included Sharon (president) and Ralston (treasurer).

But the line actually began as a defensive maneuver. Starting in 1860, Comstockers were enrapt by another transportation scheme, advanced by a former tobacco salesman who owned an amalgamating mill in nearby Dayton. This was the ubiquitous Adolph Sutro, who proposed tunneling through the mountains to drain and ventilate the mines, then installing tracks along which mules would pull cars laden with ore for delivery to mills in Dayton and elsewhere in the Carson Valley, all the while collecting various fees.

At first, the Bank Ring had heartily endorsed this scheme, but Sutro's undiplomatic way of promoting it gave them pause. (For more about Sutro and his lonely crusade, see Chapter 7.) Why let this Herr Doktor Upstart isolate the bank's mills and downgrade what had become the bank's town? Why pay tariffs to an outsider? Why shouldn't the bank itself go into the transportation business? Sharon's answer to those questions was to conceive of the Virginia & Truckee and also to reverse course: he and the bank came out against the tunnel. He pressured other mine owners and superintendents to fall in line, and he made a pariah of Sutro. Sharon coaxed newspapers friendly to the Bank Ring to make glowing predictions of prosperity to come, and the counties along the planned route agreed to subsidize the project. Ground for the V&T was broken on February 18, 1869, and the last spike was pounded into place in mid-November. Teamsters tried to hang on by cutting their rates, but Sharon ran most of them out of business.

On the strength of those subsidies, Sharon was able to fulfill a promise he'd made, to reduce regional transportation costs (the price of wood dropped from $15 to $11.50 a cord, the price of hauling ore from $3.50 to $2 per ton, and overall costs were down twenty-seven percent by the end of 1870) while still making a handsome profit for the bank. But his maneuvers did not go unnoticed. Critics charged that he and his cronies had hoodwinked the public: by one estimate, the Ring had parlayed a mere $42,000 investment into a railroad worth almost $3 million. (Sharon boasted of having "built that road without it costing me a dollar.") It was Sharon himself, though, who usually took the rap, not the Bank of California, and in any case little could be done to straighten things out now. At the same time, Sharon had grown so rich personally that in 1870 he bailed out Ralston, his overextended sponsor, by covering $4 million worth of Ralston's overdrafts on the bank. A comment (in mock-Irish dialect) published in the *Territorial Enterprise* gives a sense of how complete the bank's ascendancy now was: "Bejabers! The whole of Virginia is comprised in two blocks, and them two blocks consist of one corner, and that corner is the Bank of California." Sharon felt so giddy that, when he thought no one was looking, he left the Comstock and took up residence in San Francisco.

But the Comstock was both too big and too fragmented to be dominated by one man, no matter how canny and ruthless; and the Lode could be moody. No amount of insider knowledge, hyping of news, and jiggering of financial relationships could overcome a protracted borrasca, such as the one that gripped the mines in the late 1860s. Production dropped steadily from the $16 million of 1864 to $8 million in 1870, causing a chain reaction of bankruptcies and another bleeding of population. The region needed a bonanza, and got one. When it came, however, Sharon saw part of the profits fall into other hands.

Among the mines controlled by the Bank of California was the Crown Point, which appeared to have played out. In 1867, however, the mine's superintendent, John P. Jones, discovered a deep vein of rich ore. Bypassing the bank, he sought out one of its wealthier backers, a relative by marriage named Alvinza Hayward. Together, they bought Crown Point stock cheap, they bought it dear, and either way they bought it secretly. Sharon caught on eventually, but the predators had struck at a time when the bank was strapped (mostly thanks to Ralston, who shook it like a personal piggy bank to make ever more lavish commitments to his civic projects) and providing limited income. Jones and Hayward amassed enough shares to seize control of the Crown Point. Adhering to the Ralston–Sharon formula for success, the pair formed their own Nevada Mill and Mining Company.

But the resilient Sharon tried to salvage something from the defeat. He knew that the Crown Point abutted another previously disappointing mine, the Belcher. Reasoning that any treasure on one side might spill over into the other, he offered to sell his new rivals his interest in the Crown Point if they would sell him theirs in the Belcher. They agreed, paying Sharon $1.4 million in June of 1871, the largest amount of money ever to change hands in a private transaction on the Comstock. Sharon was soon vindicated: the Crown Point bonanza did indeed jut into Belcher territory. By all rights, in fact, it was the Belcher Bonanza: the Crown Point ended up producing $25.8 million, its "little brother" $31.8 million. And together they delivered the much-needed regional godsend. Fear that the Lode had seen its best days had been gnawing at Comstockers, but the dual bonanza revived their spirits.

Jones had almost outfoxed the master, but not quite. Sharon's next opponents were to fare better (we'll save this part of the story, in which the Bonanza Kings hold sway, for the next chapter), but in the meantime the Comstock lived. It had been a close call, though. Without the Crown Point–Belcher bonanzas, what one native son called "the darkest year in the history of the Comstock up to that time" would probably have ended with the collapse of the Bank of California, the enormous deposits in the Lode's lower levels would have gone unmined, and the Comstock saga would be far less colorful than it is.

Sharon's lapses of attention may have been accentuated by his new-found interest in Nevada politics. To say that he was not a natural politician is to be guilty of gross understatement: when the Nevada Republican Party lost its hold on the state in the 1870 election, analysts blamed the voters' dissatisfaction on anti-Sharon animus: wags were mocking him as "the Great King." But he hadn't been a candidate himself. In 1872 he decided to have that experience, announcing his bid for a seat in the U.S. Senate.

He wasn't the only Comstocker vying for the prize: his adversary Jones, the Crown Point multimillionaire, entered the race, too, also as a Republican. Despite having once lost a race for lieutenant-governor of California, Jones had a gift for politics and, like Sharon, enough scratch to bankroll a serious campaign. Until the Seventeenth Amendment to the Constitution was ratified in 1913, United States senators were elected not by popular vote but by state legislatures, so a candidate had to do two difficult things at once: appeal to the populace and court politicians running their own races. In addition to funding his own campaign, the wise senatorial candidate would help defray those lesser lights' expenses, and by the time it was all over in January of 1873, Jones had poured somewhere between $500,000 and $800,000 into the race.

The fact that the seat in question had an incumbent, James W. Nye, didn't bother the two aspirants. The *Territorial Enterprise* threw its support behind Jones, whose nickname, "The Commoner," alluded to his humble Welsh origins. Sharon retaliated by buying himself a newspaper, the *Gold Hill News*, and installing a handpicked editor, Alfred Doten.

The ensuing campaign was base even by the low standards of the nineteenth-century West. The Bank Ring played into Jones's hands by faking a discovery in the Savage mine via a familiar but dramatic technique: locking miners underground to keep news of a glorious strike from getting out (only in this case, there was no glorious strike, and the Ring very much wanted the news to get out: phony news, which would drive up the stock price). San Francisco papers were so taken in that they excoriated the Ring—and its main Comstock man, Sharon—for its "hogging game"; Sharon was being blamed, in other words, for his part in bottling up a nonexistent bonanza. Sharon retaliated by spreading a rumor about Jones and the 1869 Yellow Jacket mine fire, which had taken the lives of more than forty men. As superintendent at the time, the story went, Jones had either set the fire himself or known what was happening and done nothing to stop it, in a heinous effort to cause a stock-market crash and then buy up shares at bargain-basement prices—all of which was balderdash. The newspapers hurled charges and countercharges: Sharon had bribed Jones's accusers to implicate him; no, Jones's accusers had tried to blackmail Sharon.

Doten gave it his best, but he was no match for Joe Goodman, the *Enterprise*'s witty editor. Goodman had shown he could wield elaborate invective in an editorial that greeted Sharon on his first campaign stop in Virginia City:

You are probably aware that you have returned to a community where you are feared, hated and despised. . . . Your career in Nevada for the past nine years has been one of merciless rapacity. You fostered yourself upon the vitals of the State like a hyena, and woe to him who disputed with you a single coveted morsel of your prey. . . . You cast honor, honesty, and the commonest civilities aside. You broke faith with men whenever you could subserve your purpose by so doing.

But Goodman was even better at the quick jab. When the *News* erroneously credited Sharon with having fought for the Union army in the Civil War, the *Enterprise* referred to the banker as "William Tecumseh Sharon." The ridicule wore Sharon down. Pleading ill health, he withdrew from the race, and Jones was elected.

But Sharon was determined not to be cast aside a second time. Unable to beat the *Enterprise*, in 1874 he bought it; thereafter, it, too, hewed to a pro-Sharon line. (The ousted Goodman went west to edit the *San Francisco Post*; later he started a literary magazine and immersed himself in archaeology. His brilliance carried over to that field nicely: after seven years of study, he deciphered the Mayan calendar and collaborated on a method of dating Mayan sites which is still used today.)

With his millions to draw upon, the bank to support him, and Virginia City's most influential paper to fawn over him, Sharon ran for the Senate again in 1874. As before, he had an incumbent to reckon with: Bill Stewart, no less. Stewart had performed loyally for his chief protector, the Bank of California, but with a bank insider now in the running, he was expendable. He chose not to seek a third term. (In his *Reminiscences*, Stewart skipped over the bank's dissuading role and cited financial troubles brought on by his mining ventures, "many of which proved disastrous." True enough.) Sutro took time out from his tunneling to run as an independent populist, and Sharon had a rough time on the hustings. Speaking at the Virginia City opera house one night, he defended his campaign expenditures by saying, "You know I can't take my money with me." Someone in the audience shouted out, "If you did it would burn."

But Senator Jones closed ranks with his former enemy, money talked, and the Republicans won a majority in the legislature. Not until two weeks afterward did Sharon permit his daughter Clara to marry her fiancé, a young Nevada lawyer named Francis Newlands, in San Francisco. Had the wedding taken place before the election, it would have drawn voters' attention to the fact that William Sharon, Great King of the Comstock, didn't live there anymore.

The legislators still had to cast their votes for senator, and the *Virginia Evening Chronicle* waged an eleventh-hour campaign to deny Sharon the prize, charging that if elected he would make himself scarcer than he already was. In January the Nevada assembly debated the fine points of whether Sharon lived in the state. The Democrats may have had the facts on their side, but the Republicans had the votes. Stamping Sharon "Made In Nevada," they sent him to the nation's capital. He'd paid an estimated $800,000 for the coveted seat.

It all turned out to be a waste. Not Virginia City but Washington, D.C., was the town where Sharon made himself a stranger. He'd sought office mostly to appease his vanity, and he soon learned how insignificant a freshman senator can be. Besides, the West demanded his presence. The bank was in need of rescue, his own portfolio needed special care (he was in the process of sailing from the stormy seas of mining stocks into the calm harbor of real estate), and he could hardly be expected to dawdle in Washington, fooling around with tariff bills and whatnot. The poetical Ambrose Bierce had imagined Sharon being ignored by the Senate's presiding officer, who "only sought him when too loud he snored." But Bierce's aim was a bit off: Senator Sharon's snores were far more likely to erupt in San Francisco than in the Senate chamber. Once, when Sharon returned to Washington after a long absence, the *Carson Valley News* paraphrased a stinging remark by the secretary of the Senate: "if Sharon asks for back pay, he shall decline paying him until legally advised so to do, as no case of this kind has been presented of late years." "[Sharon's] record of inaction is unbelievable," summed up Nevada historian Russell Elliott. "He was seated at only five sessions and was recorded on less than 1 percent of all roll calls. He never introduced a bill."

The do-nothing senator did nothing for a full six years, at the end of which he faced another Comstock millionaire desirous of attaching a Senate bangle to his charm bracelet. This was the Bonanza King James Fair, who'd grown rich enough to match Sharon's expenditures dollar-for-dollar, and the dollar-matching rose to dizzying heights. "In the entire history of Nevada politics," wrote an editor of the *Carson Appeal*, "there had never been such a saturnalia of corruption." Fair ran as a Democrat not because of any particular affinity with that party ("I hardly knew which party I belonged to," he admitted), but simply because their nomination was available.

To regain the advantage, Sharon tried every tactic he could devise. Fair, he charged, "says he is an actual resident of Nevada. These words were penned at his place on Nob Hill. . . . They think he possesses the means to purchase or oppress the voters of Nevada. . . . It makes the blood curdle in my veins that a man should perpetrate such a crime." The brazenness of that almost takes the breath away, but Fair shook it off. Employees of Bonanza mines were given election day off, at full pay; they mustered out to vote for "their" candidate, and because this was before the introduction of the secret ballot, any miner who voted for Sharon's ticket would have done so at the risk of his job. Not surprisingly, the Fair ticket won. Sutro waded in at the last minute, in January of 1881, trying to deny Fair his seat by a scheme in which a state legislator would go public with details of Fair's payment for the legislator's vote: $5,000. The ensuing scandal, it was presumed, would force the other assemblymen to dump Fair and turn to Sutro himself instead. But the bribee got cold feet, and Fair was duly elected. Not that Nevada gained anything from changing horses. During his single term, Fair succeeded only in giving Sharon a good run for the title of Least Seen Senator. (The highest "compliment" ever paid Fair as a legislator was that "during his term he was industrious in endorsing and forwarding anti-Chinese legislation.")

Unlike his protégé, Ralston had no political aspirations. He was too engrossed in juggling the books of his various companies (the bank very much included), boosting and building San Francisco, raising funds for his favorite charities, and racing the choo-choo to San Jose. More impresario than true banker, he silenced doubters by charming them with his boyish enthusiasm, and he'd enjoyed a remarkable string of luck. Whenever his grandiose dealings had pushed the bank to the brink of failure, a new Comstock find or a surge in mining stocks had come along to save him. His public image was epitomized in a gushing remark made by his own lawyer: "Of all her public possessions, California owned nothing more precious than Ralston."

But Public Possession #1 suffered an interrelated series of setbacks after the intercontinental railroad linked the United States from coast to coast in 1868. The firms Ralston had founded to make San Francisco self-sufficient hadn't prospered even while enjoying a West Coast monopoly, and now trains were importing woolens and watches, furniture and tobacco and the like from the East, most of it of higher quality than the homegrown items and competitively priced. Even Ralston's real estate company was on the skids, with nearly $1 million in bills it couldn't pay. At the same time, his profligacy was making a mockery of the Palace Hotel's construction budget. Historian George Bancroft said this of the pile going up on Montgomery Street: "It was carried to completion as regardless of cost as might an Egyptian king have built a pyramid. Its foundation walls were made twelve feet in thickness, and beneath its huge central court was constructed a reservoir containing 650,000 gallons of water."

One might think that somewhere along the line the bank's directors would have fired their ebullient leader, or at least reined him in, but they sat tight: all, that is, but the bank's president, Mills, who'd had enough and resigned. Now Ralston finally assumed the office himself, augmenting his freedom to embezzle and play shell games. And later in the year, the Comstock came through for him. Thanks to Sharon's recovery of his balance in the conflict with Jones, the bank was heavily invested in the Belcher mine, which, as we've seen, went into bonanza, taking other Comstock stocks with it on a giddy upward ride.

The Bonanza Kings made their big strike in 1873, giving Ralston and Sharon another set of rivals. On behalf of the Bank Ring, the pair sought to regain the upper hand by making a replenishing find of their own. The Bonanza Kings' Consolidated Virginia Mine abutted the Ophir, and bonanzas don't recognize claim boundaries. Aiming for a takeover, Sharon and Ralston bought Ophir stock, whose price soared precisely because of its potential to decide who controlled the mine. Sharon also bought Ophir shares for himself. By December of 1874, the Ophir had become yet another Bank of California possession, and the stock was still climbing. Without telling anyone, however, Sharon switched to selling his shares. When the stock dropped as part of a marketwide trend, everybody but Sharon either lost money by selling out or was stuck with deflated Ophir stock. The Ophir's "new" deposits eventually logged in about midway between bonanza and borrasca, but the more ominous point was this: for the first time, the Comstock had failed Ralston, who may have lost as much as $3 million in the flurry of transactions. The episode marked a first for Sharon, too: never before had he acted contrary to his sponsor's interest. Nor was Ralston the only friend of Sharon's burned in the Ophir flame. On hearing the news, one of Sharon's political allies said, "If this be true, the man is a demon and deserves destruction."

Ralston was left squirming in the pit into which he'd dug himself. His latest excess was to build the family a house in San Francisco, at a cost of at least $140,000 (and perhaps as much as $350,000). His own West Coast Furniture Company had gotten so habituated to overcharging customers that it did the same to him, billing him $8,000 for work in the new house's dining room that should have cost $2,000. Ralston's whims were implacable. After quarrelling with his wife, he tried to smooth things over by having a ballroom constructed and attached to the townhouse for a special party; then, in a mission-accomplished moment the morning after the party, he had the ballroom torn down. His brothers warned him to quit taking mining-stock flyers and put his money in conservative stocks and bonds, and Sharon urged the same course. They might have saved their breath. Ralston looked haggard these days and was short-tempered with anyone who crossed him, but he was embroiled in such a frenzy of civic hoopla, cost overruns, and plundered accounts that he couldn't stop, or even slow down. A friend said of him, "The almighty had grown in him until he felt himself a god, whose shrine was set up in San Francisco."

What Sharon knew about Ralston's increasingly reckless behavior and precarious position, and when he knew it, are unclear, but he surely was put on notice in May of 1875, when Ralston tried to sell Sharon his interest in the Palace. The hotel was so dear to Ralston's heart that this could only be a late-innings move by a badly frightened man. Sharon agreed to a $1.75 million deal, then thought better of it and backed out.

In July, Ralston adapted his Potemkin-ballroom trick to banking. To cover a $2 million shortfall, he managed to borrow that amount and have it sitting in the vaults on the day when a committee sent by the board of directors stopped in for an examination. The next day the $2 million was gone, on its way back to the lenders.

Impulsive as ever, Ralston went off on a new tangent. From San Francisco's beginnings until the early twentieth century, finding sources of fresh water for a growing population was a paramount civic mission. A stopgap solution was to harness nearby streams, one of which, Alameda Creek at the bay's southeast end, became the target of the Spring Valley Water Company. Having secured the rights, the company intended to pipe the creek's water across the bay and up the peninsula to San Francisco. Ralston bought a controlling interest in Spring Valley with the expectation that the city would in turn buy it from him, giving him a life-saving profit. But the public got wind of Ralston's scheme and, already socked with the nation's highest water rates, resented it; in a rare departure from the favor he'd long enjoyed as an ostentatiously civic-minded grandee, newspapers attacked him by name. According to the *Bulletin*, the city could have had Spring Valley for $6 million in 1874, and now Ralston was asking $15.5 million for it. The Associated Press warned of gathering clouds in the California skies, and the *New York Commercial Advertiser* sounded a note of derision: "We are afraid that a good many of the Pacific Coast dollars will be found stuffed with straw before their $5,000,000 hotel, $20,000,000 water works, $100,000,000 railroads, and big bonanzas generally are all settled up." Ralston still had his supporters, especially workmen grateful for all the jobs he'd created in San Francisco, but the momentum was shifting. By the time the proposed purchase reached the city's Board of Water Commissioners, the mayor had come out in opposition. The Board voted no.

Stymied, Ralston was reduced to holding a fire-sale of his personal property and ad-libbing a series of secret transactions to keep the bank solvent one day at a time. But his position became wobbly when the stock market fell in August, and bank insiders began withdrawing their money. Next an outsider, Flood of the Bonanza Kings, sent word that they wanted to close their sizable account. (The Kings had their own bank now, the Nevada Bank of San Francisco, with offices there and in Virginia City.) Ralston talked him into holding off for a few days. Even so, by August 23 the scent of trouble had drifted into the nostrils of ordinary depositors, who rushed downtown to close their accounts. To protect the bank against the run, Ralston approached a party that had always been reliable in the past, the Oriental Bank of London. A cable went off to London, but word of the Bank of California's troubles must have already crossed the Atlantic: the Oriental didn't deign to reply. Ralston resorted to more flim-flam, as described by Sharon's biographer, Michael J. Makley:

Using the remnants of his previously incomparable influence, Ralston prevailed upon the president of a depository belonging to various companies to take all available bullion and mint it into coin. On August 25, hoping to quiet nervous depositors, Ralston piled the bank's counters high with new twenty-dollar gold pieces. . . . This time the tactic failed.

Senator Sharon, AWOL from Washington as usual, tried to cajole the Bonanza Kings into taking over the bank, but after looking at the books, their representatives declined.

Sharon himself now joined the deserters. Shortly after the stock exchange opened on August 26, he placed an unlimited order to sell his Comstock holdings. Not only did those stocks fall sharply, but observers assumed the worst: Sharon must be trying to round up cash to prop up the bank against another day's run. But that wasn't it at all; he'd just had enough of Ralston's irresponsibility. When Sharon deposited the proceeds of his sell-off in the Wells Fargo Bank, the public correctly saw this as a bailout by the ultimate insider. That same day, the line of depositors bent on withdrawing their money stretched out the doors and into the street. About twenty minutes before the three o'clock closing time, the bank ran out of cash. Employees were ordered to shut the doors early, leaving customers struggling to get in. The Virginia City and Gold Hill branches closed, too.

Ralston tried to stay upbeat. Calling his employees together, he complimented them for behaving well under pressure and told them not to worry, "for I this night enter into a contract to provide each and every one of you with a first class position." Later he confided to an old friend, "I do not expect to leave much to my children, but I do want to leave them a good name and that no man shall ever say that he lost a dollar by me." But when the bank's directors examined the ledgers, they were appalled; Ralston owed the bank $4 million. Next morning, he executed a deed of trust transferring control of all his property to Sharon, who was to use it to satisfy Ralston's creditors.

A friend who saw Ralston that morning described him as exhibiting "perfect self-possession." He insisted to the board of directors that he could lead the bank out of this morass. But when the board called him into an afternoon meeting and asked for his resignation, he complied without a murmur. Soon afterward, he left the building and headed for North Beach. On the way he ran into a friend, a physician named Pitman. When Ralston mentioned he was going swimming, Dr. Pitman cautioned against it because he seemed overheated. Ralston replied that, on the contrary, his resignation had left him feeling "like a schoolboy off for his holidays." He changed clothes in the Neptune Bath House and dived into the sea. Half an hour later, a swimmer was seen struggling in the water. When rescuers reached him, Ralston was floating facedown. Attempts to revive him failed. He was forty-nine years old.

On hearing the news, San Franciscans wept in public. The *Alta California* eulogized the dead man in Lincolnesque terms: "His was the vast vision of the Builders and his like shall never pass this way again." The *San Francisco Chronicle* charged vaguely that "Mr. Ralston, in the hour of his extremity, and at the moment when he most needed encouragement, was abandoned by those who should have felt their fortunes linked to his own." The *Golden Era* was more specific, blaming Ralston's demise on the Nevada Block (i.e., the Bonanza Kings). He'd been tricked, the newspaper charged, "induced to short the bonanza" while schemers were conspiring to drive stock prices up to lofty heights. "We all know the result. A large proportion of his immense fortune passed to the Nevada Block."

Fired up by such insinuations, a mob formed and attacked the offices of two papers that had been running Ralston down. Out on the Comstock, rumors fueled anxieties already inflamed by remoteness from the venue where these bombshells were landing. "No one, whose coin is not in his absolute possession," the *Gold Hill News* declared, "knows how much he is worth or how utterly bankrupted he may be."

At Ralston's funeral, his fiscal irresponsibility was buried under a heap of what Mark Twain liked to call "flapdoodle." A eulogist with a gift for same intoned:

> Commerce commemorates his deeds with her whitening sails and her laden wharves. There are churches whose heaven-kissing spires chronicle his donations. . . . He was the supporter of art; science leaned on him while her vision swept infinity. The footsteps of progress have been sandaled with his silver. He was the life-blood of enterprise; he was the vigor of all progress; he was the epitome and representative of all that was broadening and expansive and uplifting in the life of California.

Publicly, Sharon professed to be of the same mind. At Ralston's wake, he'd made a sweeping pledge: "All I have I owe to him, and to protect his name and memory, I will spend every dollar of it." But in a less guarded moment, according to the novelist Gertrude Atherton, a granddaughter of the bank's secretary, he delivered a gruff verdict on Ralston's demise: "Best thing he could have done." The facts of Ralston's death lend themselves equally to suicide and to a fatal heart attack or stroke, but Sharon had a point: had Ralston lived, he might have found life unbearable. Yet hadn't Sharon himself been at least partly responsible for his master's downfall?

Makley explains the apparent treachery of Sharon's sell order as an instance of *sauve qui peut*: "Facing the bank's imminent failure, he acted with disregard for his partner. Did he do it with the intent to cause Ralston's demise? The facts suggest only that he was protecting his own wealth. Nevertheless, to his discredit—whatever his motive—his actions precipitated the tragedy." Unless you subscribe to the demonic view of Sharon's character, this sounds about right. He wasn't out to destroy Ralston; he'd simply given up on the man. And that heartless "Best thing he could have done" is consistent with Sharon's card-playing mentality. As every sensible player knows, the time may come when the best move is to swallow your losses and quit the game.

The Bank of California now faced bankruptcy, with likely devastating effects on both Virginia City and San Francisco. Sharon worked assiduously to straighten things out. He put up $1 million of his own money to stave off creditors, and he browbeat Mills into doing the same. In a comforting show of solidarity, Mills also resumed the office of bank president. After Sharon had assured himself that, for all of Ralston's excesses, his estate remained quite valuable, he paid the bank $1.5 million for the dead man's assets and liabilities, with the understanding that anything left over would be Sharon's to keep. He buttonholed prominent businessmen, asking them to form a syndicate and stand behind the bank. "He appealed to the public spirit of some," recalled Sharon's son-in-law Francis Newlands. "He appealed to the pride of others. He encouraged the doubting. He threatened the cowardly." The resulting pledges totaled $7.5 million. Turning to the bank's creditors, Sharon persuaded many of them to settle for fifty cents on the dollar. The once-foundering ship began to right itself.

But some insiders questioned the purity of Sharon's motives. Harpending ran an informal tote of Ralston's assets and came up with "a conservative estimate" of $15 million in value. Another critic judged that the estate could pay all of Ralston's debts in full and still be worth $3 million. Far from it, Sharon replied: in settling Ralston's accounts, he'd been forced to make up substantial deficits. But it didn't help Sharon's credibility that he blocked attempts to inventory the estate. (Among the Ralston interests to which Sharon had succeeded was the Spring Valley Water Company, which remained a family heirloom until 1908.)

To achieve maximum ballyhoo for the bank's reopening, Sharon held it on the same day—October 2, 1875—as the grand opening of the Palace Hotel. The fear had been that the bank's doors would swing open to admit a crowd inflamed by the same desire as on the day of its closing: to get their hands on their money. But most folks showed up in a forgiving mood. "Not a man drew coin from the bank during the day," the *Chronicle* noted approvingly, "who had not immediate necessary use for it." A similar vote of confidence was registered in Comstock country, where the branches reopened to cheers and cannon-fire.

Addressing his guests at the Palace wingding, Sharon said the right things:

In the crowning hour of victory, in the presence of the grand witness of your skill in the mechanical arts in this glorious temple of hospitality, amid all this flood of light and music, I experience a sense of almost overpowering sadness. I miss, as you do, the proud and manly spirit of him who devised this magnificent structure, and under whose direction and by whose tireless energy it has mainly been reared. I mourn, as you do, that he is not with us to enjoy this scene of beauty, and I offer here with you the incense of regret and affection to his memory. Peace be to his ashes!

A cynic might have argued that the speaker deserved a good share of the blame for the reduction of that manly spirit to ashes, but Sharon was entitled to the phrase bestowed by the fellow who'd introduced him that night: "first and foremost in sustaining the credit of the city of San Francisco and the great State of California." With the bank healthy again, the Comstock was primed for another boom, and the fire that destroyed much of Virginia City three weeks later only redoubled the civic determination to march forward.

Sharon now turned his attention to the claims of Ralston's widow,

Lizzie, upon her husband's estate, which he talked her into settling for cash and property worth about $85,000. A Ralston biographer has accused Sharon of preying on Lizzie like a "tiger beetle." Be that as it may, he was now the proud owner of Ralston's beloved Belmont and the Palace Hotel, and rather than choose between them, he and his family moved into both. The hotel prospered, especially after Sharon convinced the city board of equalization to regard it not as a business but "an ornament to the city" and reduce its tax assessment accordingly. Lizzie Ralston came to regret the paltry amount of her settlement, and in 1877 she sued Ralston on multiple grounds, as set out in one of the lengthiest complaints in California judicial history. After two years of contesting the claims, Sharon forked over about $200,000 more, plus a ranch. Lizzie herself was shunted over to Little Belmont, the former residence of the estate's superintendent. Despite his grousing about the burden of Ralston's debts, Sharon ended up with nearly everything his sponsor had owned and a net worth estimated at $20 million. Essentially, he *was* Ralston now, in everything but likeability.

During the final phase of his life, not only did Sharon's deceitful nature catch up with him; he also became the first target of a new tribe of schemers bent on bilking Comstock tycoons. Perhaps the best way to start the story is to focus on a certain covered bridge on San Francisco's Montgomery Street, in the early 1880s. This was the passageway being used by one Sharon possession, Sarah Althea Hill, to sneak from a second, the Grand Hotel, into a third, the Palace Hotel. Without it, Hill would have had to use the street, where the public might have noticed her, with scandal being the likely result. A smashing beauty who came from money and old American stock, Hill didn't fit the stereotype of a hussy. But she seems to have launched her career as a flirtatious mercenary at a young age.

She and Sharon became chummy after he gave her investment

tips and she invited him back to her digs. Soon afterward she moved into the Grand and was regularly tiptoeing across that bridge, protected from prying eyes, to be with Sharon. He was a widower by then, in his late sixties, more than thirty years older than Hill, and so lovestruck that he invited her to Belmont for the marriage of the year 1880: his second daughter, Flora, had reeled in Sir Thomas Fermor-Hesketh, a British baronet whose pedigree and financial standing Sharon had vetted to his satisfaction at a cost of $10,000.

According to Hill, her interhotel visits with Sharon were not illicit, but conjugal. Earlier that year, she claimed, Sharon had paid for another, far more modest wedding, his own to her, and she had a document to prove it. This was after she'd had him arrested on charges of adultery with one Gertie Dietz, although later Hill expanded the list of co-respondents to a total of nine women. Sharon copped to the liaison with Hill, acknowledged the bridge traffic, admitted to paying her $500 a month for her expenses, but denied the marriage. As assorted criminal and civil charges wended their ways through the courts, the press dubbed Hill "the Rose of Sharon."

During most of the ensuing controversy's long life, it consisted of two main strands unrolling on parallel tracks: Hill's divorce petition in the California court system and Sharon's suit to nullify the supposed marriage contract in the federal system. (Sharon had somersaulted into the federal courts by invoking the Constitutional provision giving them jurisdiction over lawsuits between citizens of different states: Hill was a resident of California, and where else could the ex-senator from Nevada be from but Nevada?) In 1884, a state judge found for Hill, granting her a divorce and alimony in the amount of $2,500 a month, but a year later a federal judge came down on Sharon's side, declaring the marriage contract a forgery.

Behind the formal maneuvers, however, lurked a shadow-world of superstition. In her campaign to win the old man over, Hill had consulted a San Francisco sorceress named Mary Ellen "Mammy" Pleasant, one of the few persons of color associated with the Comstock to leave a mark on the historical record. Born a slave, Pleasant had obtained her freedom and then worked on behalf of the Underground Railroad. When abolitionist John Brown was captured, he had with him a letter from Pleasant promising more funding for his revolutionary plots.

While living in New Orleans, Pleasant had studied voodoo with the legendary Marie Laveau. Pleasant never lived in Virginia City, but she visited there, invested in the mines, and tried to influence events by transmitting thought-waves from San Francisco, where she kept a boardinghouse. Under her tutelage, Hill had taken part in a complex ritual calculated to win Sharon's affections. The spell she was casting directed a woman who'd set her cap for a man to wear some of his clothes for nine days and nights (Hill chose scraps of Sharon's underwear), bury them under a corpse in a freshly dug grave between midnight and 1 a.m., and wait. When the buried garb rotted, one of two things would happen: either the desired husband would propose, or he would die. The *Alta California* described an ingredient used by Hill in another ritual as a "single hair from the scanty locks which straggle over the Senatorial brow like railroad routes across a new country." The hair was meant to be sliced and scattered into an omelet that Hill and Sharon would share. (All this came out in one of the court proceedings, much to the audience's titillation.)

As the proceedings expanded and subdivided, sixteen lawyers took part in them, ten for Sharon and six for Hill. Among Sharon's ten was none other than William Stewart, representing the man who had made off with Stewart's Senate seat (nothing softens hard feelings like a fat retainer). Stewart argued that Hill and Sharon had not acted as a married couple would. "Dodging about the corridors of the Grand and Palace Hotels to secure clandestine meetings," the lawyer sniffed, "was no assumption that such meetings were lawful or proper; on the contrary, it was conduct tending to show that the marriage relation did not exist." But Hill's side could point to contrary evidence, such as her being welcomed to Flora

Sharon's wedding. (When a lawyer reminded the court that Sharon had introduced Hill to other wedding guests as a respectable woman, Sharon churlishly replied: "I spoke of her simply as Miss Hill. I said nothing about her respectability.") Testimony was given by warring handwriting analysts and an expert in all things papery, who opined that certain words in the senator's love letters had been blotted out and written over. *The Wasp*, a satirical San Francisco weekly, likened it all to a dime novel, although no hack writer would have dared frame such a tawdry and convoluted plot. The sixteen lawyers created a monster that sent out far-reaching tentacles:

> Secondary skirmishes involved several of the participants in trials for perjury, obscenity, embezzlement, disbarment, battery, unpaid bills, procuring false affidavits, desecration of a gravesite to obtain pertinent evidence, contempt of court, and criminal libel. When a witness and her son both drew pistols during the primary court battle, the judge ruled that everyone in attendance had to be searched before entering the courtroom.

For the two principals, the case became an obsession. Hill threatened more than one lesser participant with bodily harm, and Sharon was having angina pains. He even quit playing poker. His surviving children, Fred and Flora, stayed far away from the circus (Clara Sharon Newlands had died in 1882).

The California Supreme Court upheld the divorce ruling, but Sharon kept battling until his death in November of 1885; only the week before, he'd made his son and son-in-law swear they would never give in to Hill. Sharon left his estate in trust to his children and grandchildren, freezing Hill out. A month later, federal judge Mathew P. Deady, an old friend of Ralston's, affirmed the ruling that there had been no marriage. In the accompanying opinion, he laid bare, in all its smug bigotry, an underlying premise of so much nineteenth-century decision-making, legal and otherwise: Hill, being "comparatively obscure and unimportant," was more likely to have deceived the court than a rich and powerful nabob like Sharon. "Other things being equal," Judge Deady capped his reasoning, "property and position are in themselves some certain guaranty of truth in their possessor."

Now the case sank to even more sordid levels. In 1886, Hill married another much older widower, the hulking and volatile David Terry, one of her lawyers in the trial. A petition filed in federal court on behalf of Fred Sharon asked that Hill be compelled to produce the contested marriage contract for another look. The case was assigned to three judges sitting as a panel, but Hill and Terry strenuously objected to two of them: Lorenzo Sawyer and U. S. Supreme Court Justice Stephen J. Field. As far as Hill and Terry were concerned, Field was a stooge of the Sharon family; he'd been a frequent, nonpaying guest at the Palace Hotel and the recipient of a $25,000 loan from Sharon which he'd never repaid. But this hardly exhausted the ties between Field and the case. Terry had once been chief justice of the California Supreme Court, serving with Field, whom he'd sworn in as an associate justice. By today's standards— no, by any standards of impartial justice—Field should have disqualified himself several times over. But he may have given himself the benefit of the Judge Deady Equation: Powerful=Trustworthy.

Sawyer's involvement was equally infuriating to Terry, who bad-mouthed Sawyer as "a bribe-taking judge who had taken his orders from Field." And the notoriously vindictive Terry was not someone you wanted to cross. In 1859, he'd stepped down from his post as chief justice of California to challenge one of its U.S. senators, David Broderick, to a duel. Terry had shot Broderick dead. Now, in August of 1888, two weeks before the decision was expected, Sawyer and the Terrys happened to be riding the same train. Hill went over to Sawyer and pulled his hair (presumably in anger, not for an omelet). Terry was heard to say that if there weren't so many witnesses, "the best thing to do with him would be to take him out into the Bay and drown him."

The court's decision, when it came down, surprised no one: Hill was ordered to hand over that contract. Enraged, she stood up in court and accused Field of being bought. Field ordered a federal marshal to eject her. Terry knocked the marshal down. A crowd jumped Terry and knocked *him* down. Hill ended up on the floor, too. Terry drew a Bowie knife and had to be subdued. Field sentenced Hill to a month in jail for her part in the fracas, Terry to six months.

The Terrys still had a chance. Over in that parallel realm, California courts hadn't finished chewing their mouthful of Hill–Sharon goulash. But ultimately they, too, sided against Hill, citing the fact that while supposedly married to him she had written Sharon letters using the unwifely salutation "Dear Mr. Sharon." Terry denounced the decision: "The Supreme Court has reversed its own decision . . . and made my wife out a strumpet." Hill and Terry muttered of violence, and Field was assigned a federal bodyguard, David Neagle, the very marshal who had tackled Terry in court.

On August 14, 1889, the train-riding Terrys found themselves on board with enemies again, this time Field and Neagle. When the train stopped near Stockton, California, for a break, Neagle urged Field to stay on board and eat his breakfast out of harm's way, but Field entered the station anyway. Hill noticed Field sitting in the dining room and alerted her husband. Terry walked over to the judge and slapped him twice. Neagle drew a revolver and shot Terry twice; within minutes, Terry was dead. Neagle later testified that Terry had been about to strike a third blow, perhaps even to draw his knife, when he, Neagle, reacted; another witness said no, the shots had followed the slaps without a "perceptible lapse of time." The case came before—who else?—Judge Sawyer, who not only exonerated Neagle but commended him.

After losing both her claim and her husband, Sarah Hill Terry also lost her mind. She was committed to a state asylum for the insane in 1892 and remained there until her death in 1937. Shortly before his death, Sharon had admitted what a self-defeating course of action he'd followed in the Hill matter, be she a gold digger or not. That first California court had set her alimony at $2,500 a month, a mere trifle for a $20-million-man like Sharon. But he probably couldn't help himself. When challenged, he had to safeguard his money and power, never mind the cost in terms of opprobrium and ridicule. Better that he and his family should become laughingstocks and fodder for the sensationalistic press than that Bill Sharon should lose a game in which he'd staked his manhood. Wasn't he the Great King of Nevada, or California, or possibly both at the same time?

≈ SIX ≈

The Pooh-Bah Effect

Next time you're in San Francisco, you can take a crash course in Comstock dynamics. Just ride a cable car (relying on Comstock technology) to the top of Nob Hill and go to what might be called Comstock Corner, at the intersection of Mason and California Streets. On one side of Mason stands the Pacific Union Club, formerly the mansion of James C. Flood, one of the four Bonanza Kings. Dating from 1886, it's a grand, if subdued, edifice whose dark-brown sandstone exterior, blocky silhouette, and flat roof give little hint of the splendor in which it was decked out inside.

Through the middle and late eighties every Californian who read his newspaper at all attentively was familiar with the dimensions and décor of its vast rooms: a forty-foot reception parlor finished in East Indian style; a Louis XV drawing room forty-six feet long; a twenty-six-by-forty-six-foot dining-room paneled in carved San Domingo mahogany, and—not least—a smoking-room done in authentic Moorish style, with domed skylight of iridescent glass.

Around the house stretched its chief display of outer glitz, a fence composed of brass shafts interlaced with curlicues. The fence gave job security to a menial who supposedly spent his entire work week polishing it to a gleam.

Taken over by the Pacific Union Club after the 1906 earthquake, the mansion has kept little of its original interior; the fence is still there, but it has corroded to a dull green, no buffing required. To-day the house looks sedate next to the busy behemoth across the street: the multiwinged Fairmont Hotel, whose imposing outside consists of granite carved into innumerable wings, layers, pillars, alcoves, lozenges, dadoes, and tips. Another Bonanza King, James G. Fair, had bought the block now occupied by the hotel with the intention of putting up a mansion there. He aimed to outspend and outshine not just his royal brother Flood but two other neighbors as well, railroad tycoons Charles Crocker and Mark Hopkins (today the Mark Hopkins Hotel holds down another corner of the same intersection), but died before he could do so. The Fairmont was built in 1906 by Fair's daughters, Theresa and Virginia. As ex-plained in the caption to a photo displayed in the lobby, they in-tended to honor their father by putting up "a grand hotel . . . that would serve as a gathering place for the world's socialites."

As you stand admiring these paired colossi, it's almost as if a ge-nie had scooped up chunks of Nevada silver and whisked them west, kneading them into the Flood and Fairmont on the way. Nothing remotely so large or imposing as these two structures stands, or has ever stood, in Virginia City. Together, the Nob Hill giants form Exhibit A for the proposition that young Nevada was a colony of San Francisco in all but name. Or, to view the matter the other way around, if the Gold Rush made San Francisco prosper-ous, the Comstock Lode made it rich.

Flood and Fair belonged to the second wave of Comstock bucca-neers, the Bonanza Kings. Although viewed as successors to the Bank Ring, the quartet could trace its risk-taking behavior back almost to the dawn of the Lode's development. In August of 1859, a go-getter named John Mackay and his partner, Jack O'Brien, were prospecting the Mother Lode in California when they heard of a silver rush in Utah Territory. They bought supplies and hustled over the Sierra. As they crested a hill overlooking the newborn mining camp's tents and shanties, O'Brien asked Mackay if he had any money. "Not a cent," Mackay replied. "Well, I've only got half a dollar, and here it goes," said O'Brien, flinging the coin downhill. "Now we'll walk into camp like gentlemen."

The carefree pair found jobs as common miners, at the going rate of $4 a day. O'Brien went his own way, and history has lost track of him. But Mackay's brains served him so well that, a decade later, his résumé included stints as superintendent of several Com-stock mines, as well as a rewarding investment. He and a new part-ner had taken over the small Kentuck mine, which, although unproductive so far, occupied a tantalizing niche between two big producers, the Yellow Jacket and the Crown Point. Under its new management, the Kentuck lived up to its neighborhood, making Mackay and his partner a bundle. After that partner cashed out, Mackay replaced him with another former mine superintendent, James Fair, with whom he'd worked during an 1868 sojourn in Idaho. They teamed up with two money men, William S. O'Brien and James C. Flood, who'd been partners in a San Francisco lunch-room called the Auction, a seemingly unrelated business, except that the Auction was a gathering place for traders on the old min-ing exchange. The restaurateurs had listened, learned, and set themselves up as brokers specializing in mining stocks.

These four Irish-Americans—the future Bonanza Kings—had

little formal education, but they were smart, disciplined, and bold. Mackay and Fair knew the Comstock firsthand, and they meant to see what they could make of the quartet's pooled assets. Flood and O'Brien weren't miners; they were speculators, and they continued to live in San Francisco, where they could keep tabs on and meddle with the stock exchange. (Early on, there had been a fifth partner, James H. Walker, but he sold out to Mackay, who from then on had a double share in the partnership.)

The foursome's first target was an existing mine, the Hale & Norcross, which Sharon and the Bank of California had seized control of after a bidding war that drove prices as high as $10,000 a share. But the victory proved to be hollow; the mine wasn't producing, the share-price plummeted to $50, and Sharon turned his gaze elsewhere. Fair knew all about the Hale & Norcross from having been its foreman. He assured Mackay, Flood, and O'Brien that it had potential, and they agreed to mount a takeover attempt by secretly buying shares at the bargain-basement price.

By February of 1869, Sharon had got wind of a furtive campaign to wrest control of the Hale & Norcross, but not of who the stealth-buyers were. On behalf of the Bank of California, he fought back by rounding up more shares, and the contest came down to one hundred shares held by a San Francisco widow whose existence was known to Sharon but not to the four Irish partners. Sharon went to the Virginia City telegraph office and sent a coded message to Ralston, directing him to call on the woman and buy her stock. Mackay had tailed Sharon and, after Sharon left, went in and asked the telegraph agent what the message said. In common with so many others, the agent disliked Sharon; he solved the code for Mackay, who wired similar instructions to Flood in San Francisco. Next morning, Ralston showed up at the widow's door only to learn she'd already sold out to Flood at the whopping price of $8,000 a foot. Sharon tried to save face by making the new owners a patronizing offer: he would continue to manage the Hale & Norcross for them. They turned him down flat.

On their own, they transformed the Hale & Norcross into a profitable mine, making what Dan De Quille called "a snug bit of money." But another mine they invested in, the Bullion, was a bust, and their next venture seemed unexciting. The Consolidated Virginia, the name given to a welter of claims between two proven winners (the Ophir and the Gould & Curry), might look good on paper. But the territory had already been plumbed unsuccessfully to a depth of five hundred feet, and an attempt to push deeper had failed after investors lost heart. What the meek shrank away from, however, Mackay and Fair were willing to probe, and Flood and O'Brien consented. The Bonanza Kings-to-be bought the Consolidated Virginia for about $100,000 and proposed to reach its nether reaches by tunneling horizontally from the shaft of the Gould & Curry, 1,300 feet below the surface.

Almost inevitably, the Gould & Curry was controlled by Sharon, who not only erred in granting the right-of-way (for a price, of course, but a modest one). He will also forever stand convicted of hubris for the crack he made in private after publicly wishing the four partners luck: "I'll help those Irishmen lose some of their Hale & Norcross money."

For a while, however, Sharon's sneer seemed prophetic. Working at such depths was sheer punishment—this was the infernal zone in which workmen could stand the heat for only a quarter-hour at a time—and the drills' every turn only loosened more chunks of barren rock. The partners financed the operations by assessing the shareholders, and in late summer of 1872 the shareholders were balking.

What happened next comes to us courtesy of Fair. Having spent weeks haunting the leading edges of passageways like a fretful mother, in September he noticed a "knife-thin" vein of ore. "Anxious days followed," wrote a sympathetic historian, "with Fair . . . directing operations, following the thin metallic film, losing it, picking it up again, and at last seeing it begin to widen." None of his partners contradicted Fair's version. But he was an inveterate self-promoter, and when *Territorial Enterprise* editor Joe Goodman heard this account of a mineral bloodhound on the track of a geological wrinkle, he scoffed: "A blind man driving a four-horse team could have followed it in a snowstorm."

Whatever the truth as to the seam's original size and elusiveness, it kept widening. Workers sank new shafts at multiple angles, uncovering more ore. By early 1873, it was clear that the four partners had a healthy strike on their hands. No, it was a full-fledged bonanza. No, it was more than that, so humongous that no single English term could capture its magnitude. Rather, it would take a flood of hyperbole, something like the one loosed ten years later by Eliot Lord: "The lid, so to speak, of that wonderful ore-casket, termed commonly the Big Bonanza, had been lifted off. Of its magnitude and richness all were then ignorant. No discovery which matches it has been made on this earth from the day when the first miner struck a ledge with his rude pick until the present."

The partners kept their hosannas to themselves until they had a rough idea of how stupendous the formation really was. Then they called in De Quille, who wrote eye-popping articles about it for the *Territorial Enterprise*. The phenom struck him as not only prodigious but comely: "Its walls on every side are a mass of the finest silver chloride ore, filled with streaks and bunches of rich glistening black sulphurets. In the roof . . . is to be seen a quantity of stephanite, shining like a whole casket of black diamonds." He predicted an eventual payout of $360 million, but Philip Deidesheimer trumped that with an estimate of $1.5 billion (in the event, the Big Bonanza produced "only" $105 million, but that amounted to roughly a third of the entire Comstock yield, enough to make its kingly quartet very, very rich). If Sharon had anything to say—smart-assed or rueful—about the Big Bonanza and his role in enabling it, the words have been lost. His rage at being outmaneuvered again was probably tempered by the upward jolt given to mining stocks generally: the share price of the Kings' Consolidated Virginia shot up from $15 in June of 1872 to $700 in early 1875, and bank-controlled stocks catapulted to lofty levels, too. Moreover, he might have seen something of himself and Ralston in the rambunctious Kings, who, like their predecessors, gathered as much information as they could, formed hunches, and took big chances. Nonetheless, within a few years Sharon had to reconcile himself to a sobering set of returns: more than half of the Comstock's $300 million in ore production came between 1873 and 1878, and the Bonanza Kings raked in most of the profits.

Having discovered the Big Bonanza, the four Kings had finished the "clean" part of mining. What remained to be seen was how dirty they were willing to get while carrying out the other chores.

One way to answer that question is to note that the Kings' reason for rejecting out of hand Sharon's offer to run the Hale & Norcross becomes clear in hindsight: they'd already memorized big chunks of the master's playbook. Just as Sharon and the Bank Ring had expanded from the core activity of mining into milling and the supply of raw materials, so in the next few years did the Bonanza Kings. (They did not follow the Ring, however, into the railroad business.) A San Francisco weekly, the *Golden Era*, gave a sense of how the Kings made these incestuous relationships work to their advantage:

> The stockholders owned an interest in the mines, but the group contracted with themselves for the timber used in the mines, for the wood that ran the engines and for the water used in reducing the ores. It owned the mills at which the ore was worked, and not only charged its own price for reduction, but left a large percentage of the gold and silver in the tailings, which it appropriated to itself.

At each stage of the process, then, Mackay, Fair, Flood, and O'Brien were grabbing intermediate profits and deferring dividends until all bills were paid (to their own companies). In 1878, when Flood testified in a lawsuit brought by disgruntled stockholders, opposing counsel pressed him about these arrangements:

Q: Who are the owners of the Pacific Mill and Mining Company?
FLOOD: Mackay, Fair, Flood and O'Brien are the principal stock holders.
Q: Who are the owners of the Pacific Wood, Lumber and Flume Company?
FLOOD: Mackay, Fair, Flood and O'Brien.
Q: From what source does the company procure water?
FLOOD: From the Virginia & Gold Hill Water Company.
Q: Who are the trustees of the Virginia & Gold Hill Water Company?
FLOOD: Mackay, Fair, Flood and O'Brien, Hobart, Skae and Wells.
Q: Is there any other corporation from which the company draws supplies of any character of which Mackay, Fair, Flood and O'Brien are not the trustees and principal owners?
FLOOD: I don't know of any.

In less steady hands, these interlocking ownerships might have led to quandaries. As mine owners, Mackay and partners wanted to get their ore milled as cheaply as possible; as mill owners, they wanted not only to charge the highest prices the market would bear but also to keep their plants humming. Similar tensions characterized relations between the Kings' mines and their timber and water companies. But these conflicts of interest seem to have been largely theoretical; in practice, the Kings worked it all out so as to maximize their income. One might think of their various firms as aspects of a single personage, someone like Pooh-Bah in Gilbert and Sullivan's *Mikado* (1885). Pooh-Bah holds so many imperial posts—First Lord of the Treasury, Lord Chamberlain, Attorney-General, Chancellor of the Exchequer, Privy Purse, and Private Secretary—that he is continually bumping into himself. Anyone hoping to close a deal with this one-man bureaucracy had better be prepared to hand over "a very considerable bribe." Except the Bonanza Kings didn't stoop to the vulgarity of being corrupted by outsiders; in effect, they bribed themselves.

At first, they did so without attracting the bad press that had nipped at the Bank Ring. Mackay, in particular, enjoyed a reputation for level-headedness, for not getting too big for his miner's boots. When other mine owners proposed riding out slack periods by cutting wages to $3.50 a day, Mackay dug in his heels: "I always got $4 a day when I worked in these mines, and when I can't pay that I'll go out of business." He and his partners also seemed to have an instinct for public relations. In 1874, after putting out the word on the Big Bonanza, they let so many visitors descend and feast their eyes on the glitter that the miners had trouble getting their work done.

As mentioned, the Bonanza rejuvenated the mining stock market, and euphoria reigned in Virginia City and especially in San Francisco, where multimillionaires became sources of civic pride, comparable to today's baseball sluggers and football quarterbacks. In January of 1875, the editor of the *San Francisco Chronicle* exultantly rated the city's tycoons according to their balance sheets (which, in the case of the Kings, he exaggerated):

Lick, Latham, Sharon, and Hayward are all poor men. Worth $5,000,000? Well, yes, they may be worth that paltry sum. So are Reese, Mills, Baldwin, Lux, Miller, Jones, Ralston, and Stanford. These are only our well-to-do citizens, men of comfortable incomes—our middle class. Our rich men . . . are

Mackay, Flood, O'Brien, and Fair. Twenty or thirty millions each is but a modest estimate of their wealth. Mackay is worth from sixty to a hundred millions.

The delirium was so contagious that when the boom peaked in early 1875, Comstock mining stocks were valued at a total of $300 million, $110 million greater than the assessed value of all San Francisco real estate.

For all their multistage profit-taking, however, these kings weren't knaves: unlike Sharon, they didn't toss junk rock in with the ore they sent to their mills, and they maintained a flow of dividends to shareholders in their two mining firms, the Consolidated Virginia and the California. This set them apart from most other owners, who withheld dividends and repeatedly hit their stockholders with assessments. In 1876, for example, 135 Comstock mining stocks were listed on the San Francisco exchanges; only three of them, the Bonanza Kings' Consolidated Virginia and California and the Bank Ring's Belcher, were paying dividends; all the others were levying assessments.

At first, the Kings didn't much concern themselves with stock-market fluctuations. Mackay even tried to discourage the madness. In an interview with De Quille, the great miner leveled with would-be Comstock investors: "Here and in San Francisco, persons are constantly coming to me and asking me, or writing to me, to ask: 'What shall I buy?' . . . I said to all that came: 'Go and put your money in a savings bank.'"

That was sound advice because for ordinary mortals Comstock mines were a sucker's game. If the mine you selected wasn't declaring dividends, the only way you could profit from it was to buy stock at a low price and sell it sometime later at a higher one, and you couldn't count on being able to do that unless you were acting on inside knowledge, to which as an ordinary investor you were—by definition—not privy. For instance, one good bet was to find out which mines had real potential, wait until the market went into one of its periodic slumps, buy at low prices, and hang on until the market rose again, but how could anyone but the best man at a Bonanza King's wedding or the brother of a mine superintendent obtain such information?

De Quille suggested another way to play, the "simple rule" of "buying [stocks] when they are down so low that nobody appears to care to touch them, paying for them in full and then holding them for developments in the mine, and it seldom happens that there is not a time within two years when they can sell for twice or three times the price originally paid." This formula, which seems more likely to let you keep your shirt than make big bucks, might have worked until the mid-1870s (the book in which De Quille suggested it came out in 1876), but not afterward, when the Comstock had already started on its across-the-board decline.

That decline came about not just because fresh bonanzas weren't materializing. Starting in March of 1876, a group of "bear" investors led by James R. Keene systematically derided the Comstock as an investment, for a sinister reason: at the same time that their gloom-mongering was cutting the price of the Consolidated Virginia almost in half, from $440 a share to $240, they were buying short and making handsome profits as the stock continued to fall. Once Keene had squeezed out all the juice he thought he could reasonably collect, he turned around and said nice things about the Comstock, although cautioning that the Con Virginia's future depended on whether a crosscut in progress at the 1,650-foot level struck a replenishing body of ore.

Having been baited (Flood in particular took the bears' attacks as almost personal affronts), the Bonanza Kings tried to intervene in the market. But Flood's fulminating and maneuvering had no effect—the price of a Con Virginia share swooned all the way to $36 in January of 1877—until that crosscut did indeed hit rich ore. Con Virginia jumped back to $52, and hope blossomed anew in Comstock country.

Alas, it was a short-lived flowering. The new deposit turned out to be modest in size and intruded upon by a mass of worthless rock. The Kings acquired other mines and sank other shafts, but their magic touch had deserted them. The California paid its last dividend in 1879, the Con Virginia in 1880. As the group's supposed stock-market whiz, Flood had the unenviable task of trying to juggle no-show bonanzas and a deflating market. In their later years, both he and Mackey regretted that they expended so much energy in trying to control the stock market instead of just sticking to mining.

As the decline lengthened, the Kings became magnets for popular wrath. Fair in particular was easy to dislike: he'd been given the nickname "Slippery Jim" on account of such incidents as the dirty trick he played on underground smokers. To enforce the firm's no-smoking rule, he was always sniffing around in the mines, and one night in the Con Virginia, he thought he smelled tobacco. "Boys, this running around wears me out," he complained. "I can't stand it any more. If I had the whiff of a pipe it would make me feel better." One of the "boys" obliged, and Fair took a few puffs. The next morning, when he ran into the same men above ground, they told him they'd all been fired. "Ah," said Fair, "that's John [Mackay] again. I never get a good bunch of men that he doesn't lay them off." But the men knew this for the lie it was: Fair was the one who'd entrapped them, and thereby lowered the Kings' goodwill in Virginia City.

Nor were the four careful about whom they euchred in San Francisco. As we've seen, some partisans of Ralston blamed his death (erroneously) on machinations by the Kings. The *Chronicle* and the *Golden Era* mounted vitriolic attacks on the Kings after the papers' owners lost money on mining stocks and concluded that the game was fixed against them. When stockholders sued the Kings in 1878 to recover $40 million worth of allegedly unjust profits, the *Chronicle* piled up accusations into a tower of scare headlines: "The Bonanza Kings. Their Splendor Throned on Human

Misery. Rolling in Wealth Wrung from Ruined Thousands. California and Nevada Impoverished to Enrich Four Men. Plain History of Swindling Perpetrated on a Grand Scale. Colossal Money Power That Menaces Pacific Coast Prosperity."

The ensuing article, however, was light on specifics. Nor did any disaffected employees appear in court to accuse the Kings of enlisting them in outright fraud. Laws against corporate double-dealing were sketchy at the time (the Sherman Antitrust law wasn't enacted until a dozen years later), and by ordering the Kings to cough up diverted profits, a judge might have caused jitters all across the country: thanks in part to the Kings' example, the vertical monopoly had become standard practice in railroads, oil-refining, and other sectors of the economy. (Eliot Lord bought into this everybody's-doing-it excuse by granting that the Kings' managerial practices weren't ideal, then hastening to add that whether one could find better-behaving corporate officials, "except in Utopia, is gravely questioned.") In the end, the court whittled that $40 million damage claim down to less than $1 million, the amount of a single transaction that broke a state law against preferential dealing.

In good times and bad, the partners had usually acted in harmony, but in 1878 they almost fell out over an acquisition. This pivotal point in the Comstock's fortunes was called the Sierra Nevada Deal, after a mine of great promise that so far hadn't come to fruition. That summer, all of Virginia City was atwitter over a new deposit found at the mine's 2,000-foot level. Journalistic sages pronounced it the best chance for a bonanza in years, and the mine's stock rose to double, then triple, then almost quadruple its old price, jacking up the whole market with it. Fair and Flood caught the bug and invested until the four partners won control of an adjacent mine. Mackay, however, was dubious. He went down for a look at what all the fuss was about and came up shaking his head. "Fair is crazy," he wired Flood in San Francisco. When the stock market opened the following Monday, Sierra Nevada stock was "offered at forty dollars less than the previous closing figure [$260], then at forty dollars less again and then at successive declines of twenty dollars. The first sale was made at a hundred and forty and then on down, each successive sale being made at a lower figure, until it closed at eighty"; other mining stocks were dragged down with it. Many investors had bought on margin (i.e., by making a down payment to a lender, with the stock itself serving as collateral in case the investor can't come up with the balance owed), and their lenders were left holding devalued shares. The Comstock never recovered from this setback, either as an investment or a mining district. By 1881, the $300 million evaluation of its mines had shrunk to a paltry $7 million.

The Kings were all right, though. They'd followed Sharon's footsteps in yet another direction, moving their mining profits into real estate and other safe investments. The Sierra Nevada Deal inflicted a howling pain, but it didn't alter the basics. By the time the Comstock was reduced to a shadow of its former self in the mid-1880s, the Kings had made their invasion, conducted their raids, and retreated to San Francisco with fortunes more accurately estimated at $15 to $20 million apiece. At this point, their fascination for us lies mostly in how they and their families fared as plutocrats, as the dynamic shifted and greedy outsiders tried to "mine" the Kings' wealth.

Although less free with his money than Flood and Fair, John Mackay was no Scrooge, as witness an exhibit in the Mackay Mines building on the campus of the University of Nevada at Reno. There, behind glass, is housed a portion of the Mackay silver service, a gift from John to his wife, Marie. Unlike those babes-in-the-woods Bowerses, Mackay entrusted his glob of silver (more than half a ton) to a firm of impeccable standing, Tiffany and Company, which put 200 silversmiths to work on it. The resulting pieces, 1,350 in all, have so much wrought detail as to appear pebbly; they range from a splendid candelabra to a celery vase to a champagne holder in which an opened bottle will rest at just the proper angle to retain fizz. Mackay was willing to part with his money, but he demanded value in return. It wasn't enough that his silverware be ostentatious; it must also be unique, and Mackay figured out how to ensure that. He bought Tiffany's dies, so that, as a caption to the exhibit explains, "no other similar pattern could ever be made."

Mackay might know how to protect his investments, but he never made peace with being filthy rich. His wife, on the other hand, reveled in that status. A native of Brooklyn who'd migrated to the California gold fields with her parents, Marie Hungerford had married young and well: her husband was Dr. Edmund Bryant, a physician and a cousin of the poet William Cullen Bryant. They had two daughters, one of whom died, after which the promising doctor lost his career to alcohol and drugs. When he died, his still-young wife and surviving daughter were living in Virginia City, where Marie supported them by teaching French (her mother was French-born) and sewing for a local store. She and Mackay were introduced by Theresa Fair, James's wife, who rightly guessed that the struggling widow and the lonely bachelor would hit it off.

The marriage seemed happy enough, but once Marie went abroad—well, the song "How Ya Gonna Keep 'Em Down on the Farm (After They've Seen Paree)?" might have been written about her rather than World War I doughboys. She'd always carried herself "like a princess," people recalled, and now she was rubbing shoulders with genuine royalty. After the Mackays returned from their first European tour in 1873, Marie could no longer abide San Francisco, much less Virginia City. In 1876, with proceeds from the Big Bonanza pouring in unabated, she suggested that she, her daughter, and the couple's two sons return to Paris, where her parents had settled permanently. Mackay consented and moved back to Virginia City, where he took up residence in the International Hotel.

Once ensconced in Europe, Marie could hardly be pried loose. She first settled into a mansion in Paris, hoping to be accepted by its bon ton. But the French held out against this Yankee parvenu until November of 1877, when the restless Ulysses Grant and family swung through on their own European tour. Marie's glad-handing father exploited his tenuous Mexican War ties with the ex-president to inveigle him into dining chez Mackay. The event established the former Marie Hungerford of the Nevada boondocks as a social lioness.

> For the next quarter century her social triumphs were staple reading for millions all over America. It was a period when lives of rich countrymen who moved in the upper circles of European society held a singular fascination for staunch democrats from Maine to California. Paris and London correspondents regularly cabled accounts of her receptions and appended lists of her more distinguished guests. Thus John Mackay in his hotel room in San Francisco or Virginia City was often privileged to read that his wife had entertained such renowned figures as Isabella, the exiled Queen of Spain, or Marshal Marie Edme de MacMahon, survivor of the rout at Sedan and currently President of the Third French Republic.

Marie inspired a flattering character in *L'Abbé Constantin*, a popular novel of the day, and sat for a portrait by the painter Jean-Louis-Ernest Meissonier. His daub touched off an international incident. Unhappy with how he made her look, Marie asked Meissonier to retouch the canvas; he refused. Legend has it that she paid his fee, took the painting home, invited some friends over, and set the damned thing on fire. (Her granddaughter, who married songwriter Irving Berlin and wrote a family memoir called *The Silver Platter*, denied that any such thing happened. It was also rumored—no doubt falsely—that Marie had once tried to buy the Arc de Triomphe.) Whatever the truth, the flap soured Marie on France. She flounced off to London, where she bought an even grander mansion. There she scored a coup by having the Prince of Wales over for dinner.

Mackay generally crossed the Atlantic for an annual visit, but the separation seemed to bother him little, if at all. In Virginia City or San Francisco, he could work as hard as he pleased by day and attend the opera or play cards at night. His way of handling the beggars and loafers who besieged him couldn't have been simpler: he reached into his pocket and gave them money. If you sent him an importuning letter, he wouldn't bother to reply. But if you managed to buttonhole him on the street or corner him in his office, he didn't turn you down. His San Francisco business manager recalled:

> He never came [to the office] but there was a crowd of small borrowers, stretching all the way from the entrance here [at the corner of Pine and Montgomery Streets] to the entrance of the Palace Hotel. He reckoned that it used to cost him fifty dollars to walk from the Nevada Block to the Palace, and he always carried the price with him, in gold.

Mackay also lent and gave larger sums to needy friends and charities, always insisting on anonymity. And he endeared himself to the boys of Virginia City whenever he went to Piper's Opera House. Unable to afford the fifty-cents-a-head ticket fee, forty or fifty urchins would be waiting for Mackay's arrival. "How much for the bunch?" he would ask the proprietor, John Piper; the tab would amount to $20 or more, but Mackay paid without hesitation. "That is why we never envied John Mackay," recalled one of those kids. "We wanted him to live forever and always be rich."

In public, Mackay was reticent and unassuming. In private, he was steadfast. He might grouse that his father-in-law, the status-seeking Colonel Hungerford, was a "God-damned old windbag," but he went on footing the bills run up abroad by the windbag and the windbag's daughter. Once, when a hotel clerk was asked how Mackay might be recognized at a crowded bar, the clerk advised, "He'll be the one who says nothing and pays the bill." In all these ways except his love for opera, he foreshadows the tetchy millionaire papas in Hollywood screwball comedies of the 1930s and 1940s. Often played by Eugene Pallette (see, for example, *My Man Godfrey* and *The Lady Eve*), these grumblers don't like having to dress for dinner and eat French food and sit around a drawing room trying to generate repartee, but would rather cuss and take off their monkey suits and slouch around a table in their undershirts quaffing beer and playing cards with the boys, and if somebody needs a few bucks, hell, all he's got to do is ask. Mackay's most heartfelt lament had to do with the effect of immense wealth on his poker game: playing was no fun anymore, he groaned, because it didn't matter whether he won or lost.

Late in his career, he took part in several nonmining ventures, including a stab with newspaper magnate James Gordon Bennett at competing with Jay Gould in the transatlantic cable business. After a long struggle, the new partners succeeded (their company went on to lay the first transpacific cable in 1901), but Mackay suffered a great personal loss in 1895, when his older son, 25-year-old Willie, died after being thrown from a horse. Willie had been groomed to succeed his father as head of the family enterprises, and now the burden passed to his brother, 22-year-old Clarence. John Mackay himself died of heart failure at the age of 70 on July 20, 1902, leaving an estate worth an estimated $30 to $60 million, a wide range, admittedly, but his business manager cautioned against trying to be exact: "I don't suppose he knew within twenty millions what he was worth." Marie abdicated her socialite's throne and returned to the States, where she lived quietly with Clarence and his family on their Long Island estate until her death in 1928, at age 85.

O'Brien, the first King to die, was the least colorful of the lot. His value to the group lay in an easygoing gregariousness that helped keep them together. He never married, but he and his sister Kate made a handsome couple when he escorted her to public events. He let the other three Kings run the Bonanza and the Nevada Bank, preferring instead to tend to their joint real-estate investments in

San Francisco. Known as "the jolly millionaire," he gave money away freely to needy friends but didn't flaunt his wealth. One of his few extravagances was the hideous mausoleum he commissioned in anticipation of his death. That came in 1878, with his old buddy Flood at the bedside; O'Brien was only 52.

It was Flood, mostly, who took the rap once the public realized that Comstock speculation was strictly for the well connected. He combined a forbidding demeanor with a fine head for business, and he drew attention to himself by building one mansion after another, each more lavishly appointed than the last. He also knew how to fight hard without losing his sense of perspective. When Sharon heard that the four Irishmen were starting a bank, he cracked that he would "send Flood back to selling rum at the Auction." Flood retorted that if he ever poured drinks again, it would be across the counter of the Bank of California. But when the chance for vengeance dropped into his hands, Flood didn't squeeze. Aware that the collapse of such a mighty institution as the Bank of California could poison the general climate for business, he and the other Kings exercised restraint during the period when Ralston's empire fell and Sharon set about restoring confidence in the bank.

Flood diverted some of his energies toward his children, whose lives he liked to manage. When Grant and his family visited California in 1879, Flood coaxed them out to lunch at Linden Towers, his Menlo Park estate. Grant's son Ulysses Jr., nicknamed Buck, took a fancy to Flood's daughter, Cora Jane, nicknamed Jennie. An announcement of their engagement seemed imminent, but Flood went a-meddling before this could happen. The Grants had no money to speak of, and Flood wanted to spare Buck the shame of being thought an opportunist. To that end, he lent Buck some money, which in six months' time the young man parlayed into a respectable nuptial ante. But while doing so, Buck lost interest in Jennie, who waited in vain for him to call on her the next time he visited San Francisco. She sent him a note breaking off the relationship. He married someone else; she stayed single all her life.

Flood's son, Jimmy, bore up better under dad's machinations. As rich boys are wont to do, he fell in love with a fast woman, Rose Fritz, a former operetta singer who was newly broke. The two got married, but Flood wasn't about to let that technicality ruin Jimmy's life. The Floods were Catholic, and the Church knew how to deal with ill-advised elopements: annul them. Flood packed off Jimmy on a world tour and summoned Rose for a little talk. He offered her $25,000 and suggested that she act sensibly; otherwise he would cut Jimmy off without a penny. She took the money, went through with the annulment, but then stole off to Paris to meet Jimmy, who remarried her. This display of spunk won Flood over. He gave his blessing, and the young people stayed married until Rose's death in 1898.

Although generally resting on their laurels in their later years, the surviving Kings could still be tempted into action. Flood thought it might be nice to make something of their Nevada Bank of San Francisco, and when the bank's president resigned in 1881, Flood took his place.

The bank had started as a vanity vault: Ralston and Sharon had a bank, so the Bonanza Kings must have one, too; they even built its Virginia City branch right across the street from the Bank of California's. For some time, Fair had been losing patience with the slipshod way the Nevada Bank was run, and Flood's self-appointment gave Fair the excuse he wanted: count me out, he told his partners. A compromise was struck: Fair and Flood both sold out to Mackay, giving him sole ownership. Not for long, though. Mackay sold a half-interest back to Flood, who retook the helm. But as Flood aged, increasingly he entrusted the bank's day-to-day operations to an administrator, George L. Brander, a Scotsman reputed to be sound and canny.

The free rein given Brander almost proved the bank's undoing. In the summer of 1887, a broker named John Rosenfeld was making heavy purchases of California's wheat crop, which he transferred into the holds of ships. The price of wheat almost doubled, and a

picture was beginning to form: someone must be trying to corner
the market (i.e., to gain sufficient control of a commodity as to be
able to dictate its price). But who? Although Rosenfeld wasn't saying, various clues pointed to the Nevada Bank. Its owners, however,
were out of the loop. One day Flood was surprised to hear from a
friend he met on a San Francisco street that the bank's heavy borrowing was raising eyebrows. At about the same time, Mackay was
disembarking from an ocean liner in New York after a conjugal European visit and being told that New York banks were "crammed
with Nevada bank paper." The co-owners were dumbfounded: last
time they looked, their bank had been sloshing in capital—$10 mil-
lion or thereabouts—so why all the borrowing?

Flood confronted Brander, who came clean. Rosenfeld had persuaded him that wheat was cornerable, and Brander had gone for it.
But not only was 1887 a bumper year for wheat in California; gra-
naries were filling up all over the world. Every time Brander thought
he was about to nail down that corner, more wheat sprouted, waving in the wind and crying out to be bought. He committed all the
bank's playable assets only to find that, unless he came up with still
more, the tipping point at which he could unilaterally set the price
of wheat would elude him. In desperation, he snatched $1 million in
negotiable securities that Flood had salted away for his wife, to tide
her over during probate in the event of his death, along with
$600,000 in bearer bonds that Mackay had set aside for a similar
purpose. Brander seems to have meant well. As right-hand man to
two of the world's fattest cats, he wanted to make an impression,
and why pursue the safe, piddling gains that banks typically eke out
for their investors when you're managing the portfolios of titans?
To be worthy of them, an endeavor should be global, and when one
presented itself, Brander had pounced. He'd planned to act on the
q.t. and surprise Flood and Mackay with a splendid fait accompli.
But cornering wasn't as easy as it sounded, and by the time Mackay
got off the train in San Francisco, the Bank's liquid assets had
dwindled to $368.

The Bank was bailed out by prominent San Franciscans, among them Fair, who took over from Flood as president. He made no secret of his disdain for the other two as "those kindergarten bankers," and the *Chronicle* remarked: "Old Jimmy Fair has a good deal of the Indian blood in his composition, and he has waited long for a chance to get even on his old partners." Fair played Sharon's old role of bank rejuvenator, but the losses may have added up to $12 million. Flood died two years later at age 62, and it was widely believed that the wheat binge cut his life short. The Nevada Bank lasted until 1890, when Mackay sold it; at length it was resold, losing its identity in a merger with Wells, Fargo. In the interim, Brander had disgraced himself again, being indicted for filing false reports as the manager of an insurance company.

Fair, in his later years, oversaw his extensive San Francisco properties in classic slumlord style. He owned 60 acres of prime urban real estate; he took in an estimated $250,000 a month in rents; but he refused to keep up or fix up his holdings, his excuse being that high taxes left his hands tied, and anyway the city government was riddled with corruption. Like Mackay, he'd never gotten used to being super-rich, but the two grandees' reactions to their condition were quite different. Mackay lay low and did favors for people on the sly. Fair bragged of his wealth and sought recognition for it; the mansion he didn't live to build on Nob Hill was to be his way of crowning himself Biggest Spender of Them All. Once, after a bout with asthma, Fair cracked a joke into which he just happened to slip his net worth: "I wouldn't go through another week like that for all my forty millions!"

After O'Brien's death, tensions among the surviving partners could no longer be smoothed over. The animosity came out in the open when Fair's wife, Theresa, sued for divorce on grounds of "habitual adultery." Fair was serving his term in the Senate at the time, and clergymen and newspaper editors called for his resignation.

This he did not submit, but the Mackays and Floods sided with Theresa. Fair contested the divorce, but there's not much a habitual adulterer can do when his habits take the stand and testify against him. Theresa got her decree in 1883, along with almost $5 million, in its time thought to be the largest settlement in the history of marital strife. Custody of the couple's four children was awarded by sex: Charley and Jim went to the ex-husband, Theresa (Tessie) and Virginia (Birdie) to the ex-wife. Although furious with Mackay and Flood for deserting him, Fair couldn't very well divorce himself from his partners—that would have been prohibitively expensive— but he could belittle them freely. On hearing that Flood was build- ing a mansion in Menlo Park, Fair sneered: "Flood should be popular at Menlo. There's not a bartender on the Coast who can make a better julep than Jim." After Mackay entertained a troupe of actors at his place, Fair said: "John Mackay's a great admirer of ge- niuses. I wonder how much they borrowed from him."

In a ceremony to which her father was not invited, Fair's daugh- ter Tessie married the scion of a family that divided its time be- tween New York City and Newport, Rhode Island. Birdie went east to live with her sister and brother-in-law, made her debut, and was romantically linked with a European prince and then with John Mackay, Jr., who was paying the States a rare visit. Neither of these worthies won her hand, but Birdie was young yet. Her brother Jimmy, however, made short work of himself. After going through a standard playboy-heir phase, he graduated to binge drinking. One night he celebrated his release from a sanatorium by downing twenty cocktails and passing out. A doctor brought him around that time; but a year later, only 27, he drank himself to death, whether accidentally or on purpose, no one could say.

Theresa Fair died in 1891, three years before her ex-husband; she left most of her estate to her daughters but also set up a $1 million trust fund for Jimmy and Charley to share. Jimmy's death, coming five months after his mother's, left Charley as the trust's sole bene- ficiary: he was to receive a monthly allowance of $1,000 until he reached age 30, at which time he could lay hands on the principal. That milestone was still six years off, and he waited it out by hitting the bottle and playing the horses. He also got married, to a somewhat older woman who called herself Maud and had owned an establishment said to be a brothel. (Maud had gone through a number of surnames, to none of which she was legally entitled; her real name was Catherine Decker Smith.) Slippery Jim shook his head at Charley's weakness (the old man always handled these affairs expertly: jump ship before it drifts too close to the altar) but had to acknowledge that his boy had become a grown man with a will of his own. To be on the safe side, though, Fair had discussed making a will that disinherited Charley. But during the old man's final illness, Charley and Maud were faithful presences at the bedside, and this sucking-up campaign had evidently succeeded in coaxing a new will out of the dying man.

It was not a peaceful death. The aging Fair had succumbed more and more to bitterness. Sometimes he repaired to a San Rafael resort hotel where he checked into a room costing fifty cents a night and drank himself into a stupor. Near the end, he complained to a friend, "Look at me. My wife away, my children away, and everybody calls me a son-of-a-bitch." On December 29, 1894, at age 63, he breathed his last. And then the notoriety began.

Fair's last will restored Charley to favor, but not on an equal footing with his sisters. The bulk of the estate was to be split among the three siblings and held in trust for them, but if Charley died his entire share would go to Tessie and Birdie, with nothing for Maud.

Charley felt slighted, and one feature of the will rankled with all three surviving siblings: its trust provision. Like Charley, Tess and Birdie didn't see why they shouldn't be treated as adults, free to do as they liked with all of their money, and they sued to break the will. This brought on the first melodramatic twist in what became a long, tumultuous series: the will was stolen while in the custody of the county clerk with whom it had been filed, never to be seen again. While everyone was still puzzling over this, a rival will surfaced. One Nettie Craven, the principal of a grammar school, came forward with a two-page document, written in pencil and dated September 24, 1894, three days after the trust will. This one settled the estate directly on the three surviving children. When the trust will's executors declared the pencil will a forgery, Charley Fair waxed indignant. "I think I ought to know my father's handwriting," he told a reporter. Charley went on to explain the pencil will's existence as follows: Mrs. Craven had lived in the same hotel as Senator Fair, and the two had become friends. Outside the classroom, she championed legislation to set up a pension fund for retired schoolteachers. Fair had not only agreed to donate $50,000 to the fund if the state assembly created it; he'd drawn up a new will, incorporating such a bequest, and left it in Mrs. Craven's custody.

The young Fairs were delighted with the pencil will because it left them everything (save for a few small bequests) trust-free. Mrs. Craven was looking good, too; all she stood to gain from the will was a boost for the cause she so nobly espoused, succor for poor teachers in their old age. But an imp must have whispered in her ear, *Don't be a ninny. Grab something for yourself.* In time she produced more pencil-written documents: deeds that conveyed two of Fair's properties to none other than Nettie Craven. And not just any old properties: these were prime downtown lots, one of which was the site of a five-story office building, and their combined value was estimated at $1.5 million. According to Mrs. Craven, Fair had signed the documents three months before his death, again leaving them with her for safekeeping. Her late-breaking ploy couldn't have been more blatant, but what could the three orphans do? According to a newspaper account, the parties worked out a deal: if Mrs. Craven surrendered those deeds, a settlement of $500,000 would be hers. And they all still pledged allegiance to the pencil will.

Before these terms could be carried out, however, everything changed. A judicial decision came down, the outcome of that long-pending, all-but-forgotten suit to upset the trust will. And, indeed, the court ruled its trust provisions invalid. Charley's eyesight suddenly cleared up: now that he looked at it again, the pencil will was a palpable forgery, and the original will, stripped of those obnoxious trusts, was the one to rally around. Mrs. Craven's half-a-million settlement went poof.

A duffer might have given up at this point, but Mrs. Craven had fiber. She sped home, rifled through her vast archives, and emerged with yet another find: a marriage contract between herself and the late Senator Fair. Supposedly the two had taken each other for husband and wife, in private, on May 23, 1892.

As the skirmishing went on, Mrs. Craven saw no reason why she should wait to be rich: she went to court and filed a petition seeking a $5,000 per month allowance for support and maintenance. The Fair children resisted by trying to prove that their father's signature on the various Craven-favoring documents had been forged, and one of their lawyers repackaged himself as an instant penmanship expert. Introducing into evidence 1,299 checks signed by Fair, he pointed to such anomalies as that "in the marriage contract the letter 'J' is formed with two strokes. In all the 1,299 checks introduced, this formation of the letter 'J' does not occur once."

Wills, deeds, forgeries, a marriage contract, trust or no-trust, pencils or pens, one-stroke Js versus two-stroke Js, and an estate that in the meantime had been valued at $12.2 million—what better way to resolve this welter of conflicts than by waging a climactic court battle? Each side hired a battery of lawyers, with Mrs. Craven ranging so far afield as to retain George M. Curtis, a former New York Supreme Court judge known for his ability to smash wills. The *Examiner* dubbed him "The Smasher" and ran caricatures showing him laying waste to documents.

Curtis's wrecking-ball techniques might have cowed Easterners, but Californians were unimpressed. The jury seemed far more susceptible to the constant presence in the courtroom of Mrs. Craven's fetching daughter, Margaret. Reporters fussed over her in print, and The Smasher caught on and worked references to her beauty into his arguments. But this advantage collapsed near the end of the trial: having eloped with a beau, Margaret no longer sat glowingly at her mother's side. (The Smasher reckoned that her departure "cost us at least three votes.") The jury upheld the deeds by a vote of eight to four, but the lack of unanimity allowed the judge to take over, and he ruled against Mrs. Craven. She filed a notice of appeal to the state supreme court but let it be known that she was amenable to a compromise. The Fairs gave her a modest settlement, and she handed over the disputed deeds and marriage contract. The *Examiner* estimated that the fight had cost the Fairs a total of $2 million.

That wasn't all, though. The late Senator Fair had secretly married oodles of ladies and furtively fathered battalions of children, or so, one by one, they came forward to assert. But the Fair lawyers, well-seasoned by now, ran up a perfect record in fending them off. On a calmer note, in 1899 the family announced an engagement that everyone approved of: the same Birdie who had been linked with a foreign prince now chose a homegrown lad. To be sure, he was rather a prince himself, William K. Vanderbilt, the richest living American bachelor. That made Birdie a sister-in-law of the Duke of Marlborough, who had recently married William's sister Consuelo in what was touted as "the wedding of the century."

Sensation, however, had not yet had its fill of the Fairs. Back in San Francisco, Maud Fair had her hands full trying to keep Charley from falling into utter dissipation. She may have originally used her hooks for gold-digging purposes, but once she got them into Charley, she proved to be not only a good wife but also something of a Lady Bountiful, spending two afternoons a week delivering necessities to the city's poor. Charley was now engrossed in a new hobby, automobiles, which he liked to drive at high speeds, sometimes in competition with his Vanderbilt brother-in-law. In 1902, the Fairs sailed to France, where Charley bought a Mercedes-Special, capable of doing eighty-five miles an hour. After summering with the Vanderbilts in Trouville, the Fairs were about to drive back to Paris. Charley ordered the chauffeur into the back seat and took the wheel himself, determined to win a $50 bet by beating his brother-in-law's best time of two-and-a-half hours. But poor Charley lost control of the car and hit a tree; he and Maud were thrown out of the vehicle.

They died, but not right away. They were still twitching when an onlooker came up, and the order of their going became a point of furious contention. Each spouse had made a will leaving almost everything to the other, but only if he or she survived the one who died. Thus, if Maud had outlived Charley by a mere second, $10 million or so would cascade down upon her humble next of kin. If she'd expired first, however, they would get nothing.

The Fair lawsuit machine was ready to crank up again, and Maud's people, the Nelsons, were girding their own loins. California, where the couple made their home, had a rule for such a case, reflecting another of those cards-on-the-table prejudices in which the nineteenth century abounded:

When a husband and wife died of injuries simultaneously received, it was assumed, in the absence of evidence to the contrary, that the husband had survived longer. This was on the theory that, being commonly stronger than the female, the spark of life would logically remain longer in the male. But the deaths had occurred in France, and it was thought that if the expected lawsuit materialized, it would be tried in the courts of that country. No one in San Francisco could say with certainty what the law of France might be on that point.

The chauffeur, who had survived the crash, gave inconsistent versions of the couple's last moments. Another witness, the only outsider to have seen the whole thing, first said that they had died at the same moment, but then reversed herself: "the movement of the foot of the man had ceased an instant before that of the hand of the woman." The prospects for a long and juicy contest seemed excellent.

But rather than get into a bidding war for these witnesses' memories, the Fairs and the Nelsons took the eminently reasonable step of sitting down and talking things over. They quickly reached an agreement that left the Nelsons about $1 million richer. So quickly, in fact, that the bodies of Charley and Maud were just embarking on their return trip to the States as the two families went public with the deal.

The Vanderbilts had a hand in the negotiations, and possibly it was their savvy that engineered the smooth ending. Having been rich for a few generations, the Vanderbilts knew what a drubbing the press could give to a family mired in a long financial/marital dispute. In any case, for once a Comstock family had paused, weighed the likely costs and benefits, dug into its pockets, and spared itself a media circus. And with the wrapping up of the Case of the Simultaneously Dying Heirs, the secondary mining of Comstock fortunes by prospectors using the tools of seduction, marriage, and forgery came to an end, too.

SEVEN

Challengers

After acquiring mines and branching out into milling, raw materials, and transportation during the late 1860s, the Bank Ring had the Comstock in a stranglehold. But the Ring didn't enforce its will crassly: you could cross it without fear of being jumped after dark, trussed up, and dropped into a mine. Rather, the Ring made do with economic pressure and criticism planted in the newspapers it controlled, using these methods so effectively that only a few men dared challenge it. One of them, a well-meaning but incompetent crusader, got nowhere. A second, a persevering dynamo, scored a hard-fought triumph. A third, a one-shot opportunist, rebelled long enough to make a spectacular killing and then pulled his neck back in.

The crusader, Conrad Wiegand, was one of those guileless do-gooders cursed with a defect that was even more important in the old West than it is today: the inability to project manliness. He knew that people liked making fun of him, but not why, and he never hit upon the right formula to make them stop.

He worked as an assayer in Gold Hill; in his spare time, he

preached on the streets for an entity called the Humanitarian Christian Society. His proselytizing brought forth mockery from the *Territorial Enterprise*, which in February of 1868 marveled at his "singularly pure and gentle" blue eyes, in a "countenance [that] will inevitably recall to mind the likeness of the Savior." This syrupy phrasing was surely meant to bait Wiegand, and it succeeded: he took out ads in both that paper and the *Gold Hill News* complaining of the humiliation suffered by him and his family. He vowed nonetheless to treat his enemies with "unmerited kindness." The *News* struck back by coining the term "Wiegandish," defined as "anything of a particular egotistical nature."

This journalistic ganging-up was gratuitous and mean, but probably nothing much would have come of it if Wiegand hadn't gone after the Bank Ring. The other local gadfly, Adolph Sutro, was thought to have brought the Ring's misdeeds to the assaying preacher's attention by publishing a rundown of its mines' excessive profits. As Wiegand learned more about the Ring's business practices, he became irate. To air his opinions, he founded a paper of his own, *The People's Tribune*, a homely rag that Mark Twain mocked as "[a] pygmy . . . [with its] extravagant grandiloquence confined to a newspaper about the size of a double letter sheet."

Tucked among the pygmy's grandiloquence in the issue of January 13, 1870, was the observation that if righteous European standards of mine management were applied in Nevada, "not only Wm. Sharon but (with only an exception or two) his subservient mining superintendents, secretaries and foremen in the mines, would be promptly consigned to the public galleys or be locked behind the iron gratings of prisoners' cells." This was accompanied by an article urging that eleven specific allegations be pursued with a view toward criminal indictment. Two letters to the editor (one signed "A Miner" and the other "Silver Struck," although both were probably written by Wiegand himself) implied that Sharon and John B. Winters, superintendent of the Bank Ring's Yellow Jacket mine, had concealed an ore discovery in order to slap stockholders with an unjust assessment. All in all, it was a brazen edition, and while Wiegand was out distributing it, someone assaulted him.

Of what happened next, we have not only Wiegand's version but also a running commentary by Mark Twain, who devoted a long appendix to the episode in *Roughing It*. Twain had long since left the Comstock, and as far as we know Wiegand had done him no personal harm, so why make such a to-do of the assayer's shortcomings? Something about Wiegand got under Twain's skin, but let's hold off trying to specify what it was until the whole story is on the table.

Wiegand laid out his version in a long letter to the editor of the *Territorial Enterprise*, published a week after the fact (Twain reprinted it in full, and it takes up most of that *Roughing It* appendix). He starts off by complaining that he has paid dearly for his outspokenness: hardly anyone is bringing him ore to assay anymore. After briefly describing the first assault (being "felled to the ground" and "kicked" by a complete stranger) he moves on to a second one a day later. This time he knows who the assailant was: Superintendent Winters, who initiated hostilities by asking Wiegand to come to the Yellow Jacket office. (There is no evidence, by the way, that in going after Wiegand the superintendent was acting for anyone but his own hotheaded self.) After two changes of venue, the meeting took place in the *Gold Hill News* office, where Wiegand assumed he would be safe, although he prevailed upon the sheriff to come along and stand by, just in case. At this point in the appendix, Twain intrudes, snidely inviting the reader "to fancy this lamb [Wiegand] in battle."

Inside the *News* office, Wiegand faced Winters and *News* publisher Philip Lynch. Winters demanded "a retraction, in black and white, of those damnably false charges which you have preferred against me in that ---- ---- infamous sheet of yours, and you must declare yourself their author, that you published them knowing them to be false, and that your motives were malicious."

In response, Wiegand not only played it coy as to the authorship of the material being objected to but also tried to be Jesuitical about its nature. He informed Winters that the most important misapprehension which I notice is that you regard them as "charges" at all, when their context, both at their beginning and end, show they are not. These words introduce them: "*Such an investigation . . . we think MIGHT result in showing some of the following points.*" Then follow eleven specifications, and the succeeding paragraph shows that the suggested investigation "might EXONERATE those who are generally believed guilty." You see, therefore, the context *proves* they are not preferred as charges, and this you seem to have overlooked.

Not surprisingly, this windy hair-splitting did not mollify Winters, and Lynch backed him up by remarking, "If they are *not* charges, they certainly are *insinuations.*" Winters renewed his call for an apology and shook his fist in Wiegand's face. Wiegand was seated, and every time he tried to get up, Winters shoved him back down. (The sheriff had wandered off somewhere.)

In the next few paragraphs, the letter writer goes batty, as a bracketed comment by Twain makes sure we notice: "*The reader is requested not to skip the following.*" In tedious detail, Wiegand elaborates on a four-step strategy he adopted on the spot to assuage Winters, such as keeping cool and making no motion "which might be construed into the drawing of a weapon." But it's the fourth step that leaves the assayer wide open to ridicule: "I resolved to try on Winters, silently, and unconsciously to himself a mesmeric power which I possess over certain people, and which I have found to work even in the dark over the lower animals." Wiegand knows he's asking for trouble here: he quickly adds, "Does anyone smile at these last counts?" But he compounds the folly by declaring that at first his mojo seemed to be working, although in the end the lower animal in question came to his senses and struck Wiegand repeatedly with a horsewhip.

Forging on, Wiegand posits two theories as to why he was being so ill-treated, followed by four subtheories as to the intended result.

Near the end of a missive that consumes almost fifteen pages of small type, he assures the reader that he wouldn't have made all this public if Winters himself hadn't been going around blabbing about it. He finishes up by predicting that Winters will "resolve on my violent death, though it may take years to compass it."

Portions of Wiegand's letter show him in an admirable light. He refuses to capitulate to the bully, offering to sign only a watered-down semi-retraction, which reads in part, "I do not know those 'charges' (if such they are) to be true, and I hope that a critical examination would altogether disprove them." (Winters rejected the offer.) Moreover, Wiegand courageously repeats his attacks on the Bank Ring. But the letter serves up much silliness, too: the prissy language; the spinning of theories about the devious thought processes of a foe who in all likelihood was simply blind with rage; and, of course, the woo-woo stuff about mesmerism and the lower animals. Still, Twain's final kissoff (he calls the second assault upon Wiegand "the merited castigation of this weak, half-witted child") rounds out a case of writerly overkill.

It so happens that we can compare Twain's take on Wiegand with another, more measured one. Although published anonymously in the October 1, 1908, issue of the *Nevada Mining News*, the second treatment is almost surely the work of former *Territorial Enterprise* editor Joe Goodman, who knew Wiegand well.

Goodman called his article "The Tragedy of Conrad Wiegand," referring to the fact that, in 1880, a decade after his run-in with Winters, Wiegand killed himself. In the piece, Goodman praises the assayer as one of a kind, "in whom loftiness and purity were predominant forces, independent of all motives and surroundings and inseparable from every action of his life." Wiegand was aware that people didn't take him seriously, Goodman goes on, but rather than blame them for it, he "grieved to have so failed in making himself understood that it should be possible to thus misconstrue his purposes and actions."

According to Goodman, ill will between the Bank Ring and

Wiegand originated before Sutro began criticizing the Ring in public, and was quite personal. Sharon had tried to get Wiegand to "understamp" bars of bullion (i.e., mark them as being worth less than they actually were), so that after buying them the Bank of California could turn around, sell them for a price reflecting their true content, and realize a profit equal to the difference. Other Comstock assayers were cooperating, but Wiegand refused. In retaliation, the Bank Ring denied him its business. He railed against the bank in his newspaper (although apparently without mentioning the understamping contretemps), the bank put pressure on other mining firms to freeze him out, years of struggle went by, and Wiegand's troubles multiplied until he had to declare bankruptcy. He'd almost recovered, however, when he succumbed to a terrible temptation—"overstamping"—and thereby reduced himself to Sharon and the bank's level.

Goodman found out about this in the winter of 1879, when Wiegand called on the editor, who was living in the Bay Area at the time but making one of his periodic visits to Virginia City. They met in Goodman's hotel room, where Wiegand poured out his lacerated heart. Overdrawn at his bank, he had cast all his available silver into a bar worth $1,000, stamped it to reflect an additional content of $2,000 in gold, and sent it in that form to his bank. Because the bar contained no gold whatsoever, this was a fraudulent act. Having gotten away with it once, Wiegand did it again and again; he now had on deposit five mis-stamped bars, giving him a bank balance $8,000 higher than that to which he was entitled.

Thoroughly ashamed of himself, Wiegand hoped to borrow enough money to redeem the five bars. Goodman said he didn't have it to spare. Would Senator Jones be a good man to take the matter up with? Wiegand wondered. Goodman said he didn't know. Wiegand guessed he would go to Washington and find out. In the event, Jones turned him down, but relatives in Philadelphia came through, and Wiegand was able to retrieve those five bars. Peace of mind, however, proved elusive. As Goodman puts it, "He became a prey to remorse, and a few months afterward put an end to his wretched existence by hanging himself." (It was in the same article that Goodman broke the news that John Winters was a knowing participant in one of the Bank Ring's most outrageous practices. He'd mixed worthless rock in with ore being milled by the Ring's machines, and he'd confessed as much to Goodman personally.)

How much Twain knew about any of this while writing *Roughing It* in the early 1870s is unclear. What we can say for sure is that initially he'd looked at Wiegand the other way 'round, as a man deserving of praise for his honest assaying (a handwritten manuscript reflecting this approach has come down to us), only to change his mind. He tacked his revised assessment of Wiegand onto the end of *Roughing It*, according to Goodman, "in spite of repeated protests" from friends allowed to read the manuscript before publication.

In finally deciding to pillory a man who spoke out against the Ring's highhandedness, Twain was siding with the Comstock establishment. It may have come about this way. While working as a journalist in Virginia City, he'd refrained from delving beneath appearances to expose and explicate the real truth, preferring to amuse himself and his readers with spoofs and canards. Nothing dishonorable in that, but in light of what mine owners were starting to get away with at the time, Twain might have looked back on his younger self as rather a trifler. Wiegand's attempts to bring the Bank Ring to justice not only contrasted with Twain's hoaxes and "quaints"; they also threatened a group whose approval Twain had sought, won, and meant to keep, all the more so as he prepared to turn loose *Roughing It*, much of which is devoted to his Comstock days. While writing the first, pro-Wiegand draft of the appendix, Twain may have wondered why he was jeopardizing the book's potentially big sales in Virginia City and San Francisco by heaping praise on one of the Comstock's most vociferous detractors.

Another reason for Twain's ultimately harsh treatment of Wiegand may be an unconscious identification with the assaying publisher, who had got himself into trouble by the way he used words. As we will see in the next chapter, a carelessly worded item appearing in the *Territorial Enterprise* had led to a duel that Twain barely avoided fighting; he was a novice with guns, and had the firing actually commenced, there's a good chance he would have been the one to take a bullet. Like Wiegand, Twain can be considered a Western "lamb," not just a failed prospector and speculator but also one of the effete types who earn their daily bread the soft way: by putting words down on paper. True, Twain's genius had lifted him above other scribblers. But the inordinate amount of effort he put into attacking Wiegand in *Roughing It* (as Alexander Pope once asked, "Who breaks a butterfly upon a wheel?") suggests that Twain had internalized the popular notion that a writer is less of a man than the roughnecks who go down into the mines or the princes who pull the levers of capitalism. Slamming Wiegand at such length seems to have been Twain's way of distancing himself from a fellow with whom he had a lot in common.

Few men on the Comstock were less lamblike than Adolph Heinrich Joseph Sutro, whom we've encountered before as a Paiute War reporter and tunnel champion. He neglected his wife and children, scored low at "works and plays well with others," and reputedly lacked a sense of humor, but he was a paragon of energy and combativeness. Brilliant, curious, well-read, determined, he lived a life of vision and accomplishment. Mary McNair Mathews summed him up well by remarking that he seemed not to know the meaning of only two English words: "I can't." His go-it-alone, nothing-hidden-up-my-sleeve career stands in bracing contrast to the furtive machinations of those who opposed him. He repeatedly outmaneuvered the Bank Ring, and few nonmembers have had their way with the U.S. Congress more thoroughly than he.

Sutro accomplished all this as an outsider by nationality and religion. Born in 1830 to Jewish parents in Prussia, he was a passionate reader from an early age. He learned English in school but had to drop out at age sixteen after his father became seriously ill. With an older brother, Adolph managed the family business, a woolen-cloth factory, until it closed amid disruptions caused by the 1848 revolutions. Soon afterward, the family (minus the father, who had died) emigrated to America, settling in New York. Adolph, however, struck out for California, where so many men were already prospecting for gold.

While crossing the Isthmus of Panama, the young foreigner with the funny accent put the time to good use. Drawing upon an ingrained curiosity, he learned about the gold fields by pumping returnees for information; based on what they told him, he revised his plan. Mining was a crap shoot, he decided, and a better bet would be to supply goods to miners. He already had a leg up on such an enterprise, having toted along two bales of German cloth to sell. But the steamer on which he booked passage from Panama to California was crammed with cargo, and he had to leave his bales behind. He landed in San Francisco on November 21, 1850, with only his luggage and a letter of introduction. He took the letter to a shop-owner (imported glass and crockery), who hired Sutro as a watchman and let him sleep under the counter.

Just four years later, Sutro had graduated from crashing in someone else's store to running two of his own in San Francisco, one selling tobacco and the other variety goods, as well as owning a house that he rented out in the Sierra foothills. He and a cousin went partners in additional stores, one of which was memorable for the wooden Turk stationed out front: when a hidden pump was activated, the pasha took a puff and blew out smoke. (This gimmick may have been an early demonstration of Sutro's technological savvy.) It was around this time that Sutro got into a fight that resulted in his joining General Ambrose Burnside and future president Chester A. Arthur in the Great Nineteenth-Century Cheek Hair Club. The

other combatant went after Sutro with a knife, cutting him from ear
to mouth and leaving a scar that he hid by growing lush side-whiskers.
By now he was a husband and father, although he put little effort into
either role. He wasn't an adulterer (at least, not at first), just one more
Victorian-era paterfamilias who thought his duties began and ended
with keeping his wife and children in comfort.

In 1858, San Francisco was swept by gold fever again, although this
time from a faraway source. The Fraser River country of British
Columbia was lousy with gold, or so everyone said, and Sutro hur-
ried north to open a cigar store there. The rush fizzled out, and he
returned with nothing to show for himself save ownership of a
town lot in Victoria. But when news came of silver strikes in the
Washoe region of Utah, Sutro was ready to try again. In the spring
of 1860, he made the five-day trip to Virginia City: from San Francisco to Sacramento by boat, on to Folsom by rail, and to the final
destination by stage.

After climbing down in Virginia City, a town still boasting fewer
houses than tents, Sutro went into information-gathering mode.
He shared his findings in dispatches to the *Alta California*, among
them this telling critique:

> The mine-working is done without any system as yet. Most of
> the companies commence without an eye to future success;
> instead of running a tunnel low down on the bed, and thus
> sinking a shaft to meet it, which at once insures drainage, ven-
> tilation, and facilitates the work by going upwards, the claims
> are mostly entered from above, large openings made which
> require considerable timbering, and which expose the mine to
> wind and weather.

That is a remarkable observation, a tribute to Sutro's analytical
mind. In contrast to individual owners focusing on their mine only,

he sized up the whole landscape with an eye for its topography. Instead of continuing to dig down into the mountain from above and constantly lowering and lifting men and timber and machines and ore, why not tap into Mt. Davidson's depths from the side? At this point, Sutro hasn't had his great brainstorm to build a single cooperative tunnel providing access to most of the principal Comstock mines, but the idea of boring into the mountain laterally is clever. Possibly Sutro borrowed it from one of his "sources" as a journalist, but even so the above quotation hints at his perspicacity. Here he is, a Washoe resident of less than a month, already going public with a primitive form of the concept that will preoccupy him for the better part of the next two decades.

Sutro filed more newspaper reports, including his accounts of the Pyramid Lake War. Then he returned to San Francisco, where he ran another idea by a new partner, a German chemist he'd met on the boat from Panama City to San Francisco: the world needed better processes for separating silver and gold from quartz ore, and the two of them could provide one. Indeed they could, and Sutro took their recipe back to Comstock country, where he set up a mill in the Carson Valley town of Dayton. Soon the business was flourishing, with eight stamps crushing not only virgin ore but also tailings, from which the new process could tease out overlooked value. The company got a big break when the Gould & Curry mine gave it a milling contract; the result was a profit flow of $10,000 a month.

We have a verbal snapshot of Sutro from this period, courtesy of Twain, who was then at large in Comstock country. After meeting Sutro, he fingered one of the man's shortcomings in a piece for the *Territorial Enterprise*. Twain and Sutro were hanging out together one day when Twain cracked what he thought was a good joke. It fell flat. "Sutro is insensible to the more delicate touches of American wit," Twain complained, "and the effort was entirely lost on him." Yet Twain came to admire other facets of Sutro's makeup, as he was to demonstrate between hard covers a decade later:

Mr. Sutro, the originator of this prodigious enterprise [the tunnel], is one of the few men in the world who is gifted with the pluck and perseverance necessary to follow up and hound such an undertaking to its completion. He has converted several obstinate Congresses to a deserved friendliness toward his important work, and has gone up and down and to and fro in Europe until he has enlisted a great moneyed interest in it there.

If in the early 1860s Sutro had foreseen how little progress his "prodigious enterprise" would have made by the time that passage appeared in *Roughing It*, even he might have lost heart. But, lacking occult powers, he forged ahead. By 1864, he'd become rich and respected, with a seat on the Washoe Stock and Exchange Board and even a mine of his own with which to experiment. (Although Sutro never put his personal wealth on the line in his tunnel fight, having sizable assets to fall back on undoubtedly gave him confidence of a sort not available to Wiegand.) Nevada entered the Union, the Bank of California opened its branch in Virginia City, and Sutro polished his idea. Instead of advocating piecemeal tunneling as the best way for each separate company to get at its ore, he now plumped for a grand common passageway, which would solve two increasingly vexing problems—draining water out of the mines and bringing fresh air into them—while also making it easier to transport ore and waste rock out of the mountain. The prospectus he drew up called for breaking ground along the bank of the Carson River and tunneling more than three miles at a one and a half percent upward grade to intersect with the mines under Virginia City at the 1,640-foot level, then poking extensions north and south under the Lode. The main tunnel would accommodate two lanes of traffic, inbound for carts laden with supplies, outbound for carts full of ore, as well as a drainage ditch. He laid his proposal before the Nevada legislature, which granted him a franchise on February 4, 1865. Because virtually all of Comstock country belonged to the federal government and its miners were little more than squatters, the law's effect was dubious; but its enactment encouraged Sutro to incorporate and undertake surveys.

The next step was to round up private support. Going from mine to mine, explaining the project in detail, Sutro got twenty-three companies, representing ninety-five percent of the Lode's collective value, to sign agreements. Each firm would pay the tunnel firm a royalty of $2 per ton of ore extracted after the tunnel began serving its mine; additional charges would be levied as men, equipment, and ore moved through the tunnel. For his part, Sutro pledged to obtain $3 million in stock subscriptions by August 1, 1867, and to spend about $400,000 annually on the project until it was completed.

Sutro's brainchild won a key endorsement from the Bank of California. William Ralston himself signed a gung-ho letter that Sutro could wave in front of potential investors. It read in part: *"Too much cannot be said of the importance of this great work*, if practicable upon any remunerative basis. We learn that the scheme has been very carefully examined by scientific men, and *that they unhesitatingly pronounced in its favor on all points—practicality, profit, and great public utility."* Sutro could hardly have asked for a better plug, and he also signed up a bank favorite, Senator William Stewart, as the Sutro Tunnel Company's first president. With Stewart's crucial support, in 1866 Congress passed two laws almost simultaneously: the Sutro Tunnel Act, which granted a tunnel right-of-way to "A. Sutro, his heirs and assigns" and approved the concept of the mining companies' paying him royalties; and, a day later, the first general mining law, which went some way toward regularizing the crazy-quilt of Comstock claims.

Flush with these victories, Sutro traveled to New York City and called upon financiers. The Easterners listened politely but wondered why they should commit funds to a project when Sutro's friends and neighbors had yet to do so. Taking their point, Sutro asked for it in writing. He got what he wanted, a letter calling upon Westerners to pony up "say $400,000 or $500,000," in which case "we think you will find it comparatively an easy task to obtain the balance of the funds here." Signers included the powerful banker August Belmont.

Back home, Sutro took care of some housekeeping matters. The year 1866 was ending, and the August 1867 deadline for raising that $3 million in subscriptions loomed. He went to the mining companies and negotiated a year's extension. He also revisited the Nevada legislature, which at his behest passed a resolution calling on the federal government to subsidize the project: because precious metals contributed heavily to the burgeoning value of the nation's taxable property, the argument went, it made sense for the feds to help coax more production out of proven bonanzas. Next, he concentrated on meeting the New Yorkers' demand for a Western show of good faith. By May he had pledges for a total of $600,000, with prospects for more. Everything seemed to be falling into place for Adolph Sutro.

But now his rough-edged personality betrayed him. He wrote and disseminated a pamphlet predicting that a new town to be built at the tunnel's mouth—and to be given the name Sutro—would supersede Virginia City. And he let his tongue get away from him, predicting that, once built, Sutro the town would lord it over the region, while up in Virginia City "the owls would roost." This was a blunder: Virginia City had an assessed valuation of nearly $7 million even apart from the mines, and its residents weren't likely to stand by while their town was strangled. Sutro's intemperate language got Sharon and the Bank Ring thinking, and something they hadn't previously picked up on now became clear: how far away ore removed through the tunnel would end up from their mills in and around Virginia City, and how close it would be to Sutro's mills in the town of Sutro. The Bank reexamined its endorsement of the project, and the matter came to a head at the annual meeting of the Crown Point Mining Company, a bank fiefdom at the time, on June

7, 1867. In a secret gathering the night before, the bank had nixed a proposal to buy $75,000 worth of tunnel stock and called for replacement of the mine's president and superintendent. The next day, Crown Point's stockholders agreed.

The reversal took Sutro by surprise, but his fertile mind went to work figuring out where he'd gone wrong. Apparently unaware of the resentment caused by his new-town scenario, he thought the rub might be Nevada's request for federal aid. Until now the Comstockers had acted largely on their own, but if Sutro and the legislature had their way, the feds would come barging in, disrupting the bank's hegemony. He might also have noted changing conditions on the Comstock. As miners dug deeper, the most serious water problems went into abeyance; the zones now being worked were comparatively dry, and the companies had installed mightier pumps and fans since Sutro first floated the tunnel concept. Also, the bank had amassed so much power that it hated to pay royalties to anyone, and the idea of building a railroad, with which the tunnel would compete, was beginning to form in Sharon's cunning mind. Once the Bank Ring made up its mind, it acted decisively. Stewart resigned as Tunnel Company president, the rest of the promised $600,000 dried up, and Sutro found himself on the outs, with old friends in Virginia City crossing the street to avoid him.

He reacted in the only way he knew how. "He made what he called a sacred vow," his co-biographers wrote, "to devote the remainder of his life to carrying out the tunnel project. He would defend his rights as long as there was breath in his body."

Of the three places where he might turn for help—Nevada, New York, and Washington—Sutro concentrated on the nation's capital. He was just getting warmed up there when a telegram reached Nevada's senators with a terse message: "We are opposed to the Sutro Tunnel project, and desire it defeated, if possible." The lead signature was William Sharon's, followed by the names of several Comstock mine superintendents. Nevertheless, Sutro made headway with the House of Representatives, in part because he had the ear of perhaps its most powerful member, Thaddeus Stevens. But Congress adjourned without passing a tunnel bill, and Stevens died two weeks later.

In Virginia City, a disastrous fire that broke out in the Yellow Jacket mine on April 7, 1869, tipped the balance toward Sutro. Possibly started by a candle that someone forgot to douse at the end of a shift, the blaze consumed supporting timbers, leading to a cave-in that "caused . . . smoke-filled, oxygen-starved air to blast through other parts of the mine like a gale force wind of poison." The foul air spread to two other mines, the Kentuck and the Crown Point, and drove back would-be rescuers. Some miners died while trying to reach elevator cages that could hoist them to the surface; stumbling around in the dark, they fell down open shafts. The rescue effort had its share of heroics (including those performed by a future U.S. senator, John P. Jones, described later in this chapter), but in the end an estimated 45 miners were dead.

Never one to miss a trick, Sutro now added safety to the tunnel's rationales. He hoped to make his case before a delegation from the House Ways and Means Committee, which was on a field trip to have a look at the new transcontinental railroad. In San Francisco, Sharon and the bank hogged the committee members' attention, but Sutro managed to get through to them, and they promised to stop in Virginia City on their way back. There Sharon tried to shut Sutro out again, informing one committee member, "Sir, the Bank has waved its hand over the Comstock Lode and ordered Sutro away. That's the whole of the transaction as it seems to me." The pomposity of this remark backfired, causing the committee to wonder why the bank was so vehemently anti-Sutro.

Sutro went before a joint meeting of two Comstock miners' unions and made his case for the tunnel as a lifesaver. The unions pledged $50,000 to the cause, enough to start work. On September 20, Sutro explained his new rationale to a wider public in an impassioned speech-cum-magic-lantern-show, at Piper's Opera House. Daringly, he baited his opponents with a martial phrase of General

Grant's, telling listeners he had no choice but to "expose some of the doings of an institution called the California Bank. I shall tell the truth, without fear or reservation, for I have come here to 'fight it out on this line,' and I intend to do so, 'though the heavens fall.'" He lambasted the bank crowd as "the vampires that have nearly sucked you dry" and illustrated the tunnel's new additional purpose by displaying a pair of contrasting cartoons. The first one showed miners trapped in a fiery shaft while outside, at the top, their wives and children agonized over their fates; in the second, the Sutro Tunnel was in place down below, the miners were escaping through it, and their euphoric loved ones were waiting to embrace them at the tunnel's mouth.

As Sutro finished, some members of the audience were ready to charge out and string somebody up. Sutro calmed them down and sat back to wait for newspaper coverage of the event; the *Enterprise* obliged by reprinting the speech in its entirety, giving it the whole front page and two columns inside.

Speaking out seems to have been therapeutic for Sutro: he was living up to his self-image as a crusader. A month later, he staged the ceremony of swinging the first pick; the tunnel project was now underway. The *Gold Hill News*, a captive of the Bank Ring, took a dim view of the event: "His first pick has been heretofore, is now, and ever will be, a pick at the pockets of all honest workingmen and others, whom he can 'bamboozle' into supporting him like a gentleman at other people's expense." But the editor of a more influential paper, Horace Greeley of the *New York Tribune*, read Sutro's speech and came out in favor of a federal loan to finish the tunnel.

The Bank Ring now stooped to subterfuge. It sent its attorney to Washington, where he and Nevada's congressman drafted a handwritten bill to repeal the tunnel rights and buried it among the papers on the Speaker's desk. The idea was to get the thing passed before anyone knew what it meant. Learning of the gambit, Sutro rode the transcontinental railroad to Washington, where he had the hidden bill printed and circulated at his own expense. Ways and Means Committee members who'd been on that Western trip recalled Sharon's arrogance and spread the word. The bill was defeated.

But all Sutro had done was quash an attack; his project was no closer to being fully financed. Confident in the soundness of his position, he hatched the idea of a special congressional commission to investigate and report on the tunnel's feasibility. On April 4, 1871, President Grant signed into law a bill to that effect. From late June to late August, the three commissioners (two officers of the Army Corps of Engineers and a professor of mining engineering) conducted their field work.

True to form, the Bank Ring tried to control what the commissioners saw and heard. Comstock superintendents chaperoned the commissioners around, steering them to trouble-free mines and peppering them with upbeat comments about how smoothly the work was going, with no serious impediments, not even the aqueous kind. Sutro managed to pry the visitors away for a tunnel tour, but to him they seemed meek in their questioning. In the end, they chose to believe the supers: the tunnel, they said in their report to Congress, was "not a necessity."

Sutro was flabbergasted. The tunnel already ran 2,000 feet into the mountainside, but now it might be stymied by the incompetence of three so-called experts. He could flag obvious weaknesses in their report (who but a dolt would put stock in such observations as "the miners with whom we conversed did not complain," made when their bosses were standing right there?) but Congress might be too busy to look past the bottom-line recommendation. The plain truth, he moaned, was that the three men were "not quite up to the rascalities of that bank ring out there. . . . They took many things for granted which these men told them; took it all for gospel; thought it was just so. They were not sharp enough for them at all." But how could Sutro make that case on the Hill? Almost in desperation, he envisioned a kind of verbal jousting match in which the commissioners would have to defend their conclusions against the tunnel's most knowledgeable proponent: himself. He managed to sell the idea to the House Committee on Mines and Mining.

The hearings began on February 12, 1872, and lasted until the end of March. Sutro was a forensic virtuoso throughout. He tripped up the three commissioners on figures, forced them to admit they'd relied on the superintendents' rosy claims without checking them against the companies' records, and nailed the professor as one of those irritating academics who qualify their every statement with "perhaps" or "possibly." The bank's lawyer, left flat-footed by these attacks on the careless commissioners, could do little more than carp about all the speeches Sutro was being allowed to make. (The lawyer would not even acknowledge whom he was working for; he kept insisting he was appearing on behalf of the whole Comstock, whatever that was.)

Sutro delivered a masterful closing argument, as effective in its own way as his Opera House speech in Virginia City, and had it published as a slender book with red-leather binding and a pick-wielding miner embossed on the cover. A distillation of Sutro's mind in action, the volume still makes for rousing reading, with subheadings such as "RING RASCALITIES," "HIDING ORE," "CERTAIN RUIN TO OUTSIDERS," and "THEIR OWN LETTERS CONDEMN THEM." Sutro flays the Bank Ring throughout, as when he claims that "the Bank of California rules and runs that country. They owned almost everybody in it, and anybody that refuses to bend the knee to them they drive away." He finishes up by pointing out that it was Comstock miners who donated funds to start the tunnel, and who continue to support it: "Now, I say, will the Government consider the interests of these laboring men?" The House Committee said yea to that: rejecting its own commission's report, it recommended passage of a bill to lend the Sutro Tunnel Company $2 million to finish the project.

The Senate balked, however, and the federal loan was never

made, but in the meantime Sutro had lined up $1.4 million in private loans from McCalmont Brothers and Company, a British investment firm, and other European sources. His workmen drilled and excavated as fast as he could drive them (over a two-year period, the tunnel advanced an average of three hundred eight feet a month), and he got started on Sutro, his town on the banks of the Carson, which he'd carefully planned so that, unlike haphazard Virginia City, it formed an orderly grid. He also found time to help with the successful reelection campaign of C. W. Kendall, a sympathizer who was now serving as Nevada's lone congressman. And if you suspect that Sutro wasn't paying all that much attention to the tunnel itself while keeping so many other balls in the air, consider the good use he made of a subtle observation about equine behavior.

> Early in the history of the tunnel horses were tried for pulling the cars loaded with waste rock, but when anything touched a horse's ears the horse would throw up his head, hit the overhanging rock, and hurt his skull. Mules, on the other hand, would drop their heads and avoid injury. Although steam, compressed air, and finally electrically driven (storage battery) locomotives were tried, it was always [mules] who were called back and did the work.

One thing Sutro did skimp on was letter-writing to his family when he was absent from home, which was most of the time. He dictated his messages to a secretary, who took them down in shorthand, then wrote them up in longhand, and sometimes even signed them for the boss. Sutro's brother Hugo needled him about this practice, once suggesting that if Adolph couldn't pay a personal visit, "send your substitute; he can bring us a shorthand conversation." But Sutro's single-mindedness was paying off: his dream was becoming a reality at last.

The Bank Ring wasn't yet done with Sutro, though. In the Sharon-friendly *Gold Hill News*, Doten called him "Shylock Sutro" and mocked his accent with phonetic spelling: "Mine friends, de baper vots brinted in dis town—der GOLT HILL NEWS—is der vorsht and meanest of dem all," and so on. (A rival newspaper accused the *News* of having "Sutro on the brain.") A friendly Ophir stockholder warned Sutro of a movement afoot: Comstock mining companies were ganging up to levy assessments with which to fund anti-tunnel lobbying. The underlying strategy was Byzantine: for some time, the firms had been refusing to take their claims to patent (i.e., to comply with the new federal rules for obtaining ownership of the land described in a claim) because the patents for Comstock claims would specify that royalties had to be paid to the owner of the Sutro Tunnel. Rather than suffer this indignity, the mining companies supported a bill to make their foot-dragging universal by stopping all ongoing patent proceedings in their tracks.

Sutro's countermove was to have a friendly Congressman introduce a bill to give Comstock mine owners a choice: perfect their claims within six months or lose them. This passed the House and went to the Senate, where Sutro scored perhaps his greatest coup of all. The bill fell under the jurisdiction of the Committee on Mines and Mining, whose new chairman was John P. Jones, the victor over Bill Sharon in the 1872 Nevada Senate race. Although not beholden to the Bank Ring, Jones was a mine owner himself, and he no more wanted to pay royalties to Sutro than they did. Appearing before the committee, Sutro brazenly questioned Chairman Jones, who admitted that he owned a Comstock mine. Sutro then requested that the bill be referred to a different committee, one whose chairman had no such conflict of interest, and after much debate the committee so agreed. Successfully challenging a committee chairman in the clubbiest of American governmental bodies on a point of honor is an extraordinary feat, but it was only one of several instances when Sutro essentially told Congress how to run itself. The challenge brought success of a kind: the Senate ultimately decided not to meddle in the controversy, leaving it to be worked out by the parties or settled by the courts, and the status quo was fine with Sutro.

To consolidate his victory, Sutro thought he'd better keep Sharon out of the Senate. Hence, after Sharon announced his candidacy for Stewart's seat in 1874, Sutro entered the race as an independent. Sharon owned the *Territorial Enterprise* by now, and it dutifully slammed his opponent under the headline "Sutro Annihilated—His Contracts All Violated—His Robberies Exposed." To combat these slurs, Sutro returned to Piper's Opera House for another stemwinding speech, again complete with a lantern slide-show, but this time it didn't work. Not only did Sharon win handily; he even carried Storey County—Comstock country.

The tunnel, however, was getting a bit longer every day. Sutro introduced the more efficient diamond drills, his mules kept their heads down, and the death of two men in a dynamite blast proved to be only a temporary setback. (In all, Sutro claimed, only twelve men were killed while working on his tunnel. For comparison he cited the Hoosac, a five-mile railway tunnel in Massachusetts, which had cost one hundred eighty-five workers their lives.) But progress varied according to the texture of the rock being tunneled through. Whenever the workmen hit clay, delays were likely. The procedure was to bore through the clay, move it out on the rails, put up stabilizing timbers, and prepare to move on. But the remaining clay matrix would swell and ooze, lifting the ground and putting pressure on the timbers. "On one occasion," Sutro's biographers note, "48 feet of clay floor swelled as much as $7\frac{1}{8}$ inches one night and the track in that portion had to be relaid three times."

Even so, by the spring of 1878 Sutro's crews knew they were nearing their goal: they could now hear noises from the mines toward which they were probing. But foul air and oppressive heat were slowing them down. Consider, for example, the experience of an engineer who manned the blowers at one of the ventilating shafts. When he went down for his first underground visit, he buckled under the conditions. "[He] sat down on a rock only to jump up. He swore that he would never sit down in there again; he said it was so hot he had been burned. He promised to send in the other three engineers so that they too could experience the heat and understand the absolute necessity for keeping those blowers going."

Ice rations had to be increased, mules were dying, but the Savage mine was getting tantalizingly close. The big question now had to do with the physics of the breakthrough. All observers but one predicted that air from the mines would rush down through the tunnel; the lone holdout was (naturally) Sutro, who insisted it would blow the other way around. On September 1, 1878, contact was made, nine years after the kickoff date. Although the workmen were 20,489 feet from the starting point, they broke through a mere eighteen inches away from the spot Sutro had aimed for, an astounding achievement given the era's tools and measuring devices. But this was only a puncture, not the big blow that would decide the directional issue. So sure was Sutro of his ground that he sent a wire to caution the Savage's superintendent against rashly widening the new aperture: "Should your men succeed in knocking a drill hole through, let them stop and not enlarge it until I am fully notified. There should be ample time given for your men and ours to retire, for I am afraid a column, several thousand feet in length, of hot, foul air, suddenly set in motion, might prove fatal to the men."

Savage miners chopped away at the opening anyway, and the currents behaved more or less as Sutro had predicted. In fact, the incoming air was so fetid that the Savage men made a dash for their ventilation shafts; now they had some sense of the conditions in which the tunnelers had been working so long. Later that night, joined by his daughters Rosa and Kate, Sutro stepped through the opening and exulted in his triumph: eighteen years had gone by since he first had the idea, $3.5 million had been spent, but he'd overcome lopsided odds by applying his own brains, eloquence, and indefatigable zest for a fight.

With the tunnel nearing completion, Sutro still had to wrangle with Comstock mining companies. Some were holding back royalty payments on the niggling ground that he hadn't fulfilled the original agreement to the letter. The ill will coalesced around a dispute over lingering problems of water disposal. The Savage and Hale & Norcross owners were threatening to pump water from their mines into the tunnel before Sutro could finish cutting the ditch needed to accommodate it; for his part, Sutro was threatening to shut them out by installing a bulkhead. The Savage people went to court and got an anti-bulkhead injunction. A failure of communication led to the arrest of several tunnel workers for disobeying the injunction, and two weeks later, on February 16, 1879, one-hundred-thirty-degree water from the Hale & Norcross was sent without warning on its scalding way into the tunnel. Tunnel workers and their mules fell back, then broke into a sprint, barely making it out of the tunnel before the water caught up with them. Cave-ins seemed likely, and the tunnel's very survival was in doubt. But everybody took a deep breath, the tunnel stabilized, and on April 2 Sutro and the mine owners struck a deal: he had ninety days to finish the drainage ditch, but his royalty payments were cut in half, to $1 a ton of ore removed from the mines unless it assayed at more than $40 a ton, in which case the old rate of $2 per ton would apply.

A new wave of workmen came in to finish the tunnel, and the town of Sutro enjoyed a brief period of growth. Adolph Sutro oversaw its construction at such a level of detail that he ordered a supply of frogs for its pond. (The aide taxed with carrying out this assignment explained that "there is no difficulty at all in finding them—but no one can tell the male from the female—so that we would have to chance it as to sex.")

Unfortunately, however, the tunnel was perfect in every way but the vital one of timing. Sutro may have hit the mark he'd been aiming at, but in the meantime the action had gone elsewhere. When the tunnel came on line in 1878, the working level at many mines had dipped 1,000 to 1,500 feet beneath it, greatly reducing its ability to help with drainage or ventilation. Nor did the tunnel open up any new bonanzas, for the simple reason that there were none. Nobody knew it yet (although the Bonanza Kings, with their crack intelligence system, had an inkling), but the Comstock was just about played out. One expert on the Comstock argues that Sutro's freelance approach had all but doomed the project from the start: "If the mining companies wanted to prospect and drain the Lode at great depth they should have formed a corporation and taken stock and financed it by assessments. In that event it would have been finished in time to be of use."

But having accomplished what he set out to do, Sutro didn't brood on its shortcomings. In fact, he was indulging in some relaxation now, including a dalliance with a Mrs. Allen, known as "the $90,000 diamond widow" for the splendid jewelry pinned to her black weeds. Whether she and Sutro were anything more than chums is unclear (Sutro insisted not), but Leah Sutro, Adolph's wife, had no doubt about it. On surprising the two at dinner one night in Virginia City's International Hotel, she bopped her husband with a champagne bottle. Adolph was so embarrassed that he skipped a gala event the next day: ex-president Grant's visit to the Comstock, complete with a tunnel tour. Leah missed the occasion, too, having decamped to the couple's San Francisco house.

Whatever the truth about the diamond widow, the Sutros' marriage was now beyond repair. There was no divorce, but the couple lived apart until Leah's death in 1893. Adolph continued to do well by her and the children financially and rewarded himself with a mansion, complete with elaborate garden and statues, at Sutro Heights, on cliffs above the Pacific. (There is an amusing photo of Sutro stretched out in a rocky niche among those cliffs, a live statue with top hat: he may have had a sense of humor after all, though more visual than verbal.)

The tunnel royalties were not going directly into Sutro's pockets, but into the account of the Sutro Tunnel Company, of which he was a minority owner. Early in 1880, he began selling out. One historian regards this as a shabby exit. In his view, Sutro knew or should have known that his tunnel had come on line too late to be of much use; for once in his life, the great loner disregarded his conscience and "adopted the code of the Comstock." But Sutro's co-biographers give him the benefit of the doubt. "Who could blame him," they ask, "if he chose at this time to turn his tunnel stock into cash and let eager new shareholders reap whatever profits (or losses) operation of the tunnel might bring?"

By spring, in any case, he'd liquidated most of his share for just over $700,000 and stepped down as tunnel superintendent, although he retained his seat on the board of trustees. His co-biographers conclude that Sutro "got out just in time; his stock was sold for more money than could have been realized at any later period." This is an understatement, because it wasn't long before the stock, bought by McCalmont Brothers and small speculators, had lost all its value. The tunnel remained in service for fifty years, mostly as a gigantic drainpipe (it drains the Comstock to this day), but the burg of Sutro withered until it joined the ranks of Nevada's many ghost towns.

Sutro was only 48 when he walked away from the tunnel, and Nevada. After moving to San Francisco, he is not known to have ever set foot in the Silver State again. During Act Two of his life, he engaged in three pursuits: buying and developing San Francisco real estate, book-collecting, and politics. He was eminently successful in the first two. He purchased land until he owned an estimated one-twelfth of the city. His urban projects included a street railway and two pleasure grounds on San Francisco's seaward edge: the Cliff House resort and the Sutro Baths, the latter consisting of an enormous glass-paneled pavilion, five saltwater pools, and one freshwater pool, which together could host 10,000 bathers at a time. His bibliomania took him to England, where dealers called him "the California Book Man"; many of his holdings, estimated at 125,000 volumes before some were destroyed in a fire, are now housed in the Sutro Library at San Francisco State University.

In politics he started off well. He spoke out against the Big Four railroad magnates (Mark Hopkins, Leland Stanford, Collis P. Huntington, and Charles Crocker), who were lobbying Congress to defer for ninety-nine years their repayment of a federal loan to build the Central Pacific Railroad. This time, Sutro wasn't the lonesome Lochinvar of the tunnel fight. William Randolph Hearst was on his side, as was Hearst's star columnist, Ambrose Bierce, who referred to the Big Four collectively as "the railrogues" and Stanford in particular as "$tealand £andford." The railrogues lost.

But in the final phase of his career, the paladin who had bested the Bank of California and dictated procedure to Congress was undone by elective office. He let representatives of the People's Party, an arm of the populist movement, talk him into running for mayor of San Francisco in 1894, when he was 64. He won, but the give-and-take of politicking was beyond him, and he and the board of supervisors repeatedly clashed. At the same time, Sutro's heavy investment in city property ensnared him in conflicts of interest that made Senator Jones look like a piker, and San Francisco's antiquated city charter saw to it that the mayor was constantly being pestered to make petty decisions. When it was all over, two years later, the *Examiner* summed up the experience this way: "He passed his term in a state of exasperation." Sutro agreed with that verdict. "I have always been master of my situation," he reminisced. "I have always had a number of men under my employ, and they did as I told them. I could not manage the politicians."

The experience may well have shortened Sutro's life. He suffered from diabetes during his brief retirement, and his mind became clouded. He died in 1898, at age 68. The Sutro Baths decayed into ruins; along with a successor to Cliff House (two earlier structures were destroyed by fire), they are now part of the Golden Gate National Recreation Area. Along with the Sutro Library and certain boulevards that lead to the city's ocean neighborhoods, they still make for an impressive legacy, nearly all of it built for or since opened to the public. In this way, too, Sutro operated as a loner, the only man to make a fortune on the Comstock and devote a large part of it to civic improvement. In one respect, though, he was a brother to the Bank Ring and all the Bonanza Kings except Mackay: other than laying out a town that barely made it out of the starting gate, Sutro gave nothing back to Nevada.

The opportunist who broke out of the Ring was John Percival Jones, who has already found his way into these pages as a mine superintendent and U.S. senator from Nevada (he abided through five consecutive terms while Sharon and Fair came and went, and Stewart went and came again). Jones was born on the English side of the border with Wales in 1829, the fifth of a stonemason and his wife's thirteen children. John was still young when the family immigrated to the States, settling in Cleveland. Having graduated from high school there, in 1849 he was marking time as a bank employee when he came down with what he called "California fever." He and one of his brothers booked passage on a boat that went around Cape Horn and landed them in San Francisco.

John drifted north to Trinity County, where after failing as a prospector he went to work in a general store. A contemporary described him as

> ruddy-cheeked, and with a sparkling eye and a careless disposition, you would predict of him that his sole ambition was to pass leisurely and unostentatiously through the world. He was possessed of a large fund of good nature, with a soft and unag-

gressive manner, that won upon all with whom he was brought into contact.

Young Jones could also call upon remarkable sangfroid, as he showed while minding that store during a blizzard. When the citizens of Weaverville awoke the morning after, they heard a terrific crash. They ran outside to see that the store had collapsed under the weight of piled-up snow, with Jones presumably inside. They called out to him as they removed snow and debris but got no answer. They dug all the way down to the store's counter, under which they found Jones, wrapped in blankets, "taking it as easy as a clam at high tide." The rescuers gave Jones a bawling-out, wanting to know why he hadn't responded to their calls. "If I had answered you and let you know that I was not hurt," he replied, "you would not have dug me out of the snow, and then I would have had all the work to do myself."

Yet behind that sluggish exterior lay an inquisitive mind: Jones was famous in Trinity County for the number of books he bought and read. Wishing to put his mind to work, and despite having no legal training, he ran successfully for justice of the peace in 1856 and again in 1858. Three years later, he was elected sheriff of Trinity County. The next stop in his political climb was Sacramento, where he represented the county in the state senate from 1863 to 1867. Although he'd started out as a Union Democrat, he was now a Republican, and to appeal to rural voters the party nominated him for lieutenant governor in 1867. As a campaigner, he could marshal anecdotes gleaned from all that reading, and voters liked him. The Democrats won both offices, but Jones outpolled his running mate by over 4,000 votes. Some observers thought the ticket might have won if he'd been at the top of it.

Out of office, newly married, and with no immediate prospects, Jones was about to forsake the West (he'd already bought a boat ticket for New York) when he ran into an old friend, Alvinza Hayward. As Jones told the story, "I was the very man he wanted to see.

He wanted me to go and take the superintendence of a mine that he thought might have a good stake in it. He offered me a fair salary, which I accepted." This was a Comstock mine, and Jones was on his way to a new life in Nevada.

Jones performed well in his new field, and nobly, too. His disputed role in the 1869 Yellow Jacket fire has already been mentioned, although in truth it was a one-sided dispute: Bill Sharon got nowhere with the insinuation (made during the 1872 Senate race) that Jones had set the fire in order to game the stock market. According to Eliot Lord, Superintendent Jones had in fact been a hero at the time. After all hope of finding miners alive was gone, he and a young miner named Nagle were trying to cut off the steam being pumped into the Crown Point, to which the fire had spread, so that bodies down below might be more easily recovered. Their precise goal was to drive a sheet-iron plate through the steam pipe. As Lord tells it,

[the pair] worked for fifteen minutes to close the conduit in an atmosphere so foul that a bunch of nine lighted candles gave scarcely the usual light of one. Nagle was soon dazed and breathing heavily, but the superintendent, a man of unusual chest compass, suffered little, though he was conscious of an increasing intoxication. The blows of his sledge-hammer fell wide of the mark, striking the plate unevenly; yet he was so expert a miner that he could ordinarily cleave a fly on the wall with his pick. Still the work was nearly completed when the faint flame went out, leaving the workmen in total darkness. Nagle, half delirious, jumped upon the cage at the instant, and the superintendent had scarcely time to follow before the unnerved miner jerked the bell-rope violently, and the cage was dragged up through the warped timbers of the shaft at a rate of speed which terrified the men upon it, who expected to hear the strained cable snap momently. Half way up Nagle fell fainting against his companion, who held him tightly until the shaft mouth was reached, when he dropped the insensible body on the floor and staggered out of the cage, drunk as never before, nor since.

Jones's great chance came in November of 1870, when the Crown Point was back in service and he learned of a promising new vein. The natural thing to do—the stolidly Jones-ish thing—would have been to pass this news on to his bosses in the Bank Ring. Instead, Jones shared it with Hayward, the very man who'd lured him to Comstock country three years earlier. As we've seen, Hayward, a few other speculators, and Jones combined to seize control of the Crown Point by quietly buying its stock without Bill Sharon catching on until it was too late.

Shortly after the takeover, the Crown Point went into bonanza, and its stock price leapt from $2 a share to $1,800. Jones seems to have left no record of his thoughts as he went around his employers' backs, but for once in his life the amiable plodder had behaved like a bird of prey. (What we can say is that he and Hayward knew exactly what they were doing: almost their first act after the mine came through for them was to emulate the Bank Ring by launching a milling business.) Suddenly and ducally rich, Jones invested in far-flung enterprises and contemplated reentering politics. Nevada's Republican Party was thinking along the same lines: then as now, a candidate with a fat purse was a decided asset, and Jones was an experienced campaigner. This happened to be the year when Sharon went after the same seat, campaigning so ruthlessly that he leveled his incendiary charge at Jones. But Jones kept his poise, and Sharon ultimately dropped out of the race.

For all the rancor they traded back and forth, however, Sharon and Jones didn't take long to make up. Two years later, when Sharon ran for the Senate seat Bill Stewart was vacating, Jones endorsed him. Given Jones's well-known affability, reconciliation probably came naturally to him. As for Sharon, he saw eye-to-eye with Jones on the sanctity of laissez-faire capitalism, and they also shared a personal interest. On his original voyage to California, Jones had entered into a shipboard flirtation with one Maria Malloy. Nearly a quarter century later, Jones was invited to the Sharons' house for dinner, and when he was introduced to Mrs. Sharon, who should she be but Maria? From that moment on, Jones was an ego-stroking reminder to Sharon that he'd won the prize to which both men had aspired.

In addition, Sharon was nothing if not strategy-minded, and the Jones he now encountered was a different man from the underling of old. The new Jones had proved adept at Sharon's own game of high-stakes gambling and had played the part of a nouveau elitist by moving into a palatial residence in Santa Monica, California (thereby also conforming to the pattern of representing Nevada in Congress while living elsewhere). For all these reasons, Sharon was willing to admit his erstwhile foe into the inner circle of Western plutocrats. Jones was happy to be admitted, as he showed after the Bank of California closed and Ralston swam to his death in the ocean: Jones made a $200,000 pledge to help save the institution.

It was rumored that Jones and Sharon were even collaborating on a business venture, a railroad from Nevada to Salt Lake City. Such a line would take patronage away from the Central Pacific, and Jones posed a thorny problem to its owners because they considered him too rich to be bought. Collis P. Huntington and his partners wrote one another hand-wringing letters discussing possible moves to foil the alleged plan, but in the event Sharon and Jones settled upon a quite different and far more modest route, just from Los Angeles to the Pacific, nothing for the Central Pacific to fret about. Besides, it turned out that Jones could be bought: a gift of some railroad bonds locked up his vote for the "railrogues" in the matter of postponing repayment of their federal loan. "Jones is very good natured now," the reassured Huntington wrote a colleague, "and we need his help in Congress very much, and I have no doubt we shall have it." That they did, and in return Jones was able to count on the railroads scratching *his* back throughout the rest of his career.

No, there wasn't much doubt about Jones anymore. After making a fortune by outmaneuvering the bank on that one dramatic occasion, he slipped back into character, seldom to make waves again. Throughout his five terms in the Senate, he toed the establishment line, serving on low-profile committees and providing a reliable vote for the rich and powerful. The only issue that could get a rise out of him was silver, when it surfaced from time to time. One notable occasion was in the early 1890s, as the Sherman Silver Purchase Act was in the process of being repealed. Along with his colleague Stewart, Jones mounted a pro-Sherman filibuster:

> Dressed in a long black coat and easily recognizable with his flowing white beard, Jones delivered his longest and most important oration on silver in October 1893. His verbosity on this occasion was unprecedented for the easygoing senator. Requiring large portions of eight days over a two-week period for delivery, Jones's stupendous speech occupied more than 100 pages in the *Congressional Record*, and topped 450 pages when printed.

Despite their longwindedness, the cause espoused by Stewart and Jones lost, and the uproar in Nevada was such that each was obliged to switch from the Republican to the Silver Party. In 1896, Jones even backed William Jennings Bryan, the Democratic candidate for president, as the man who would "[restore] silver to its constitutional place in the history of the Republic." But after winning the election, William McKinley had the good sense to award Nevada's federal patronage to Stewart and Jones, and by the end of the decade both renegades were back in the Republican fold.

After retiring in 1902, Jones withdrew to his Santa Monica estate, where he died in 1912. He wasn't a slug; unlike Sharon and

Fair, he actually showed up regularly in the Senate chamber and took care of his committee work. But when you measure his thirty-year tenure in the Senate against what he accomplished there, you can hardly avoid rating him as one more place-holding Comstock graduate who nonrepresented Nevada on every issue but what to do about silver.

EIGHT

Washoe Giants

In 1864, both Nevadans and Californians had rejoiced in the election of William Morris Stewart as one of Nevada's first two U.S. senators: Nevadans admired him, and Californians believed they could rely on him. Stewart quickly cut a figure on the Hill, as noted by a contemporary journalist:

> Perhaps none of the younger members of the Senate attract so much attention as Wm. M. Stewart of Nevada. He is 38 years old, a large and good-looking man, has a light complexion and a very long sandy beard and mustache. . . . On the floor he is usually quiet and noticeable from his youthful appearance and heavy beard. . . . He is a man of executive force and will and deserves much credit for raising [sic] from humble life to great wealth and an honorable fame in national councils.

Stewart and another Comstock alumnus, Mark Twain, deserve a chapter of their own because they each had a profound influence on the shaping of American values. The two men knew each other well, crossed paths repeatedly, and in time suffered repercussions from their frontier days. They both felt their relative fiscal inferiority so keenly that it came to poison their lives; they went badly astray as a result, and their later careers point to the baleful effects of an atmosphere such as the Comstock—in which even dunderheads can become millionaires if luck falls their way—on men justly proud of their formidable talents.

Mr. Stewart reached Washington in time to befriend President Abraham Lincoln, whom he called "the wisest, kindest, most impartial, and most just man I ever knew." The freshman senator may have been the recipient of Lincoln's last letter. As Stewart tells it in his *Reminiscences,* he dropped by the White House on the fateful night and sent in his card. Back came a note: "I am engaged to go to the theater with Mrs. Lincoln. It is the kind of engagement I never break. Come . . . tomorrow at ten and I shall be glad to see you." By the time the note's importance had become clear, it was too late; Stewart says he'd thrown it away.

Elsewhere in his *Reminiscences* (published in 1908, the year before he died), Stewart elaborated on the hurry to get sparsely populated Nevada into the Union: "Washington was anxious that . . . her Senators and Representatives might assist in the adoption of amendments to the Constitution in aid of the restoration of the Southern States after the Union should be vindicated by the war." In 1868, Stewart helped make good on the deal, agreeing to review multiple drafts of a proposed Fifteenth Amendment, guaranteeing the vote to former slaves. He chose wording submitted by Senator John B. Henderson of Missouri, perfected it, defended the revised language against objections raised by conservative Democrats and radical Republicans, and was appointed to the House–Senate conference committee that guided the amendment to passage. He then successfully urged the Nevada legislature to ratify his handiwork. (In 1870, when news reached the Comstock that enough other states had ratified the amendment to give it the force of law, about one hundred fifty "colored people" paraded from Gold Hill to Virginia City, where according to Alfred Doten they "held exercises at Athletic Hall, oration, poem, etc.")

In addition, Senator Stewart's knowledge of mining allowed him to fill a sizable gap in federal law. When he took office, there was plenty of mining on federal land but no statute to govern it. In Europe and colonial America, the sovereign had traditionally retained ownership of mineral-rich lands but leased them to prospectors, who paid a "royalty," typically a percentage of the value extracted. To encourage commerce and settlement, the United States experimented with "free mining," or the treasure-hunt method: whoever claimed and developed an ore deposit on federal land got to keep it and the land encasing it, up to and including the surface. This was a glorified form of squatting, although often upon tracts high on nobody's list of sweet places to live. Naturally, miners themselves favored free mining, and the California gold rush had taken place without laws to constrain it.

A decade-and-a-half after the California rush, some members of Congress were eyeing the enormous wealth generated by the Comstock and other strikes as an opportunity to add to the federal treasury. The minerals were being chipped out of public land, after all, so why shouldn't the public derive a share of the benefit? George Washington Julian, a congressman from Indiana, sought to devise an orderly system to divide and sell federal land with mining potential. The vast majority of such tracts were located in the West, and beneath the debate lay a long-simmering conflict over how that region should be parceled out. A Radical Republican with strong Jeffersonian leanings, Julian had once favored a West divided into small holdings on which slavery would not be economical. "The freedom of the public lands," he'd declared a decade before the outbreak of the Civil War, "is therefore an anti-slavery measure." After the war, he recast his prescription in populist terms, railing against "large estates, slovenly agriculture, widely-scattered settlements, popular ignorance, and a pampered aristocracy lording it over the people."

Stewart and his Western allies argued that no one could improve upon the rules improvised by miners themselves under the aegis of free mining, and the Senate passed a bill very much to his liking. Julian, as chairman of the House Public Lands Committee, refused to move that bill, but Stewart was not to be outmaneuvered. He seized upon a measure to give private canal-owners rights-of-way over public land, gutted it, and inserted his mining bill instead. Sent over to the House, this Trojan horse went not to Julian's committee but to the one on Mines and Mining, where Julian couldn't tamper with it. During the House debate, a backer of the Stewart bill remarked that it was acceptable to Nevada and California. "Why, undoubtedly it is acceptable to them," Julian sneered. "I should deem it marvelous if they did not accept a free gift of the gold and silver to be found interspersed over a million square miles of the richest mineral land on the globe."

Julian's sarcasm didn't sway enough votes. In 1866, the House passed Stewart's bill, and it was signed into law. With amendments in 1870 and 1872, it still applies today, a hoary holdover from the old don't-mess-with-me West. Unlike federal laws controlling oil and gas development, which use a leasing system, the mining law grants fee title to first-come claimants who meet a few modest requirements and pay nominal prices, from $2.50 to $5 per acre. And once a miner owns a formerly federal tract, he's free to do with it as he likes, which is why conservationists keep trying to revamp the mining law.

Granted, little of this was foreseen. Conservation was hardly an issue in 1866; establishment of Yellowstone, the first national park, still lay six years in the future. But as preserving pristine lands became a cause and then a crusade, federal land managers devised ways to blunt the Mining Law's sting. One solution is for either the president or Congress to withdraw scenic or ecologically valuable properties from the law's application, thereby putting them off-limits to miners. The writer of this book first encountered Bill Stewart's brainchild while working as an Interior Department lawyer in the 1970s, writing statutory language to protect the national parks—one park at a time—from the giveaway provisions of a century-old law.

Stewart's senatorial career lasted twenty-nine years, but he never equaled his enviable first-term performance as a legislator: setting mining policy for the nation—or, to be more precise, giving nationwide application to customs that had grown up around mining in Nevada—and brokering the final version of an amendment designed to safeguard a fundamental American right. Those twenty-nine years fell into two stretches, 1865 to 1875 (the timing of Nevada's entry into the Union reduced Stewart's first term from the normal six years to four) and 1887 to 1905. As we've seen, Stewart pretended that the hiatus was voluntary: he chose not to run again in 1874, he explained, because of a need to replenish his finances. But unless he wanted to leave the Republican Party, the matter was taken out of his hands by a rival: William Sharon. The Bank of California had been a reliable Stewart supporter (and vice versa), but as a bank insider Sharon was assured of exclusive access to its coffers. Stewart was enough of a realist to bow out of the race and bide his time.

There is no evidence that the Emma silver mine scandal played a part in Stewart's first retirement, but it did call his integrity into question for years to come. Located in Little Cottonwood Canyon, near the town of Alta, Utah, the deposit had been discovered by two prospectors in 1868. They took on another partner, James E. Lyon of New York, who paid their expenses in return for a one-third ownership interest. After Lyon returned to New York, the onsite partners seemed to forget all about him. They borrowed money from two other men, allotted them each a one-sixth share without reducing their own, and began sending ore to Great Britain for reduction. Lyon sued to regain his one-third interest, hiring Stewart as his attorney on a contingency basis. Stewart promised to press his client's case "under any circumstances unless you get $500,000. You will, without doubt, get that." In the event, Lyon failed to get a third as much.

American speculators bought Emma stock hoping to make handsome profits by reselling it in overseas markets. At the time, Britons were swept up in a mania for wildcat American investments, especially in mines, timber, and railroads, a trend portrayed in Anthony Trollope's caustic novel *The Way We Live Now* (1875). While still representing Lyon, Stewart sailed to England with one of the speculators, Trenor W. Park. They were preceded by a federal official's pronouncement that the Emma was "one of the most remarkable deposits of argentiferous ore ever opened." Soon they were waving around a bullish report on the Emma's future by a mining engineer from Yale (for which he was paid a princely $25,000) and failing to mention other, less sanguine assessments. The English brokers, Stewart wrote Lyon, "are crazy about the mine." They went even crazier after the Americans signed up a figurehead: their compatriot Robert C. Schenck, U.S. ambassador to the Court of St. James and a greedy standout even in an administration (Grant's) that became a byword for corruption. By promising Schenck a fat return, the insiders induced him to buy into the Emma Silver Mining Company Ltd. and to lend his name to its prospectus.

The next thing Lyon knew, Stewart had crossed the line from pitching the mine to representing its officers, even joining the company's board of directors. After $100,000 was deducted for legal fees, Lyon was offered $150,000 for his interest. He took it but, on learning more about Stewart's machinations, concluded he'd been gypped. To lay out his case, the fulminating ex-client wrote and had printed an eighty-page pamphlet, "Dedicated to William M. Stewart, My Attorney in the 'Emma Mine' Controversy in 1871. Sad Commentary on the Honesty and Conscientiousness of a Lawyer and Ex-United States Senator, etc." In it, Lyon summed up his indictment as follows:

That [Stewart] has ever been of any service to me to the slightest degree in any stage of this Emma Mine business, from its discovery to its final sale in London, I have it yet to learn, but on the contrary he was as a millstone around my neck, preventing me from the exercise of my honest judgment, and was using the unlimited confidence I placed in him to cheat and defraud me of my just dues, and to appropriate them to his own use.

If Stewart replied to this diatribe, the volley is lost to history, and the Emma scandal goes unmentioned in his *Reminiscences*. While paying regular dividends (which some observers believed were trumped up in order to make the stock look like a winner, thus boosting its price and allowing early-buying speculators to sell at inflated prices) the company's directors denied rumors that the mine had suffered a cave-in and that its workers had been poaching on another outfit's claim. By and by, however, the directors had to admit that both reports were true. Finally, they announced what they should have seen coming long before: the Emma was played out. Trenor Park had been using his own savings to help pay the dividends, although he made sure to dispose of his shares before the Emma bubble burst. And burst it did, the price per share dropping from $23 to near zero. A British magazine editor called the affair "one of the boldest and most impudent swindles attempted in modern times." An anonymous pamphleteer updated an American patriotic standard: "Yankee Doodle sold a mine/ Which wasn't worth a cent, boys/ To Johnny bull for a million pounds,/ And back to Vermont went, boys."

Fallout from the scandal forced Ambassador Schenck to resign in 1876. This didn't keep him from being slammed by a House committee, but Stewart got off more easily. Called to testify, he was asked if he hadn't enmeshed himself in a conflict of interest by representing Lyon and the speculators who eventually bought him out. "I was not for both at the same time," Stewart insisted.

The committee took this denial at face value, but Stewart's biographer, Russell R. Elliott, reaches a different conclusion: "In spite of Stewart's testimony to the contrary, it seems quite clear from the House report, that his own interests, and not those of his first client, Lyon, were given priority in the negotiations leading to the settlement of the Lyon claim." Lyon thought so, too: he hounded Stewart with letters for years afterward. Not until 1893 was the last lawsuit arising from the case settled, in Stewart's favor. In the interim, freelance miners had been making sporadic attempts to revive the Emma, but in 1895 these ceased for good.

Virtually nothing of the Emma Mine is left, but remnants of the other silver-mining enterprise that tarnished Stewart's name can still be found in the ghost town of Panamint City, California. Wedged into a narrow valley high in the mountainous backcountry of Death Valley National Park, Panamint City is accessible only to hardy hikers and riders of sure-footed horses. Nearly all of the town's original fixtures are long-gone, including the Hotel de Bum, a big tent in which many of the original miners made their beds; an aerial tramway for transporting ore; Martha Camp's bordello; the San Francisco Chop House; and Galeron Hypolite's French Restaurant and Saloon. The bulk of what remains—scattered cabins with weathered boards and sheds with creaking doors—dates from later periods, when prospectors moved in and puttered around for a while, eventually to slink away in defeat.

But at least two substantial items go back to the roaring 1870s: a fill, consisting of meticulously laid stones, that shores up an old roadway as it crosses a gulch on the valley's north side; and the towering red-brick smokestack that dominates the scene. In the words of historian Richard E. Lingenfelter, the Surprise Valley Mill and Water Company's twenty-stamp mill, which the smokestack vented, was "an inspirational monument that instilled an overwhelming faith in the wealth of Panamint everlasting. It was the closest thing to a church Panamint ever had." These days, however, the church bears marks of sacrilege: bullet holes in the smokestack's walls, which the Park Service blames on potshot-taking yahoos.

Stewart's official status (part one of his Senate career was still in effect), along with that of his colleague Senator Jones, was crucial in launching the Panamint Boom in the fall of 1874. The news that the two gentlemen from Nevada and a third partner (none other than Trenor Park of Emma infamy) had bought several claims in the valley, for a total of more than a quarter of a million dollars, set off the rush that flung Panamint City into existence. Touting the area as a "California Comstock," Stewart became general manager of the new company, at a salary of $25,000 a year.

Central to Stewart's success in the past had been his ability to find the right words—to sway juries, to win over fellow lawmakers, and to lever himself out of tight ethical spots. But at the height of the Panamint craze, he shone by taking the perfect action. Wells Fargo had refused to carry bullion out of the valley because its narrows were riddled with holdup sites. "It was an admirable place for outlaws," Stewart recalled, "and it had not been overlooked." As manager, it fell to him to devise a solution. He and the crooks knew each other, and the two sides bantered and bragged about the fate of the next shipment. When the bandits went to pull their heist, they found that Stewart had played them a cunning trick. The silver had been smelted into a 400-pound cube, impossible for them to steal.

Otherwise, Panamint was a rehash of the Emma affair, with the same overhyping of limited assets, the same selective use of engineers' reports, the same flameout of hopes. The prospects had once seemed immense: the *Panamint News* had called for creation of a new Panamint County, and the public had been offered a hefty $50 million in stock. But the reality turned out to be puny, with workmen taking out a mere $500,000 worth of ore.

By the spring of 1875, the valley's population had dwindled from a peak of 2,000 to about 600. The emigrants were moving on to the next big things, the nearby silver at Darwin and the more distant gold at Bodie. The mill closed, the newspaper folded, the town withered away. For all their machinations, Stewart and Jones not only failed to make a profit but may have lost as much as $100,000 between them. Collectively, investors who had placed their confidence in a scheme headed and ballyhooed by two U.S. senators were out at least three times that much. Along with the Emma affair, the Panamint fiasco is a prime example of what Stewart's biographer calls "unethical and dishonest behavior unbecoming a leader of his political stature."

Somehow Stewart weathered these scandals: their complexities were hard for the public to fathom, he covered his tracks well, and his powers of persuasion remained intact. Indeed, his reputation seems to have taken on luster as he aged. Grant Smith, a Virginia City native who wrote a demythologizing history of the Comstock, remembered the impression Stewart made on him as a boy in the 1880s: "His hair and luxuriant beard were white as snow and he walked like a cathedral in motion, always alone. He was only fifty-five."

During his first stint in Washington, Stewart had been dubbed the Silver Senator; he was reputedly the richest man in the upper body then, and unquestionably the one with the longest beard. The beard spoke for itself, but its owner lived up to the other superlative by pouring his fortune into a Second Empire mansion designed by Adolph Cluss. In doing so, he redoubled Lyon's wrath. "The house you have built and furnished is with my money, and you know it," Lyon wrote in one of those nagging letters.

Erected in 1873 and known as Stewart Castle, the mansion looked out upon Pacific (now Dupont) Circle. Along with other mining millionaires, Stewart had invested in land around the Circle, which took on the nickname "The Honest Miner's Camp." (A few years later, Comstock money colonized another part of the Washington area: Nevada politician Francis Newlands, son-in-law of William Sharon, financed the development of Chevy Chase, Maryland, which grew into one of Washington's toniest suburbs.) Pacific Circle was then in the boondocks, and the castle's on-the-fringe location gave it an alternate nickname: "Stewart's Folly." As catalogued by James M. Goode in his *Capital Losses: A Cultural History of Washington's Destroyed Buildings*, the house's trappings conjure up a vision of baronial splendor: "five-story central entrance tower with carriage porch," "projecting corner pavilions with . . . octagonal bays at first-story level," "octagonal lantern above . . . fish-scaled mansard roof," "five floors of teak furniture and Aubusson tapestries," "a ballroom seventy-five feet long." For all its remoteness, in its day the castle rivaled the White House as a tourist attraction.

That day was not exceedingly long. Even after pocketing his Emma lucre, Stewart was overextended: besides maintaining the castle, he had to pay for European sojourns by his wife and two daughters. In 1886, a year before returning to the Senate, he leased the castle to the Chinese legation. Next he had to sacrifice its furnishings, a humiliation described by an amused historian:

> For three days the castle contents were auctioned off to gaping Washington. Forth and out went the big mirrors, the oil paintings that had been bought by the yard and the tremendous walnut bedsteads. Forth went the table silver pounded out of Comstock and Panamint metal. Down the imposing staircase and out beneath the gas-lit arched entrance went the outmoded bric-a-brac.

Even with these setbacks, however, in 1895 Stewart had the wherewithal to buy another substantial property: a horse farm in nearby Loudon County, Virginia. Four years later, he sold his original Folly to another senator with a mining fortune. Two years later, that worthy tore it down. The site is now occupied by a branch of the PNC bank.

When not perpetrating mining frauds, Stewart had spent his years out of office practicing law in San Francisco. In 1880, his first successor in the Senate, Bill Sharon, lost his bid for re-election to a Democrat, the Bonanza King James G. Fair. As we've seen, neither Sharon nor Fair showed a particle of interest in the job (as opposed to the title) of senator, and both were excoriated for their missed votes. Sensing an opportunity in 1886, Stewart moved back to Nevada and entered the race. To answer charges lingering from the Emma affair, he rented a Virginia City opera house for a speech in which he pleaded innocent and produced Lyon's signed receipt for the sale of his Emma holdings (which, of course, was hardly conclusive). What probably mattered more was the backing Stewart got. Since his last incumbency, the jointly controlled Central Pacific and Southern Pacific railroads had succeeded mining interests as the dominant force in Nevada politics. Stewart had done legal work for the railroads, and they'd counted him as one of their own since at least 1869, when Central Pacific magnate Collis P. Huntington wrote in a letter to his colleague Mark Hopkins, "Stewart is a *trump* and *no mistake*." A little later, Huntington summed up Stewart as follows to another colleague: "He has always stood by us. He is peculiar, but thoroughly honest, and will bear no dictation, but I know he must live, and we must fix it so he can make one or two hundred thousand dollars. It is to our interest and I think his right." In 1886, Fair surely caught wind of the railroad's solicitude for Stewart's "rights": he opted not to run again, and Stewart was returned to office.

In his second chance at lawmaking, Stewart focused on two subjects: the remonetization of silver and irrigation, which he hoped might deliver Nevada's economy from its monolithic dependence on mining. While advancing the cause of irrigation, he briefly found himself in sync with a great American visionary, John Wesley Powell. A veteran of the Civil War, famous for having made an epic exploration of the Colorado River, Powell was head of the U.S. Geological Survey. In that capacity, he hoped to work something of a revolution, in which government informed by science would give shape to the arid West, with boundaries drawn to follow the terrain's natural features, especially watersheds, rather than the straight lines favored by surveyors. (The traditional rectilinear style of surveying might be tolerable in the East and Midwest, which had ample water and not too many mountain chains; in the mountainous and water-poor West, right-angled ownership defied geographical sense.) The science of hydrology was still in its infancy, and Powell and his employees coined such terms as "runoff" to describe what they observed in the field. Their novel method was to inspect a region closely; group the slopes on which rain fell, and the streams and basins into which runoff flowed, into a manageable whole (a hydrographic province); and then to apply this concept across the West. In the words of Powell's biographer Donald Worster, "The purpose now was to see the entire region as a mosaic of interconnected watersheds, as integrated units of water and land, not to deepen geological understanding so much as to guide settlement."

As an agrarian populist, Powell worried about the tendency of banks and railroads to bully small ranchers and farmers, and he hoped his survey would motivate citizens to come together and form irrigation districts on their own. "Hold the waters in the hands of the people," he urged, aligning himself with the anti-monopolist camp of Stewart's early opponent George Washington Julian. Powell also preached realism, insisting that dryness was a permanent condition in much of the West and pooh-poohing the myth that rain follows the plow (i.e., that the very act of farming somehow works changes in the weather). Westerners didn't like hearing the harsh truth about their parched landscape; sometimes, when Powell told it in public forums, they booed him.

Stewart, with his background in the no-restraints world of mining, had little use for populism or rationalized settlement. As Worster memorably puts it, "He wanted a West that would be wide open to men of large ideas and heavy pockets, a West that would be developed fast, where fortunes could be made tomorrow," a West, in short, tailor-made for the kind of man Stewart himself had aspired to be. But some degree of planning was essential to irrigation, and at Stewart's urging the Senate created a Select Committee on Irrigation and Reclamation of Arid Lands, with himself as chairman. As the Senate debated whether to direct the Survey to prepare a grand topographical map of the West as the first step toward building a series of reservoirs, Stewart defended the idea and its would-be implementer against skepticism from Eastern lawmakers. Powell, he declared, was "a very competent and enthusiastic man." Congress authorized the mapping project in 1888. The following summer, at Stewart's behest, Powell accompanied the Select Committee on a field trip. It was during that junket that the two men began to notice the gulf between their concepts of not only how the West should be won, but how fast.

When their falling-out came, however, it was more lawyerly than philosophical: a dispute over a narrow provision. The law authorizing the mapmaking had included a measure to thwart speculators, who could be expected to dog surveyors' footsteps and snap up land near prospective reservoirs: all such choice parcels were to be taken out of circulation. Stewart was, of course, sympathetic to speculators, who complained to him about the clause's dampening effect on their manipulations, but he couldn't very well espouse their cause openly. Their complaints reached Powell's superior, the Secretary of the Interior, who asked his in-house lawyer for an opinion on the protective clause's meaning. The response was that Congress had frozen not just irrigable tracts but all federal lands within the vast region to be mapped, for as long as it took to complete the work. The Secretary adopted that reading, and even ordinary settlers cried foul. These were cries to which Stewart could hearken.

After Powell voiced his support of the blanket land withdrawal, Stewart turned on him. At a Senate hearing, Stewart questioned

Powell so relentlessly that the latter couldn't finish his answers. When Stewart charged that Powell had reserved "the whole country," Powell took offense: "I have not done it. I never advocated it. That reservation was put into the law independently of me. Yet you affirm here and put it in the record that I had it done." Stewart asked, "Are you in favor of its repeal?" "No, sir," said Powell. "I think it wise." Asked by another senator about the wisdom of appointing the federal government as Western water czar, Powell replied, "I think it would be almost a criminal act to go on as we are doing now, and allow thousands and hundreds of thousands of people to establish homes where they can not maintain themselves."

After the hearing, Stewart kept up his attacks on Powell. The erstwhile "very competent and enthusiastic man" was now "drunk with power and deaf to reason," "his greed for office and power unsurpassed." Stewart even resorted to character assassination: "I have made some inquiry and find that [Powell's] habits with women are scandalous." Powell countered that such charges were the product "either of utter recklessness or of a disordered mind" and took his case directly to the people of the West. To his surprise, they sided with Stewart, preferring untrammeled settlement and unregulated use of natural resources, as if despite its aridity the land held plenty of everything for all. "Apparently [Powell] underestimated the capacity of the plain farmer to continue to believe in myths while his nose was being rubbed in unpleasant facts," wrote historian and novelist Wallace Stegner. Congress canceled the irrigation survey, but that wasn't enough for Stewart. He succeeded in cutting the Geological Survey's budget, year after year, and continued to harry Powell until he resigned in 1894. With no survey and limited funds, the agency was powerless to implement Powell's dream of a West settled and managed according to scientific principles.

Stegner went on to paint the Stewart–Powell battle in epic terms, crediting the outcome with having sentenced the West to "another half century of exploitation and waste." The wonder is not that Stewart and Powell ended up disagreeing so vehemently but that two men with such divergent outlooks had ever found common ground at all.

Stewart's election to his last term in the Senate, in 1898, was a cliff-hanger with a twist. Nevadans had acted on their conviction that unlimited coinage of silver would revive the state's stagnant economy by forming a new Silver Party, which was now the dominant one in the state. Stewart jumped to the Silverite ticket, and his slate won the popular vote (Senator Jones made the same switch in his successful bid for reelection two years later). But Stewart faced a belated threat from Nevada Congressman Francis Newlands, who reneged on a pledge not to oppose Stewart by announcing his candidacy after the November election but before the legislature had made its choice.

The possibility of Stewart's defeat brought cheer to the pages of a Chicago newspaper: "the long-winded silver orator who has imitated Cato of old and tacked on a plea and warning in behalf of silver to any speech on any subject he has ever had to treat in the senate may be relegated to privacy and to other forums than the national senate." But the Stewart forces sank to the occasion, reaching into their slush fund and hiring tough characters to enforce the pledges they extracted (one henchman was the infamous David Neagle, the bodyguard who shot and killed David Terry during the Sharon–Hill controversy) and somehow ensuring that one pro-Newlands legislator missed the vote in the Nevada Assembly, which Stewart won by a margin of fifteen to fourteen. He'd already prevailed in the Senate, so that was that. "Stewart rules," Alf Doten wrote of the vote-buying and thuggery. "Wicked as usual." "The 1898 campaign," Stewart's biographer sums up, "was certainly the most corrupt senatorial election in Nevada's history to date." Two years later, Stewart rejoined the Republican Party. (Newlands went on to win a Senate seat in 1903, succeeding Senator Jones, who had declined to run again.)

His last term proved to be uneventful. In 1904, nearing his eightieth birthday, he declined to run again after learning that his fat-cat supporters were throwing their favor to someone else. A contemporary glimpse of him printed in a San Francisco paper, however, suggests that he still commanded attention:

> Though fortune forsake him, though death snatch from him his nearest, though the favored of Plutus intrigue for his toga, though the wand of age has changed his tawny hair and beard to silver, his steel blue eyes have not lost their glitter, nor his port its erectness, and he springs to the front of Senatorial debate as vigorous and alert as when he engaged in the contest of the court-room forty years ago.

Toward the end of his *Reminiscences*, the retiree observed wistfully, "The Comstock did much to build up the city of San Francisco, but nothing is left in Nevada to bear testimony to the millions furnished by the great mine." But with that, he dropped the matter: it seems not to have occurred to him that his own steadfast championship of California bigwigs, often at the expense of his own constituents, might have had something to do with the disparity. In the book's final paragraph, Stewart put the best face on what seems to have been a frittering old age (his law practice was languishing, his investments were not prospering). "At the present time," he wrote, "I am engaged in my profession of the law, and acquiring interests in mines and assisting in their development. The fascinating business of mining is a perennial source of hope. It inspires both mental and physical vigor, and promotes health and contentment."

That was a doughty and poignant farewell. But a photo taken of Stewart in his last years—stout, beard longer than ever, sitting on muleback—is apt to bring to mind the dotty old miner who has outlived his time in Walter Van Tilburg Clark's poignant short story "The Wind and Snow of Winter." Dan De Quille had once commented on this phenomenon in a letter to his sister: "Once a man becomes thoroughly infatuated in the chase for mines and saturated with the spirit of prospecting, he will rove on as long as life is left in him. On this coast we frequently meet with old men tottering on the verge of the grave who are still prospecting—still hoping to hit upon something that will make them rich in a day."

Stewart was just such an infatuated old man. Mining had provided him with a more than generous income as a lawyer, but it had also exposed him to temptations he couldn't resist, revealing deep flaws in his character without ever granting him the windfall he considered his due. Even so, he stood by the industry to the end. If not mining's most shining exemplar of rectitude, he was at least its most ardent champion.

When twenty-five-year-old Sam Clemens arrived in Carson City, Utah Territory, on August 14, 1861, he was no literary virgin. Most recently, he'd worked as a steamboat pilot on the Mississippi, but before that he'd been a printer, a trade that virtually begged its practitioners to take a stab at writing. The pre-Western Clemens's few, scattered appearances in print were negligible: travel sketches and satires, some of them couched in fractured spelling that has the effect of a warning label: "CAUTION: Contains Regional Dialect." No contemporary reader of these japes would have discerned in Clemens the makings of the man whom his editor and friend William Dean Howells was to call the "Lincoln of our literature."

Clemens came rattling up in a stagecoach with his older brother Orion, whose campaigning for the Lincoln of our politics in the 1860 presidential election had landed him a plum appointment: secretary to the governor of Nevada, which was in the process of being spun off from Utah as a separate territory. Sam got to tag along as (unsalaried) secretary to the secretary because he paid Orion's fare; soon the younger brother set out on his own to make a killing in precious metals. But before doing so, he wrote his mother in St. Louis a letter in which you can begin to detect his genius. Take, for example, this scene-setting passage, in which he evokes Western aridity in the rhythms of a wordsmith: "It never rains here, and the dew never falls. No flowers grow here, and no green thing gladdens the eye."

After that warmup, he describes Carson City as seen from a distance, capturing the astonishing clarity of dry air acting upon the elongated vistas of the basin-and-range province:

> I said we are situated in a flat, sandy desert—true. And surrounded on all sides by such prodigious mountains, that when you gaze at them awhile,—and begin to conceive of their grandeur—and next to feel their vastness expanding your soul—and ultimately find yourself growing and swelling and spreading into a giant—I say when this point is reached, you look disdainfully down upon the insignificant village of Carson, and in that instant you are seized with a burning desire to stretch forth your hand, put the city in your pocket, and walk off with it.

Clemens has just walked off with something else in his pocket: a newfound ability to see and describe the vividness around him. The soul-inflation he refers to is par for flatlanders on first encountering outsized Western landscapes (and before this trip, Sam Clemens had never been west of Missouri). As your eye traces mountain ranges receding to infinity and interspersed with Lilliputian clusters of civilization, you feel that only now, for the first time in your life, is your eyesight living up to its potential. Clemens has not only been sharp enough to notice this phenomenon; he's also found the words to do it justice. He's hardly set foot in the West, and already it has galvanized him.

At large in Utah Territory and eastern California, Clemens failed as a prospector and, as we've seen, became a wage-earner in an ore-processing mill, work that he summed up as "hard and long and dismal." Having accumulated a little capital, he began speculating in mines, an occupation that proved easier on his constitution but no more rewarding. After a year of exercising what was to be a signature trait and ultimately a tragic flaw—the ability to persuade himself that, if only he kept the faith and sacrificed more of his savings to the latest sure thing, a strapping payoff was bound to arrive—he packed it in and went to work for *The Territorial Enterprise*, Nevada's oldest newspaper, being published under new ownership in Virginia City. One of the co-owners was a brilliant twenty-four-year-old, Joe Goodman, a native New Yorker who doubled as editor in chief. Clemens had been contributing sketches to the *Enterprise* under the pen name "Josh," and Goodman admired the freelancer's sense of humor. When a temporary vacancy opened up, Goodman brought Clemens on to fill it. That temp job became the launching pad for a great career.

The man whose place Clemens took was a reporter whose observations have been quoted often in these pages: William Wright, better known as Dan De Quille (say it out loud, and it grows into a corny pun, referring to the kind of instrument its owner liked to be thought of as wielding). By the time De Quille returned from his leave, Clemens was entrenched at the paper, but the two men worked side by side, became friends, and even roomed together in Virginia City. (Years later, De Quille accepted an invitation to hole up in an outbuilding on Mark Twain's Hartford estate, where the visitor wrote his book on the Comstock, *The Big Bonanza*.)

Clemens published under his own name for a while, but a pseudonym was almost expected of newspapermen then, as a way to distance yourself a bit from the often scurrilous copy you turned out. Clemens first used the byline "Mark Twain" in the *Enterprise*, in February 1863, and its origin has long been disputed. Residents of Virginia City were sure it derived from a local barkeep's way of recording a two-drink bill: chalking two parallel lines on a board. Clemens said no, he'd simply appropriated a boatman's term meaning that a vessel was drawing two fathoms, or twelve feet. But there could be truth in both versions: perhaps he first heard "mark twain" on the river, and when it came up again in Virginia City, it struck a chord. Whatever its roots, by the time he adopted it, he was not just a reporter but a licensed fabricator of hoaxes.

By the 1860s Americans could point to a longstanding tradition of frontier humor, peopled with extravagant characters like Paul Bunyan and Mike Fink, and larded with exaggeration and sass. Originally oral but increasingly being committed to paper (the jumping-frog story that made Mark Twain famous evolved that way, from something overheard to a calculated work of art), the tall tale was a defiant celebration of several facets of the American scene: everyday life was rougher than in most European countries; manners were plainer; and the setting was bigger, grander, and wilder, with vast mountain ranges and hellacious deserts to cross, rampaging rivers to navigate, violent storms to endure, recalcitrant Native Americans to fend off, strange homegrown sects to conjure with, and ex-slaves and immigrants from just about everywhere to assimilate. Out West, where these conditions applied all the more, the tales only grew taller. (By contrast, the landscapes of Europe looked dinky when Mark Twain and other writers got around to touring them: "It is popular to admire the Arno," Twain wrote a few years later in *The Innocents Abroad*. "It is a great historical creek with four feet in the channel and some scows floating around. It would be a very plausible river if they would pump some water into it.")

So frontier newspapers accommodated a rowdy form of writing, the printed hoax or brag, and if readers couldn't always tell how much of a story was true, that was *their* problem. Goodman cut his hired hands plenty of slack, and De Quille took advantage of it to create a kind of reported fable that he called the "quaint." One such item told of a fictitious collection of magnetic stones that came together and pulled apart of their own volition in a desert valley. Another had to do with "solar armor," topped off by a helmet with

built-in air conditioning. The tale ended with the contraption mal-
functioning and freezing its wearer to death despite an ambient
temperature of one hundred seventeen degrees Fahrenheit.

When Clemens came on board, De Quille was the *Territorial
Enterprise*'s star writer. Indeed, Joe Goodman told Mark Twain's
first biographer:

> If I had been asked to prophecy which of the two men, Dan
> De Quille or Sam, would become distinguished, I should have
> said De Quille. Dan was talented, industrious, and, for that
> time and place, brilliant. Of course, I recognized the unusual-
> ness of Sam's gifts, but he was eccentric and seemed to lack
> industry; it is not likely that I should have prophesied fame for
> him.

The extent to which De Quille's "quaints" directly influenced
Clemens is unclear, but they give you a sense of what was tolerated
in the pages of *The Enterprise*. And even before joining the paper,
the young Missourian had hit the right tone of voice. The opening
of one of the freelance pieces signed by "Josh," a satire of a windbag's Fourth of July oration, sounds like a blend of "The Ballad of
John Henry" and Walt Whitman's "Song of Myself": "I was sired
by the Great American Eagle and foaled by a Continental Dam."
Once on staff, Clemens scored an early success with a "quaint"-like
article about a petrified man, found in the desert with his hand
pressed to his face in such a way that alert readers got the joke: the
stiff was thumbing his nose at them.

Baiting other journalists was also kosher. After Twain was dispatched to Carson City to cover the territorial legislature, he and
Clement T. Rice, a reporter at another Virginia City paper, traded
friendly jibes in print, with Twain invariably referring to his rival as
"the Unreliable." (This was a clear case of projection: it took a while
for Twain to master the intricacies of legislative procedure, and at
first Rice had it all over him in terms of reliability.) With Western

journalism heavily biased toward audacity, Twain fit right in—even when the worm turned, and he became part of the story. In his *Reminiscences*, Stewart recounts one such occasion, when "the boys" put on masks and held up a stagecoach carrying Twain from Carson City to Virginia City. "When the stage lumbered by a lonely spot they swooped out, and upset it, and turned it upside down, and dragged [Twain] out and threw him in a canyon, and broke up his portmanteau, and threw that in on top of him." Twain's first reaction, Stewart charged, was to be "the scaredest man west of the Mississippi," but later he reshaped the tale to make himself its victim-hero.

Twain's colorful style—when he got rolling, he was virtually incapable of writing a dull sentence—was ideal for the Comstock, a lode not just of silver and gold but also of peculiar denizens and vivid incidents. Virginia City was a toddlin' town, almost literally so when Sam Clemens showed up (it was about two years old). A decade later, in *Roughing It*, he recalled it as

the "livest" town, for its age and population, that America had ever produced. The sidewalks swarmed with people—to such an extent, indeed, that it was generally no easy matter to stem the human tide. The streets themselves were just as crowded with quartz wagons, freight teams and other vehicles. The procession was endless. So great was the pack, that buggies frequently had to wait half an hour for an opportunity to cross the principal street. Joy sat on every countenance, and there was a glad, almost fierce, intensity in every eye, that told of the money-making schemes that were seething in every brain and the high hope that held sway in every heart.

Joy may have sat on every countenance, but brutality was afoot, too. We've already heard Twain's assertion that "the first twenty-six graves in the Virginia cemetery were occupied by *murdered* men." Like a twenty-first-century urban gangland, Comstock country was a topsy-turvy world in which killers were men of substance and "the desperado stalked the streets with a swagger graded according to the number of his homicides."

Those who settled their scores the civilized way—the bringers of lawsuits—stepped into an arena of payoffs and chicanery, as Twain made clear in an *Enterprise* piece about his and the Unreliable's road trip to San Francisco in the spring of 1863. In Twain's exuberant telling, the Unreliable went around "locating" rooms in their posh hotel much as a prospector locates claims, and when management took offense, the Unreliable cried out for the presence of a certain Virginia City stalwart to defend him:

> If Bill Stewart had been down here, Mark, I'd have sued to quiet title, and I'd have held that ground, don't you know it? . . . Bill Stewart!—thunder! Now, you just take that Ophir suit that's coming up in Virginia [City], for instance—why, God bless you, Bill Stewart'll worry the witnesses, and bully-rag the Judge, and buy up the jury and pay for 'em; and he'll prove things that never existed—hell! What won't he prove!

This cornucopia of bustle and greed, of mayhem and corruption, was a godsend to a journalist, especially one as attuned to the extravagant as Twain. He went on blossoming in Virginia City, which fed him material galore. It also provided him with a surprisingly sophisticated audience. Virginia City had pretensions, and the bearers of culture were stopping in to perform there. The town boasted some of the finest restaurants outside New York City, while at the same time it was flush with gambling dens. On a given night, you might have a choice between attending an art-song recital and watching hurdy-gurdy girls in your favorite saloon. It was a rich stew of high and low that gave reporters ample opportunity to develop their gifts.

Perhaps the most important thing that Nevada gave Mark Twain was an appreciation for—and eventually a lust to adapt and deploy—

its inhabitants' libertine ways with the English language. Or, rather, the American language. He built a whole chapter of *Roughing It* around the contrast between the sautéed English of the educated classes and the raw patois of the common folk. It's the story of Buck Fanshaw's funeral, a tour de force of misunderstandings between a slanging roughneck and the proper man of the cloth who is being importuned to conduct the rites for the deceased. By way of introduction, Twain acknowledges the verbal treasure trove he'd lucked into in Comstock country:

> Now—let us remark in parenthesis—as all the peoples of the earth had representative adventurers in the Silverland, and as each adventurer had brought the slang of his nation or his locality with him, the combination made the slang of Nevada the richest and the most infinitely varied and copious that had ever existed anywhere in the world, perhaps, except in the mines of California in the "early days."

Hearing this polyglot and having grown up among the multiple dialects of Missouri and mastered the argots of print shops and riverboats, Twain began to assemble shards of outcast lingo and brash boasting and verbal inventiveness into a new mosaic: the vernacular American style that culminated in Huck Finn's earthy, heartfelt narration of his own *Adventures*. It hadn't occurred to Twain's predecessors—Irving or Hawthorne or Melville or even Whitman—to adopt the untutored voice of a backwoods naïf, whose ignorance of grammar and scorn for refinement lend his storytelling authenticity and directness and force. "I was powerful glad to get away from the feuds," Huck reflects at the end of Chapter XVIII, "and so was Jim to get away from the swamp. We said there warn't no home like a raft, after all. Other places do seem so cramped up and smothery, but a raft don't. You feel mighty free and easy and comfortable on a raft." After assimilating a bookful of such sentences, American prose was feeling mighty free and easy and comfortable, too.

That pungent, demotic writing—and the declaration of independence from Old World standards of suitable diction and acceptable subject matter that it entailed—started a revolution, as Ernest Hemingway noted in his famous assertion that "All modern American literature comes from one book by Mark Twain called *Huckleberry Finn.*" It was in "the Silverland" that Twain discovered not just his calling but how he might express it in his best works. The Comstock served him as both life-changing academy and copious thesaurus.

By 1863, Twain had become a regional star, writing stories about Virginia City for San Francisco papers and stories about San Francisco for his Virginia City paper, with some of each being picked up and reprinted in the East. A visiting New Yorker called him "that Irresistible Washoe Giant [who] imitates nobody. He is in a school by himself." To one of his California editors he was one of the "Wild Humorists of the Pacific" (it's unclear just how many Wild Ones there were, but Twain's friend Bret Harte was certainly another). Mark Twain was getting too big for Virginia City, but he might have stayed longer if not for a fiasco that almost added him to the town's grim graveyard.

It started with another of his hoaxes. On the heels of a successful local money-raising drive for the Sanitary Fund, which went to the care of wounded Union soldiers, Twain wrote a piece alleging that money raised in Carson City for the same purpose had been diverted "to aid a Miscegenation Society somewhere in the East," and that Virginia City's contribution was likely to suffer the same fate. Not only was this false; it also probed the tender subject of race. De Quille counseled against publishing it, and Twain agreed. But he and De Quille walked out of the office that night without destroying the item; the composing-room foreman found it and assumed it was meant to be printed. Its appearance in the next morning's *Enterprise* led to a feud between Twain and the editor of the *Virginia City Union*; they traded insults in print, and the prankster foolishly challenged the editor to a duel.

Twain was a poor shot, but he caught a break at the dueling ground. When the editor happened not to be looking, Twain's second tested the pistol by firing a shot that took off the head of a sparrow. Thinking quickly, the second pointed to the decapitated bird as evidence of Twain's marksmanship. Faced with the undeniable evidence of that headless sparrow, the editor called off the duel. Damage, however, had been done. Under Nevada law, Twain was liable to be arrested for fomenting a duel, and he fled to San Francisco. There he found another newspaper job, albeit one in which he was expected to stick to the facts, not spin fables.

He didn't stay on the coast for long. In 1865, a New York newspaper published "Jim Smiley and His Jumping Frog," better known as "The Celebrated Jumping Frog of Calaveras County," the carefully wrought tall tale that brought Mark Twain national fame, and he packed up and went East. With his curly auburn hair and droopy mustache, his ever-present cigar, and his rolling gait (the white suit came later), he was on his way to sharing with Buffalo Bill Cody the distinction of being our first mass-market celebrity.

Twain's progress wasn't unbroken, though. He'd already gathered "The Jumping Frog" and other tales and sketches into a book, launched his lecturing career, and traveled to Europe and the Holy Land with a deal to write about it for a pair of New York newspapers when, in 1867, he took a job as secretary to the other Washoe Giant, Bill Stewart, now serving his first term in the Senate. Twain could use the money and reckoned he might meet important men and pick up useful insights into Washington mores; Stewart wanted the younger man as a trophy aide: an up-and-coming literary type on the payroll was a sign of prestige. The collaboration, as both parties soon recognized, was a misfire.

This is understandable. Of the three kinds of writing that a political aide is likely to be assigned, at least two are hostile to flair. A reply letter to an importuning constituent should express sympathy for every complaint, no matter how carping, and appear to take seriously every request, no matter how absurd, while in the end promising little more than to "look into the matter." Draft legislation must be utilitarian and to the point, heavy on the boilerplate and hold the flourishes. Only in speeches can you show off a bit, and even this opportunity may be curtailed if you aren't working for a bold politician elected by a landslide.

In May 1868, shortly after he'd quit, Twain spoofed his two months with Stewart in an essay called "My Late Senatorial Secretaryship." Disguising Stewart as "James W. N**" (Nye, that is, the other U.S. senator from Nevada), Twain recounted being summoned to the senator's office one day to find his boss in disarray: "His cravat was untied, his hair was in a state of disorder, and his countenance bore about it the signs of a suppressed storm." What was the trouble? A constituent had written asking for a post office to be built in his rural community. The secretary had penned a tactless reply—"What the mischief do you suppose you want with a post-office at Baldwin's Ranch? What you want is a nice jail."—and signed it on his master's behalf. The piece goes on in the same irreverent vein, with the senator waving around a copy of another letter in which a constituent was told that a proposal of his is "ridiculous." "Leave the house!" the senator commands at the end. "Leave it for ever and for ever, too!"

Stewart had a rather different take on Twain's Washington stint. The senator wrote about it at the end of his life, long after Twain had ribbed him in the *Enterprise* for bribing juries and raked him in *Roughing It* for reneging on that promise to hand over mining stock, so his memory may have been colored by pique. In his version, not job performance but Twain's uncouth habits and childish pranks drove the two men apart. Stewart introduces his scribe-to-be as "the most lovable scamp and nuisance who ever blighted Nevada" but who is immediately out of his depth in Washington: "disreputable-looking . . . arrayed in a seedy suit, which hung upon his lean frame in bunches with no style worth mentioning . . . [and]

an evil-smelling cigar butt, very much frazzled, [protruding] from the corner of his mouth." (Each man's emphasis on the other's dishevelment may reflect the honest truth: Twain was still a bachelor in 1867, and Stewart's wife and daughters, off living it up in Paris, were unavailable to police his grooming.)

Stewart had offered Twain the job while he was still abroad, but Stewart omits that detail. In his version, this slob from his past just shows up at his rooming house one day (the Silver Senator is ensconced in pre-Castle digs), looking for something to tide him over while he collects and pads various newspaper pieces into a book about his just-completed Grand Tour. Suppressing his memory of Twain as a friendless liar in Virginia City and fending off his request for a loan, Stewart hires him and suggests that he move into a vacant room across the hall.

Enter the two men's soul-of-respectability landlady. It doesn't take her long to find Twain's habits deplorable: the coming home and banging around late at night, the smoking in bed, and the incessant teasing of her. She gives Stewart an ultimatum: get rid of "that man" or she will throw them both out. Stewart calls Twain on the carpet, not for the first time, and promises him a "thrashing" if he doesn't desist. Twain promises to reform and is allowed to stay a while longer. He begins to write *The Innocents Abroad* in Stewart's room, reading portions of it aloud to the senator as they are finished. "I was confident that he would come to no good end," Stewart finishes up mock insultingly, "but I have heard of him from time to time since then, and I understand that he has settled down and become respectable."

Stewart's fooling around hardly disguises his annoyance with Twain, who had reentered his life while the senator was busy drafting the Fifteenth Amendment. Having to tear oneself away from Constitutional repair work to discipline a boisterous underling must have been galling, but the episode did pay off in the end: Stewart devoted a whole chapter to it in his *Reminiscences* (from which the above quotations are drawn), and it's the most amusing part of a book that otherwise runs on for scores of pages without cracking a smile.

Twain himself fared better, getting everything he wanted out of his Washington sojourn. Presumably Stewart paid him his salary; he met Ulysses Grant, with whom he was to make a mutually advantageous publishing deal a decade afterward; and he took notes on national politics, which stood him in good stead six years later, when he and Charles Dudley Warner lampooned Washington in their novel *The Gilded Age*. A sly touch in that book surely reflects one co-author's personal knowledge of the D.C. rental market. When a newcomer applies for a room in a boardinghouse, we are told, the landlady's first question is liable to be whether he's a member of Congress. If the answer is yes, she will scowl and announce that the house is "full." Why? Because she has been burned: "The person and property of a Congressman are exempt from arrest or detention, and . . . she has seen several of the people's representatives walk off to their several States and Territories carrying her unreceipted board bills in their pockets for keepsakes."

Twain's Washington notebooks, which have been published, are well worth dipping into. Here, for instance, is his skewering of Ben Butler, former Union general and current Radical Republican congressman: "forward part of his bald skull looks raised, like a water blister. . . . Butler is dismally & drearily homely, & when he smiles it is like the breaking up of a hard winter." Seldom has a young writer put in a Capital stint as fruitful as Mark Twain's.

Twain, of course, is far better known than Stewart, and there's no need to detail the whole of his literary career. Ahead of him lay the masterpieces on which his reputation is based, all of them harking back to his early years in Hannibal, Missouri, and to the river that flows by: *The Adventures of Tom Sawyer* (1876), *Life on the Mississippi* (1883), and *The Adventures of Huckleberry Finn* (1885). But it's worth spending a bit more time on *The Gilded Age* (1873) because of its connection with his Comstock days.

In this bestseller, which gave its name to a generation of corruption and ostentation—the era of robber barons and oil trusts, of palatial houses and $100,000 debut parties, of American pork and beer heiresses being wooed by penniless European aristocrats—Twain and his co-author poke fun at what might be called The Windfallers. These are investors who take flyers on vacant land or untapped minerals or iffy inventions, then fret and connive and perhaps tender bribes in hopes of gaining the bonanzas on which they've been banking. For one family in the novel, the elusive pot of gold is the potential value of a large tract of land in Tennessee, a plot point that comes straight out of Clemens family history. Just as the book's Colonel Beriah Sellers never fails to make the wrong decision when it comes time to sell or hang on to the land, so did Orion Clemens fumble every chance to make a profit on the Tennessee holdings entrusted to him by his late father as the family's ace in the hole. ("Cling to the land and wait," John Marshall Clemens had intoned on his deathbed; "let nothing beguile it away from you.")

Other opportunities in the novel center on inventors and their backers. Early on, Sellers takes an interest in a perpetual-motion machine, which he is sure needs only "one more little cog-wheel" to crank out "oceans of money." After that comes to naught, another character mentions his "invention for making window-glass opaque" and his "plan of coloring hen's eggs by feeding a particular diet to the hen." Yet another fellow is always bringing big talkers home to dinner, where they bore the family with windy pitches for their pet causes: "to build a road, or open a mine, or plant a swamp with cane to grow paper-stock, or found a hospital, or invest in a patent shadbone separator, or start a college somewhere on the frontier, contiguous to a land speculation." The family's shrewd daughter observes that her father attracts such dreamers "as naturally as a sugar hogshead does flies." One night the featured enticement is the Tunkhannock, Rattlesnake and Youngwomanstown railroad, which early investors can ride, as it were, to a certain point and then cash out on, with no worries as to whether it ultimately fulfills its promise.

What's remarkable about this grab bag of schemes—some ludicrous, others halfway plausible—is that they are barely distinguishable from ones Mark Twain actually pursued. The egg-dying process, for example, calls to mind a plan scrambled up by Sam Clemens when he was piloting steamboats on the Mississippi: buying eggs by the thousands of dozens in St. Louis and hauling them downstream to sell at (he hoped) a tidy profit in New Orleans. Trouble was, he had no way of knowing what the price of eggs in New Orleans would be, and ended up losing money.

This was only the beginning. Twain wasn't content just to write and lecture, even though both occupations consistently paid him well, and sometimes munificently. Like every other member of his family, he'd been infected by a virus incubated on that Tennessee land; in his *Autobiography* he calls it "the heavy curse of prospective wealth." Of all the places he could have lived in as a young man, the Comstock may have been the likeliest to reinforce his sickness, as indeed it did, persuading him that manna regularly sifted down from the American sky to drop at the feet of the sharp-eyed and the well connected—and wasn't he both?

What's more, he considered himself clever with his hands. In fact, he invented at least three items: an Adjustable and Detachable Garment Strap; Kaolatype, a process that used clay to make engraved illustrations better and faster; and a Self-Pasting Scrapbook (which, unlike the other two, actually turned a modest profit). When not anticipating that stock fictional character, the barmy inventor, Twain bought Nevada mining stocks and found fellow tinkers to invest in—or, more often, they and their wares found him. There was the watch-manufacturing company that turned out to be a fraud. There was the steam-powered whiskey still. There was a more sensible investment for a writer, majority ownership of Charles

L. Webster & Company, a publishing firm whose list included Twain himself, his friend Grant, and Pope Leo XIII, although not even this illustrious trio could keep it from eventually going bankrupt. Most of all—the bane of Twain's middle age—there was the Paige Compositor, a typesetting machine eternally being invented by James William Paige.

A native of Rochester but living in Hartford when Twain met him there in 1880, Paige had a near-deific ability to inspire confidence, at least in Twain, who called him "the Shakespeare of mechanical invention." Young Sam Clemens had labored in the vineyard in which Paige intended to make a killing—printing—but this background only seemed to lull the grownup writer into a false sense of up-to-date expertise. Paige hoped to revolutionize printing with his patented Compositor, which set type faster than anything else available, but only when it worked right, which was hardly ever. High-strung and temperamental—you would be, too, if you weighed 9,000 pounds and had 18,000 moving parts—it was always breaking down.

Or being late. Twain talked a group of investors headed by his old Comstock friend Senator John P. Jones into taking an interest in the machine, and they came to Twain's Hartford house (of which more below) for a demonstration. Much depended on this meeting, notably a $50,000 pledge from a banker, contingent on Jones's thumbs-up. (That, at such a critical juncture, Twain should call on an old silver buddy for support is another indication of how deeply his Comstock years had affected him. As for Jones, he was probably sick of being begged for loans and hit with schemes to invest in: we've seen Conrad Wiegand trying to put the touch on him, Alf Doten regularly pelted the wealthy senator with requests for loans and gifts, and who knows how many other pleas have gone unrecorded?) But Paige lost track of the time that day; instead of a working typesetter, the visitors walked in on what Twain biographer Justin Kaplan calls "a crazy tangle of gears, keys, cams, wheels, springs, cogs, levers and other hardware." Jones was gracious enough to stop by again, on a better day, make a $5,000 investment, and take out an option to manufacture and sell the Compositor. But Paige had more kinks to iron out, and Jones finally declined to exercise his option on the quite sensible ground that another, more reliable machine, Mergenthaler's Linotype, had overtaken Paige's. Twain was crushed. "For a whole year you have breathed the word of promise to my ear to break . . . my hope at last," he anguished in an unsent letter to Jones. "It is stupefying, it is unbelievable."

Equally stupefying and unbelievable is that Twain didn't end his commitment to Paige then and there. But the glib inventor knew his man, as his man had to admit: "He could persuade a fish to come out & take a walk with him." Twain was that fish, a dupe of what economists call the fallacy of sunk costs: basing a decision on how much time and money you've already invested rather than on the actual merits (the idea of throwing in the towel now and letting all those years and thousands go to waste is all but unthinkable). Time after time as you read a Twain biography, you tense up as he and Paige reach another crossroads: will the patsy dig into his pockets and ante up again (because that's how a gambler postpones the dreadful admission that he's been a fool), or will he finally grit his teeth and fold?

The protracted seduction finally ended in 1895, fifteen years after its start, and then only because a desperate Twain relinquished control of his finances to a friend, a Standard Oil magnate named Henry Huttleton Rogers, with permission to consolidate, reorganize, and slash at will. Twain estimated his total loss to the machine at $150,000, but in fact it may have been twice that amount. (Of the two complete models of the Paige that were built, one was scrapped for its metal during World War I; the other—the mighty Wurlitzer of typesetters—now displays its zany complexity in the museum attached to Mark Twain's Hartford house.) The Paige affair contributed mightily to the financial woes, culminating in bankruptcy, that plagued the Clemenses; in the early 1890s, the family absconded to Europe, where the living was cheaper and creditors couldn't get at them, and stayed away eight years. And even then, while Rogers was righting the good ship Clemens at home, Twain kept feeding his investment habit. True to his preference for risky young businesses over blue chips, he took out a $1.5-million option on an Austrian carpet-weaving machine. That chance he ended up letting go, only to pour $50,000 into a dietary supplement called Plasmon—a total loss.

In making his overheated assessments of the Compositor and other contrivances, Twain had to blind himself to his own gullibility and deafen himself to his role as cheerleader for a team of one: himself. His self-deception becomes all the more astounding when you read what he wrote about speculation in his soberer moments. Not only did he and Warner burlesque those foolish investors in the text of *The Gilded Age*, but Twain summed up its theme in his preface to the British edition: "In America, nearly every man has his dream, his pet scheme, whereby he is to advance himself socially or pecuniarily. It is this all-pervading speculativeness which we have tried to illustrate in *The Gilded Age*. It is a characteristic which is both bad and good, for both the individual and the nation." In practice, Twain resolutely closed his eyes to the bad side of high-risk investing.

To return to *The Gilded Age* family that is offered the chance to buy into the Tunkhannock, Rattlesnake and Youngwomanstown railroad, the thoughtful daughter asks the pitchman a pointed question: "Well, what would become of the poor people who had been led to put their little money into the speculation, when you got out of it and left it half way?" This was the very trick pulled by Bill Stewart and his cronies in the Emma and Panamint scandals, and it's quite possible that Twain had the Emma in mind as he and Warner wrote their novel. In any case, for all their sparring, the two Washoe giants had a great deal in common.

For one thing, the Hartford house to which Jones and company

repaired for Paige performances was a cousin to Stewart's Castle.
Fred Kaplan uses that very noun to describe it in his Twain biography: "a large turreted three-story building, 105 by 62 feet, with
nineteen rooms, a combination manor house, steamboat, and castle,
built in burnished brick and wood, with sloping roofs and over-
hangs for each segment, a large covered veranda curving around
the south end and an octagonal tower on the west side," plus a
Tiffany-decorated interior to complement the bravura outside. The
place cost $55,000, which Twain said came out of his wife's inheri-
tance; if so, this only gave him more leeway to gamble with his
book royalties. And to that figure must be added the greenhouse he
tacked on and adjacent acreage he bought for $12,000 in the early
1880s, and the $10,000 renovation of the house he contracted for
during the same period. Castle-owning might come naturally to
American beer barons and oil tycoons, but a senator and a writer—
the one a public servant, the other dependent on the fickle tastes of
his readers—were ill-suited for such magnificence and its upkeep.
At one rare high point in his finances, Twain had indulged in a
frontier-style boast, calling himself "one of the wealthiest grandees
in America—one of the Vanderbilt gang, in fact." The Vanderbilt-
ian pretensions of both Stewart and Twain derive from a formative
experience they shared: rubbing shoulders with sudden and excessive wealth on the Comstock.

Like many other normally sensible American men, Stewart and
Twain had lost their bearings amid the vast extent and enormous
bounty of nineteenth-century America. Hamilton Fish, President
Grant's secretary of state, summed up the mind-set this way: "The
continent spills its riches for everybody; everybody is grabbing his
share; 'I must get mine'—so men argued. Why be overscrupulous
in making money when it is so plentiful? Why should politics be
more honest than business, or business than politics, or Tom than
Dick and Harry?" This was a milieu in which the number of American millionaires swelled from 350 in 1860 to more than 2,000 in
1880, with many of the nouveaux riche being miners. Twain and

Stewart were hardly the only prominent men to chase the chimera of a mineral fortune and be emotionally ruined by their failure to bag it. Clarence King, first director of the U.S. Geological Survey, made a bad mining investment that contributed to his ultimate mental breakdown, and even a dignified academic like University of Pennsylvania paleontologist Edward Drinker Cope took the plunge, much to his regret. While hunting dinosaur skeletons and fossils all over the West, he kept running across mining opportunities. Having seen fortunes accrue to what he dismissed as "illiterate Irishmen," he couldn't see why the same might not happen to him. A friend described what befell Cope after he mortgaged his house in Philadelphia to invest in two mines:

> He was almost immediately hit with losses which alarmed and confused him. Instead of accepting these as severe warning that he was entering upon unknown dangers and withdrawing on the best terms available, with a diminished but still handsome fortune, he plunged deeper and deeper and lost so heavily that his whole subsequent life was harassed and even the moderate requirements of himself and his family were inadequately met.

In this way, Cope was a soul brother to Bill Stewart and Mark Twain.

In 1890, Twain's mentor and friend William Dean Howells published a novel called *A Hazard of New Fortunes*, but King and Cope and Twain and Stewart had run afoul of a prior hazard: the desperate urge to acquire a new fortune. Picture the latter two in Silverland in the early 1860s, making a decent living (in Twain's case) or even a handsome one (Stewart's) while their inferiors all but backed their way into bonanzas. When Twain and Stewart measured themselves against the lucky bastards getting filthy rich in Virginia City (or, more likely, in far-off San Francisco), it was no contest. The two old comrades, whose keen intellects and quick wits could lift men and women out of themselves, moving them to laughter and indignation and political action, were plainly more deserving of the gods' largesse than the average Comstock millionaire, whose talents ran more to schmoozing and acting on inside tips. Why, Sandy and Eilly Bowers were no better than hillbillies, and look how much money had run through their fingers! Surrounded by so many second-rate possessors of instant wealth, the immensely gifted Stewart and Clemens yearned for membership in the club.

But as jackpots continued to elude them, Twain and Stewart weakened, making wretched investments and, in Stewart's case, committing fraud. Twain never went that far. To the contrary, he punctiliously paid off all his creditors (it took him years). Something he wrote toward the end of his career, in "Pudd'nhead Wilson's New Calendar," a collection of maxims published in his last travel book, *Following the Equator* (1897), gives tart expression to the lesson he finally learned: "There are two times in a man's life when he should not speculate: when he can't afford it and when he can." But until his keeper, Rogers of Standard Oil, reined him in, Twain's lust for super-wealth had been as extreme and almost as unbridled as Stewart's.

It's hard to know which of the Washoe Giants paid more dearly for his Comstock habit. Stewart seems to have been unruffled by the corners he cut and the people he cheated in trying to strike it rich; there's not a line of breast-beating or second-guessing in *The Reminiscences*. But no fiscal fixer came to the Silver Senator's rescue. At the turn of the century, he was still gripped by what his biographer calls his "almost compulsive drive to invest," and he owed "substantial sums" to many of his friends. He spent his last years occupying a dowdy house in the nowhere town of Rhyolite, Nevada—a far cry from his Castle-on-the-Circle existence.

To be a tragic hero, a man must come to grips with his flaw, and Stewart never did. Nor did he live long enough to witness the full effects of his every-man-for-himself approach to Western development: once-booming mining towns going bust, natural resources from buffalo to timber being either wasted or used up heedlessly, farms and ranches failing for lack of water, and the rural West beginning to empty out. Today a small fraction of Virginia City's peak population survives there by exploiting the town's silvery past; Rhyolite is a ghost town.

Twain, with his keener vision and profounder sensibility, owned up to his follies, and by the time he died in 1910, he and his guru had put his house in order. The bitterness didn't go away, though—too many Clemens family members had died by then, including his wife and favorite child—and, picking up what he called "a pen warmed up in hell," he poured his rancor and alienation into late writings that partake of fable, nightmare, and screed. He left many of these unfinished—brilliant fireworks that sputter out prematurely—but did complete a caustic little masterpiece about avarice and mendacity, "The Man That Corrupted Hadleyburg" (1899). Another story, the striking "$30,000 Bequest" (1903), hews even closer to the bone: in it, a husband and wife amuse themselves by blathering endlessly about the imaginary riches that accrue as they daydream about investing the eponymous amount, which has been promised them by an aged relative upon his death. "The $30,000 Bequest" is a raw slice of psychodrama, with a final twist that turns it into one last expression of Twain's flair for literary practical jokes.

That, in the end, was the difference between the two Washoe Giants. When Bill Stewart's high-flying days were over, he had nothing to show for them but memories, which he prettied up and at times falsified in print. Mark Twain, in the end, faced the truth squarely and transformed his failures and regrets into art.

NINE

The Big Borrasca

By the late 1870s, the Comstock had dried up to such an extent that a conspiracy theory was making headway there. According to the complainers, more glittering stuff was down underground—deep down, at the mines' remotest levels—but the owners were sitting on it, keeping mum until they could consolidate their control. Nonsense, said Alf Doten in an 1883 letter to the *Territorial Enterprise* from Austin, Nevada, where he was temporarily working. As any veteran Comstocker knew, secrets don't last long in that hothouse environment. And don't forget, he added, that in the recent Sierra Nevada Deal, "too much was known—or unknown—for more insiders than outsiders were slaughtered" (even including some of the Bonanza Kings). Look to "the upper portion of the lode," he advised, "above the level of the Sutro tunnel, where all past bonanzas have been found."

High up or down low, however, the bonanzas failed to show, and mines either shut down or reduced their workforce. The laid-off miners, naturally, packed up and left. Wherever they went—Butte, Montana; Leadville, Colorado; Tombstone, Arizona—their reputation for toughness and skill preceded them. The biggest single draw was the gold-rush town of Bodie, California, near the Nevada border 50 miles south of Lake Tahoe. Its population of 10,000 was less than half of Virginia City's in its prime, but Bodie could brag about its more extreme location, a couple of thousand feet higher, and an all-star cast of roughnecks. Gunslingers such as Three Fingers Jack and Johnny Behind the Rocks had the run of the place, along with whores such as Big Nell and Bull Josie; in one hellish year, one hundred fifty murder charges were filed, and "I'm a bad man from Bodie" became a national catchphrase. But Bodie ultimately weighed in as a disappointment: the good times lasted only about five years, from 1877 to 1882, after which the place emptied out fast. (The ghost town of Bodie is now a California park, whose surviving buildings are maintained by the state in what it calls "arrested decay.")

The Comstock-wide borrasca affected San Francisco, too, where even residents savvy enough to stay away from mining stocks learned that the nexus between the two locales had a downside. A newspaper commentator pointed out that during the Comstock's stagnation in the late 1870s, deposits in San Francisco's savings banks dropped by $25 million, presumably as investors withdrew money to pay for speculations that were going nowhere and to satisfy nonstop assessments. The same writer went on: "Capital, no longer generally distributed, is concentrated in colossal fortunes, which may be numbered upon the fingers. Manufactures have lessened in number, and those that still exist struggle for life."

Yet the troubles in Nevada actually boosted one sector of San Francisco's economy: the stock market or, rather, its brokers. The Bank Ring and the Bonanza Kings had ruthlessly squeezed spectacular profits out of mines, but stockbrokers proved that you could get rich off the Comstock by using gentler methods: dangle the prospect of whopping returns to hook small investors and churn the market so as to generate a steady stream of transactions. Smooth-talking brokers got so good at their jobs that they attained tycoon status themselves. On a tour of the San Francisco waterfront in the 1870s, an observer marveled at the berths full of lavish yachts. His guide began ticking off the owners and their occupations: a remarkable number were stockbrokers. "Where are the customers' yachts?" the visitor wondered aloud.

With the Bank Ring long gone and the Bonanza Kings no longer a force on the Comstock, brokers joined hands with mill owners and politicians to keep the place artificially alive. The mill owners were happy to be paid to grind up rock regardless of its worth, and what sort of politician would pull a long face and predict that the legendary Lode was a goner? The brokers didn't care one way or the other about the underlying reality; for them the Comstock was little more than a pretext for commissions. Thanks to this odd alliance, thirty or so mines still remained open, if just barely, in the late 1880s. Each had a superintendent, foreman, and so on, but few actual miners, and little or no work was being done.

Some brokers went a step further, employing a tactic called "bucketing," the last great fraud in the Comstock's impressive arsenal. Bucketing targets those who buy stocks on margin, that is, in a credit transaction by which the client hands over only part of the purchase price but gets ownership of the stock, although the broker holds on to the certificates. Typically, the Comstock investor put down half in cash and signed a promissory note to pay two percent a month interest on the balance, but a bucketing broker simply filed the buy order away and did nothing. Because from all indications the stock was going nowhere but down (we're in the dismal mid-1880s now, and Con Virginia and California, the company recently formed by a merger of the Bonanza Kings' two leading mines, can be had for as little as $2 a share, down from a top price of more than $700 apiece), the shamming broker had little fear of getting caught. When ordered to sell, he could count on getting hold of the missing stock at a lower price than what the client had paid for it. Meanwhile, the broker had invested that fifty-percent-down in something safe and collected the interest paid by the customer on the balance owed. When the mine levied assessments (and how else could it keep going?), the broker drew up a bill and sent it to the unwitting customer exactly as if he owned the stock; and when those assessments were paid, the broker, in the position of middleman, simply kept the money for himself.

James L. Flood, son of the famous James C., found out about bucketing and in 1886 teamed up with several mine managers to launch what might be called a "punish-fraud" against the brokers. The conspirators leaked the market-dampening news that they intended to shut down the last deep-mining operation on the Comstock—true, but a diversion. In the bearish climate that resulted, with brokers reassured as to the continuing wisdom of bucketing, Flood et al. quietly went into buying mode. On the strength of their purchases, Con Virginia and California shot up from $4.50 at the end of October to $55 in early December, and other stocks followed its lead. The rise happened to coincide with the U.S. Senate race in which Bill Stewart was making a comeback after a dozen years out of office. "Politics red hot, & stocks up," Alf Doten noted in a journal entry, and it was easy to believe that Nevada and its beloved Comstock might be reverting to form. It wasn't, but the rise was what so many investors had been waiting for, and they bombarded their stockbrokers with orders to sell. Which meant, of course, that the bucket brigade was screwed.

The more unscrupulous brokers reacted by piling deceit upon deceit. According to a historian of the San Francisco Exchange, a "Negro porter" anxious to sell was invited into his broker's office for a chat during which the porter mentioned that he was acting on a tip provided by Dick Dey, John Mackay's San Francisco business manager. "Why you poor sucker," said the broker, "don't you know that Dey advised you to sell so Mackay could pick up your stock?" The porter changed his mind, and lost his entire investment. Tricks like that could accomplish only so much, however. One day so many orders to sell caught so many brokers with empty buckets, as it were, that the president of the exchange closed it down early, and brokerage houses failed in both Virginia City and San Francisco.

For Comstockers, the most shocking failure was that of their own L. B. Frankel, reportedly $1 million in the red after "not purchasing & filling orders during the present boom—couldn't either buy or sell so had to bust—great excitement—The Frankels filed petition in insolvency with list of creditors & skipped out for San Francisco." Or so Doten assumed in his journal; a few days later, however, he noted that "At 7 this evening [December 11, 1886], Sol Frankel was arrested at his rooms, where he has been concealed, right across the way from mine, since his bust up—He was badly dilapidated, mentally & physically and almost starved—Took him to jail." The following April, having spent the intervening months behind bars, Frankel was about to stand trial for embezzlement when the prosecutor dropped the charges. Frankel was freed and put on a stage out of town. For their handiwork, young Flood and his co-conspirators might deserve a round of applause, if it weren't for the likelihood that their vigilante action hurt not just dishonest brokers but a number of innocent investors as well.

Young Flood and his co-conspirators followed through on their plan to end deep mining on the Comstock in part because underground conditions were worsening: not just more water at the lower levels, but hotter water. As one historian noted, "Men had almost reached the limit of endurance." Starting in late 1886, however, Doten and other look-higher-in-the-Lode optimists were vindicated by the discovery of low-grade ore near the surface, among the holdings of the Con California and Virginia. Several dormant mines opened again, stockbrokers perked up, in 1887 a bold fellow named Captain J. B. Overton built one last Washoe Pan Process mill (it was run by electricity), and the Comstock enjoyed a mini-revival for the better part of a decade. By 1895, however, these deposits, too, were played out. Things were so bad that the *Territorial Enterprise* had ceased publication in 1893, its last words being a euphemistic reference to the tough times: "For sufficient reasons we stop."

Writing a year later, historian Charles Howard Shinn painted a grim picture of the unraveling mining district:

> Wreck, decay, abandonment, make the dominant note of the scene. Many of the great mills stand idle over their vast gray waste heaps, rotting slowly down to death and chaos. Inside, the stamps hang rusting in long rows, "hung up," as the miners say. No clang and clatter is heard—no strong, deep roar of the massive machinery that filled the canyons and the crowded streets in bonanza times with constant undercurrents of thrilling, pulsing sound night and day alike while millions of dollars' worth of bullion poured out of the smelters.

The region stayed afloat in the first two decades of the twentieth century as more low-grade ore was found, as open-pit mining was introduced and as entrepreneurs in other Nevada mining boomtowns took advantage of Virginia City's existing infrastructure to ship ore there for milling. But by 1930 the population of Storey County had dipped to six hundred sixty-seven, and the Comstock's future as a mining district looked so irreversibly bleak that scavengers were dismantling the old structures and machines for scrap. Their cannibalizing speeded up the rotting process described by Shinn, and today most of the mighty sheds and mills once standing on the side of Mt. Davidson are gone.

The fortunes of one Comstocker rose and fell in synchronicity with the Lode itself: Alf Doten, the indefatigable keeper of a massive journal whose later entries present an almost clinical record of public and private decay. Born in Plymouth, Massachusetts, in 1829, he went west as a 49er; later he was a farmer and reporter. An 1863 letter to a newspaper called the *California Ledger*, written after Doten had visited the Comstock but before he'd moved there, reflects the characteristic youthful exuberance of that buoyant period:

> In mining stocks, of course, there is the greatest kind of chance for wild speculation, and many a fortune is won and lost at it; but investments in the stock of a really good mine, the reputation of which is fully established, are really good; for the stock increases in price, as the mine turns out better. The "Gould and Curry" mine, for instance, at Virginia City, on the far-famed "Comstock" ledge, is now sold at over six thousand dollars per foot or share, which three or four years ago went begging at five dollars per foot.

Doten's strengths as a journalist were accuracy and thoroughness, but he wasn't clever, and once settled down in Comstock country, he found himself outshone by Mark Twain and Dan De Quille. Yet Doten stayed put, plugged away, and was named editor of the *Gold Hill Daily News* in 1867, a coup that he celebrated in a short but exultant entry: "I hoisted my name to the head of the columns today as *Editor* of the News." With backing from Bill Sharon, Doten took over as publisher in 1872.

But as the Big Bonanza hollowed out, both Doten and the *News* were left on shaky ground. In an entry from January 26, 1879, he notes that Western Union has "shut [him] off from all press telegrams" for not paying his bills. (In the next line, he confesses to cribbing the missing news from the *Territorial Enterprise* and San Francisco papers.) In April of the same year, he notes the closing of the Bank of California's Gold Hill branch; from now on, anyone having business to transact with the once-mighty institution must amble up the road to Virginia City. Rutherford B. Hayes, not an ex-president like Grant but an actual sitting chief executive, pays the Comstock a visit in 1880, but a platitude he tosses out from the balcony of the International Hotel can bear an ominous interpretation: "All people

are fond of treasures, but good health is a treasure beyond all price."
What might sound like standard political blah-blah anywhere else
takes on an unfortunate second meaning in the context of the
Comstock's sickly economy.

A few months later, Doten records a development that encapsu-
lates the regional doldrums as almost nothing else could: Virginia
City is down to its last two-bit saloon; all the others have bowed to
economic reality by reducing the price of a drink to one bit. By the
end of the year (1881), he has sold the *News*, left it entirely after
fourteen years' service, and relocated with his wife and four children to Austin, Nevada, where he edits the *Reese River Reveille*.
Without him, the *News* bumps along for a few more months before
ceasing publication on April 8, 1882. The paper's last owner blames
the euthanasia on "the great depression in business interests of this
town, the stagnation of mining industries in the district and unfa-
vorable prospects for the near future."

Doten leaves the *Reveille*, sells life insurance for a while, and
takes any freelance writing job that falls his way. On his sixtieth
birthday, he observes that he is "poorer financially than I ever was
in all my life." A few weeks after that, he learns that the Gold Hill
house he'd built years earlier, at a cost of $8,000, just sold for $300.
He becomes an alcoholic, works fitfully, returns to Virginia City
from time to time but can't land a secure position there, separates
from his family at his wife's insistence, rents humble Carson City
digs while using a hotel lobby as his "office," even to the point of
writing his letters on their stationery, so eccentric a figure as to be
rather a laughingstock.

At one point, he runs into an old acquaintance who sizes him up
cruelly but not inaccurately: "You never amounted to much." This
"snub" wounds him, and his financial woes try his patience, but he
pulls himself together to write an informative series of reminiscences and updates on the Comstock for various newspapers and
magazines. With his freelancer's income, such sums as he can fina-
gle out of friends, and regular donations from his wife and children,

he gets by, and always he perseveres with his journal, a touchstone in an otherwise amorphous life.

Many entries are humdrum, and Doten almost never engages in self-analysis, but some lines crackle with the wonder of life in the ever-changing nineteenth century. For example, in 1887 he writes with unusual fervor about his first sight of electric lighting, in downtown Reno: "About a dozen of them in saloons and hotels, & 2 or 3 on street—Bright white light transcending all others—Even made the moon look yellow and gas lights & coal oil lamps looked like 'pumpkin lanterns.'" In 1891 he puts his finger on Nevada's future by describing the pervasive, irrepressible urge to gamble as personified by a young man named Leo Hechinger. Hechinger takes out ads in the local papers announcing his willingness

> to wager from $100 to $500 that I can shoulder an eight-gallon keg of beer, not to weigh less than 105 pounds, and pack it to the flagstaff on the top of Mount Davidson, and return, from the corner of Union and C streets without any artificial means of support or any rest. My weight is 146 pounds. Should I slip or fall without outside interference, so that the keg touches the ground, I lose my wager.

A big crowd turns out, and the enterprising jock makes it up and down the mountain—a three-mile round trip—in two hours and twenty-five minutes. "There was much betting," Doten notes, "$4000 or $5000 changing hands on the result."

In a poignant entry from 1897, Doten bids farewell to his old friend De Quille, who is suffering so badly from rheumatism that he must move back to Iowa to be cared for by relatives:

> [He] is racked with it from shoulders to knees, back humped up double and is merely animated skin and bone, almost helpless—can only walk about the house a little, grasping cane with both hands. . . . Looks to be 90 yrs old, yet was 68 on the

9th of May last—2 months & 10 days older than I am. . . . Poor dear old boy Dan—my most genial companion in our early Comstock reportorial days, good bye, and I think forever personally on this earth. . . .

After Mackay's death in 1902, Doten is one of a dwindling band of old-timers. He stays true to the journal until the very end, jotting a final entry a few hours before his own death on November 12, 1903.

We owe the survival of Doten's journal to his family, who saved the seventy-nine notebooks he filled with it. We owe its accessibility to the labors of a far better writer, the novelist Walter Van Tilburg Clark, who spent almost ten years winnowing it down (to about half the original length) and supplementing it with Doten's published writings.

Born in New York in 1909, Clark had grown up in Reno from the age of eight on, after his father assumed the presidency of the University of Nevada. In 1940, the young writer published a novel, *The Ox-Bow Incident*, that probes the psychology of a lynch mob without sprinkling in solo heroics or a cavalry charge to save the day. Written in defiance of the cowboy-as-knight-errant myth launched by Owen Wister in *The Virginian* and perpetuated by Zane Grey and hundreds of Hollywood Westerns, the book became an instant classic. Clark published two other novels, including an allegorical Western called *The Track of the Cat*, and critics entertained great hopes for him. But what was to be his last book, *The Watchful Gods and Other Stories*, came out in 1950, when he was barely 40. Much of his time thereafter was consumed by teaching. Not only was he a perfectionist; he also had lofty ambitions (he worked sporadically on a trilogy of novels about the boom-and-bust American West), and the combination gave him an incurable case of writer's block. "I'm as inspired as a sawdust dummy," he once complained.

The original plan was for him to mine Doten's journals for a biography, while historian Russell Elliott edited the documents themselves, but as Clark read the material he saw a great deal of himself in the frustrated, aging Comstocker. "I have become Alf Doten," he began telling friends. He dropped the biography idea in favor of a novel based on Doten but couldn't get that going, either. Finally, he accepted an offer from the University of Nevada to become a writer-in-residence and take over editing the journals for publication.

In common with many other academics, Clark had been a nomad, teaching in Iowa, Montana, California, and other places, but he liked Virginia City, and he moved there to work on the journal. In so doing, he was returning to a place where he'd lived once before, in the 1940s. During that earlier sojourn, he'd been present for the kindling of a new blaze of Comstock glory, when a number of East Coast expatriates fetched up in Virginia City and formed an artists' colony. Their bellwether was dilettante and writer Lucius Beebe, who in 1940 had breezed in as part of a train tour promoting a new movie, *Virginia City*, starring Errol Flynn. The film, Beebe admitted, was a "real stinker," but he found the town so congenial that he and his lover, Charles Clegg, moved there and revived *The Territorial Enterprise*. Other writers and artists gravitated there for the cheap living and plentiful carousing, outsiders temporarily in Nevada to take advantage of its liberal divorce laws stopped by, and upon his return Clark found himself enjoying the newcomers' sparkling company. Yet he held himself apart (in a group photo, he's down on one knee in the foreground while behind him other members of the Comstock rat pack cluster in front of a gambling wheel) and he disapproved of Beebe's cavalier way with facts. (After reading Beebe's slapdash *Legends of the Comstock Lode*, one dips into the relentlessly factual *Journals of Alfred Doten* with a sense of relief.)

Beebe's fable-telling helped Virginia City reinvent itself as a tourist town, but when the mythmaker died in 1966, Clark was still hard at work on setting the record straight. He'd almost finished the editing project when he died himself, of cancer, in 1971. Some years earlier, he'd offered his take on Doten in a letter to the journals' publisher, the University of Nevada Press:

> [The journal] presents in graphic and often moving detail the tragic course of a single representative life through the violent transformations enforced by the predatory and essentially amoral life of the California Gold Rush and the Nevada Silver Rush. . . . It is so perfectly the whole, inevitable rise and fall that even in form, within the journals themselves, it practically assumed the structure of classical tragedy. Even with violent, elemental accompaniments. Hard to believe, but [Doten's] very first entry is made twelve hours out of Plymouth [Massachusetts], in flying scud and violent squalls, and his very last, made the night he died, is concerned chiefly with the house-shaking, dust-hurling violence of the winds which have kept anybody from coming to see him all that day.

With an introduction by Clark's son Robert, the journals appeared in three handsome, slipcased volumes in 1973.

Novelist Wallace Stegner came up with a theory as to what besides writer's block might have kept his friend Clark from producing more fiction. Just as American literature as a whole had slogged through a long adolescence until the country was mature enough to appreciate novelists as sophisticated as Hawthorne and James, Stegner suggested, so writing in and of the American West might have to bide its time until the rest of the regional culture catches up with it. In other words, the part of the country from which Clark drew his subjects and inspiration may not have been ready for what he had to say.

Stegner went on to sum up Clark's oeuvre in a way that applies with special force to the last project: "His books are on the permanent shelf, and I do not mean the shelf of mythic, easy, deluding westerns. His theme was civilization, and he recorded, indelibly, its first steps in a new country." Doten's journal details that civilizing process in Nevada, and Clark's work on it can be seen as a substitute for the final, elaborate fictional scheme that he wasn't able to carry out. *There it is*, Clark seems to be saying of this mammoth dual record of a troubled Western life and a mercurial Western boomtown, *it will have to do.*

Virginia City still hangs on as a tourist destination, a role it's been playing so long that the last of the weathered-board facades nailed up in the *Bonanza* era to make C Street look more like its TV incarnation has just about earned historic status itself. Yes, those unpainted vertical boards on the Bonanza Casino are inauthentic (in the old days, the buildings along C Street were made of brick or painted, horizontal boards), but the false note captures an era. The Comstock Historic District Commission, a state body, has come into being to ensure that what goes on in Virginia City nowadays doesn't destroy the remaining historic ambience, and the town is well worth visiting. But be advised: it looks both gaudy and tatty. What you have to keep in mind, though, is that this is the nature of mining towns. Unlike, say, historic Williamsburg, today's Virginia City lacks smooth uniformity and ironclad integrity. It's a thrown-together hodgepodge, just as it always was.

Barring some unexpected new bonanza, the Comstock will go down in history as having yielded roughly $300 million in ore, a total that holds up well against the $500 million reached by its more famous predecessor, the California Gold Rush. But Alexander del Mar, a mining engineer who directed the U.S. Bureau of Statistics more than a century ago, reckoned that overall the Comstock cost five times what it contributed to the economy, with hapless small investors suffering most of the losses. "Five times" sounds high, but it's quite possible that when you factor in all the wrongful assessments and the myriad losses in a rigged stock market, the number appearing on the Comstock's bottom line has a minus sign in front of it. In any case, the Lode was a precursor to the gambling economy that has dominated Nevada ever since. Just as deposits of gold and silver gave royal rewards to the Comstock's favored few—the Ring, the Kings, and a few others—while thousands of commoners were parted from their savings, so legalized games of chance and lotteries hand over big returns to a small number of winners at the expense of the great majority of players.

The Comstock nabobs also have a lot to answer for because of their ingratitude to the state that allowed them to fleece it. On this subject, the last word might go to a colorful local figure named James "Kettle Belly" Brown, who'd served as Virginia City's first paid fire chief. In an 1893 interview with the *San Francisco Examiner*, Kettle Belly was told of a rumor that John Mackay might finance an effort to pump out the mines and get them working again. The news (which turned out not to be true) brought forth this tirade of hope mixed with resentment:

I'll stand on C Street . . . and welcome back the prodigals. Where would the Palace Hotel be, I'd like to ask, if it hadn't of been for the bullion of the Comstock Lode? Where would the Nevada Bank get off, and what would become of the Flood Building? Wasn't the Mills Building put up with profits from the Virginia and Truckee Railroad, and didn't the Comstock furnish all the ore and most all the freight to give those profits? Who made Sutro Heights? The Comstock. What built those lordly palaces of architectural splendor on Nob Hill? The Comstock. Who put the postal cable lines across the continent and under the ocean? The Comstock. What gave Uncle Sam his piles of gold to buy ammunition and hard tack when the ark of the nation was buffeted by the war billows of the greatest rebellion ever known in history? The Comstock. What kept the Bank of California from going up the flume? The Comstock.

But perhaps that's too resentful a note on which to end. Virginia City may be a tarted-up facsimile of its old self, but unlike many a mining town, at least it's still alive, with surviving buildings, museums, a multitude of photos and drawings, and the voluminous writings of an unusually talented group of journalists to suggest how grand and enthralling it once was. And isn't there something to be said for a town—and later a whole state—that opts out of the puritanism that has gripped America through most of its history? The fun index of any given place is hard to quantify, but I think it's hard to read extensively in Comstock history without getting the impression that on the whole its dramatis personae—miners, plutocrats, newsmen, suppliers, gamblers, entertainers, women, children, perhaps just about everybody but the Chinese and the Paiutes—had a hell of a good time producing silver and gold and partying and writing down stories about themselves.

In that vein, a better envoi might be this line from *The Travels of Jaimie McPheeters*, a 1958 novel of the Old West by Robert Lewis Taylor: "Money for nothing," says a fictional miner. "I wouldn't have missed it. It's what we live for—the incomparable boon of not being bored."

❧ NOTES ❧

1. The Perfect Monster

2: "of medium height": Shinn, Charles Howard, *The Story of the Mine as Illustrated by the Great Comstock Lode of Nevada*, Reno: University of Nevada Press, 1980, p. 27.

2: "get[ting] a couple of hundred dollars": quoted in Lord, Eliot, *Comstock Mining and Miners*, San Diego: Howell-North, 1980, p. 26.

3: "perfect monster": Ibid., p. 27.

4: "In the first burst": Ibid., p. 29.

4: "I feel very lonely": Ibid.

5: "lie down and die": Ibid., p. 31.

5: "From daybreak till noon": Ibid.

6: "When visitors came": De Quille, Dan (William Wright), *A History of the Comstock Silver Lode & Mines*, Virginia City, NV: F. Boegle, 1889, p. 37.

6: "'Old Virginia' was out one night": quoted in De Quille, Dan (William Wright), *The Big Bonanza*, New York: Thomas Y. Crowell, 1969, p. 32.

8: "An almost continuous string": quoted in Watkins, T. H., *Gold and Silver in the West: The Illustrated History of an American Dream*, Palo Alto, CA: American West, 1971, p. 74.

8–9: "sold two hundred dollars worth": Shinn, *The Story of the Mine*, p. 52.

9: "half of them were dead": Young, Otis E., Jr., *Western Mining*, Norman: University of Oklahoma Press, 1970, p. 240.

9: "knew nothing of underground mining": Lord, *Comstock Mining and Miners*, p. 60.

10: "something like a singed cat": Twain, Mark, *Tales, Speeches, Essay, and Sketches*, New York: Penguin, 1994, p. 9.

10: "[mining] is all this Territory is good for": Doten, Alfred, *The Journals of Alfred Doten: 1849–1903*, three volumes, Reno: University of Nevada Press, 1973, vol. 1, p. 714.

10: "Such a wind": Shinn, *The Story of the Mine*, p. 64.

10: "hats, chickens, and parasols": Twain, Mark, *Roughing It*, New York: Penguin, 1985, p. 179.

11: "On a slope of mountain": Browne, J. Ross, *A Peep at Washoe and Washoe Revisited*, Balboa Island, CA: Paisano Press, 1959, pp. 64–65.

12: "Nevertheless, it is true": Mathews, Mary McNair, *Ten Years in Nevada, or Life on the Pacific Coast*, Lincoln: University of Nebraska Press, 1985, p. 126.

12: "I have just heard five pistol shots": quoted in Sanborn, Margaret, *Mark Twain: The Bachelor Years*, New York: Doubleday, 1990, p. 189.

12–13: "The first twenty-six graves": Twain, *Roughing It*, p. 346.

13: "Little stacks of gold": Lord, *Comstock Mining and Miners*, p. 73.

13: "raged without check": Ibid.

15: "They will come like the sand": quoted in Egan, Ferol, *Sand in a Whirlwind: The Paiute Indian War of 1860*, New York: Doubleday, 1972, p. 102.

15: "Horrid massacre": Ibid., p. 109.

15: "There is no longer any use": Ibid., p. 103.

16: "teaching the red devils a lesson": quoted in Lord, *Comstock Mining and Miners*, p. 68.

16: "There has been a vast deal of talk": quoted in Egan, *Sand in a Whirlwind*, p. 113.

16: "a sort of pleasure excursion": De Quille, *The Big Bonanza*, p. 77.

16: "An Indian for breakfast": quoted in Egan, *Sand in a Whirlwind*, p. 116.

17: "had charged through an open gate": Ibid., p. 138.

17: "to cut their way through": Ibid., p. 141.

18: "Drop down as if dead": Winnemucca, Sarah Hopkins, *Life Among the Piutes: Their Wrongs and Claims*, Reno: University of Nevada, 1994, p. 72. On page 152 of *Sand in a Whirlwind*, Ferol Egan attributes this action and speech to Numaga, but he cites Sarah Winnemucca as the source, and she says it was her brother who tried to spare Ormsby's life.

18: "trains of people and stock": quoted in James, Ronald M., *The Roar and the Silence: A History of Virginia City and the Comstock Lode*, Reno: University of Nevada Press, 1988, p. 40.

18: "pieces of scrap iron": De Quille, *The Big Bonanza*, p. 80.

18: "When the explosion": Ibid.

19: "Amongst the killed": quoted in Stewart Robert E. and M. F. Stewart, *Adolph Sutro: A Biography*, Berkeley: Howell-North, 1962, p. 35.

20: "The Indians were admirably posted": quoted in Egan, *Sand in a Whirlwind*, p. 235.

20: "the Jerusalem of our crusade": Ibid., p. 239.

20: "I will look hard at you first": Ibid., p. 265.

20: "Is it not better": Ibid., p. 267.

21: "rather a fine looking Indian": Doten, *Journals*, vol. 2, p. 1450. Numaga was also known as Young Winnemucca, which is how Doten refers to him in this article.

21: "were welcome to use": Ibid.

21: "The Indians' orchards about Como": Ibid., p. 1451.

21: "became willing participants": James Ronald M. and C. Elizabeth Raymond, eds., *Comstock Women: The Making of a Mining Community*, Reno: University of Nevada Press, 1998, p. 245.

22: "We're one of the few tribes": Interview with the author, July 17, 2007.

22: "He said that he was about 35 years of age": Mooney, James, Fourteenth Annual Report (Part 2) of the Bureau of American Ethnology to the Smithsonian Institution, 1892–1893, reprinted in Hittman, Michael, *Wovoka and the Ghost Dance*, Lincoln: University of Nebraska Press, 1997, p. 241.

24: "The Indian troubles greatly assisted": De Quille, *The Big Bonanza*, p. 85.

2. Heavy Metal

26: "wind-sails were used": De Quille, Dan (William Wright), *The Big Bonanza*, New York: Thomas Y. Crowell, 1969, p. 385.

28: "the object with many inventors": quoted in Paul, Rodman Wilson, *Mining Frontiers of the Far West, 1848–1880*, Albuquerque: University of New Mexico Press, 2001, p. 67.

29: "The dilemma was a curious one": Lord, Eliot, *Comstock Mining and Miners*, San Diego: Howell-North, 1980, p. 89.

30: "Imagine [the mine]": quoted in Brechin, Gray, *Imperial San Francisco: Urban Power, Earthly Ruin*, Berkeley: University of California Press, 1999, p. 67.

30: "was strained like a fiddle string": Doten, Alfred, *The Journals of Alfred Doten: 1849–1903*, three volumes, Reno: University of Nevada Press, 1973, volume 2, p. 826.

30: "like peas in a hot skillet": Ibid.

31: "Fully 600,000,000 feet": Lord, *Comstock Mining and Miners*, p. 351.

32: "the form of the Greek cross": Ibid., p. 124.

32: "to stand for years": Smith, Grant H., *The History of the Comstock Lode 1850–1997*, Reno: University of Nevada Press, 1998, p. 85.

34: "George Hearst was probably": quoted in Robinson, Judith, *The Hearsts: An American Dynasty*, Newark: University of Delaware Press, 1991, p. 73.

34: "You know how fond": Ibid., p. 119.

35: "watched for three weeks": Ibid., p. 105.

35: "a turnip upside down": Ibid., p. 110.

35: "I never sold": Ibid.

36: "plethoric purse": Ibid., p. 185.

36: "a squealing pig": Ibid.

37: "Senator George Hearst": Ibid., p. 233.

37: "I could name a score": Ibid.

37: "The first five years": Ibid., p. 55.

38: "a ball of glass shaped like an egg": Dwyer, Richard A. and Richard E. Lingenfelter, eds., *Dan De Quille, the Washoe Giant: A Biography and Anthology*, Reno: University of Nevada Press, 1990, p. 90.

38: "What I now want": Ibid.

38: "always asserted": Ibid., p. 92.

39: "the prize Christmas shoppers": Paine, Swift, *Eilley Orrum: Queen of the Comstock*, Palo Alto, CA: Pacific Books, 1949, p. 129.

39: "We've lost the vein": Ibid., p. 192.

40: "What boy or girl": Smith, *The History of the Comstock Lode*, pp. 233–234.

40: "second sight": quoted in Paine, *Eilly Orrum*, p. 250.

40: "She may be consulted": James, Ronald M. and C. Elizabeth Raymond, eds., *Comstock Women: The Making of a Mining Community*, Reno: University of Nevada Press, 1998, p. 165.

40: "prepared to tell the PAST": Ibid., p. 177.

41: "distinguish the jingle of a quarter": Doten, *Journals*, vol. 2, p. 1477.

42: "a staggeringly complex enterprise": Watkins, T. H., *Gold and Silver in the West: The Illustrated History of an American Dream*, Palo Alto, CA: American West, 1971, p. 119.

3. The Nature of the Beast

44: "the millionaire and the mendicant": quoted in Shinn, Charles Howard, *The Story of the Mine as Illustrated by the Great Comstock Lode of Nevada*, Reno: University of Nevada Press, 1980, p. 145.

45: "For the purposes of speculation": Ibid., p. 150.

46: "a heavy owner in the best mines": quoted in Sanborn, Margaret, *Mark Twain: The Bachelor Years*, New York: Doubleday, 1990, p. 212.

46: "When the California papers": Dwyer, Richard A. and Richard E. Lingenfelter, eds., *Dan De Quille, the Washoe Giant: A Biography and Anthology*, Reno: University of Nevada Press, 1990, p. 208.

46: Sketch of Stewart and following quotations: Twain, Mark, *Roughing It*, New York: Penguin, 1985, Ch. XLIV.

47: "Our millionaires": Dwyer and Lingenfelter, eds., *Dan De Quille: The Washoe Giant*, p. 30.

49: "as costs . . . to be paid": Stewart, William M., *Reminiscences*, New York: Neale, 1908, pp. 98–102.

49: "a ban on intelligence": Twain, *Roughing It*, p. 349.

49–50: "Have you ever had any occupation" and following quotations: Stewart, *Reminiscences*, pp. 112 ff.

50: "everbody's spurs": quoted in Shinn, *The Story of the Mine*, p. 127.

51: "nine companies had 359 cases": Smith, Grant H., *The History of the Comstock Lode 1850–1997*, Reno: University of Nevada Press, 1998, p. 66.

51: "Two evils": Browne, J. Ross, *A Peep at Washoe and Washoe Revisited*, Balboa Island, CA: Paisano Press, 1959, p. 381.

53: "[Stewart] compared Hereford": Lord, Eliot, *Comstock Mining and Miners*, San Diego: Howell-North, 1980, pp. 147–148.

54: "faithfully dishonest": Browne, *A Peep at Washoe and Washoe Revisited*, p. 381.

54: "You little shrimp": quoted in Smith, *The History of the Comstock Lode*, p. 67.

55: "Yellow Jacket miners cut a drift": Lord, *Comstock Mining and Miners*, pp. 136–137.

56: "most honest, upright": quoted in Ostrander, Gilman M., *Nevada: The Great Rotten Borough 1859–1964*, New York: Knopf, 1966, p. 31.

56: "Hon. J. W. North": quoted in Elliott, Russell R., *Servant of Power: A Political Biography of Senator William M. Stewart*, Reno: University of Nevada Press, 1983, p. 28.

57: "No other reason could induce": Ibid., p. 31.

57: "one of those who believe": Ibid., p. 32.

57–58: "The goose that lays the golden eggs": Doten, Alfred, *The Journals of Alfred Doten: 1849–1903*, three volumes, Reno: University of Nevada Press, 1973, vol. 1, p. 763.

58: "The A No. 1, full-rigged ship": quoted in Elliott, *Servant of Power*, p. 33.

58: "This was my triumph": Ibid., p. 34.

58: "probably the most ignorant man": Stewart, *Reminiscences*, p. 153.

58: "drinking, quarreling": quoted in Lord, *Comstock Mining and Miners*, p. 159.

59: "written at the bottom of each article": quoted in Elliott, *Servant of Power*, p. 38.

59: "severe & protracted illness": Ibid.

60: "was read aloud": Stewart, *Reminiscences*, p. 162.

61: "wrong and unjustifiable": quoted in Elliott, *Servant of Power*, p. 45.

61: "lower[ing] his dignity": quoted in Lord, *Comstock Mining and Miners*, p. 163.

62–63: "The Ophir on the Comstock": Ibid., p. 133.

63: "Comstock methods look like the work of amateurs": Smith, *The History of the Comstock Lode*, p. 70.

4. Working Low, Living High

65: "The body of a man falling": De Quille, Dan (William Wright), *The Big Bonanza*, New York: Thomas Y. Crowell, 1969, p. 149.

66: "green hand": Doten, Alfred, *The Journals of Alfred Doten: 1849–1903*, three volumes, Reno: University of Nevada Press, 1973, vol. 2, p. 862.

66: "dashed from side to side": De Quille, *The Big Bonanza*, p. 149.

67: "to flatten their bodies": Ibid., pp. 146–147.

67: "complained but little": Ibid., p. 147.

68: "All are naked to the waist": Ibid., p. 248.

69: "In July 1877": Lewis, Oscar, *Silver Kings*, New York: Ballantine, 1971, p. 13.

69: "He was held a close prisoner": quoted in Mathews, Mary McNair, *Ten Years in Nevada or Life on the Pacific Coast*, Lincoln: University of Nebraska Press, 1985, p. 303.

69: "Shielded by their heavy gum clothing": Ibid.

70–71: "We had to turn out at six": Twain, Mark, *Roughing It*, New York: Penguin, 1985, pp. 262–263.

71: "By the law of ancient Rome": Lord, Eliot, *Comstock Mining and Miners*, San Diego: Howell-North, 1980, p. 185.

72: "never to work": Ibid.

72: "if labor isn't king": Ibid., p. 188.

72: "We remarked day before yesterday": Ibid., p. 189.

72: "car men, wheelbarrow men": Doten, *Journals*, vol. 2, p. 940.

72: "It would seem to work a little injustice": Ibid.

73: "Some recklessly assert": Ibid., p. 1063.

73: "When [the roadbed] is completed": quoted in Lord, *Comstock Mining and Miners*, p. 356.

74: "During the bonanza period": Elliott, Russell R., *History of Nevada*, Reno: University of Nevada Press, 1987, pp. 148–149.

75: "that class denominated 'fair but frail'": quoted in Goldman, Marion S., *Gold Diggers & Silver Miners: Prostitution and Social Life on the Comstock Lode*, Ann Arbor: University of Michigan Press, 1981, p. 88.

75: "16 carriages": Ibid.

75: "This is the first instance": Doten, *Journals*, vol. 2, p. 932.

77: "Look here, where they approached the knob": James, Ronald M., *The Roar and the Silence: A History of Virginia City and the Comstock Lode*, Reno: University of Nevada Press, 1988, p. 191.

77: "Life was . . . a great adventure": Smith, Grant H., *The History of the Comstock Lode 1850–1997*, Reno: University of Nevada Press, 1998, p. 232.

77: "a mere sordid lust for gold": Marye, George Thomas, Jr., *From '49 to '83 in California and Nevada*, San Francisco: A. M. Robertson, 1923, p. 63.

77: "few people ever enjoyed": Mathews, *Ten Years in Nevada*, p. 8.

77: "The business part of the town": Browne, J. Ross, *A Peep at Washoe and Washoe Revisited*, Balboa Island, CA: Paisano Press, 1959, p. 181.

78: "scores of angular, barracks-like boxes": Lewis, *The Silver Kings*, p. 20.

79: "When [a traveler] started out": Marye, *From '49 to '83 in California and Nevada*, pp. 128–129.

79: "a sort of Washoe midsummer night's dream": Ibid., p. 129.

80: "It claimed a population of fifteen thousand": Twain, *Roughing It*, p. 310.

80: "you gravely come forward": Twain, Mark, in Berkove, Lawrence I., ed., *The Sagebrush Anthology: Literature from the Silver Age of the Old West*, Columbia: University of Missouri Press, 2006, p. 350.

81: "Montgomery Queen's great show": James, Ronald M. and C. Elizabeth Raymond, eds., *Comstock Women: The Making of a Mining Community*, Reno: University of Nevada Press, 1998, p. 186.

81: "Good play": Doten, *Journals*, vol. 3, p. 1838.

81: "heavy shoes": Lewis, *Silver Kings*, p. 18.

81–82: "roomy smocks": Ibid.

82: "That's as close to hell": Ibid., p. 17.

83: "a cornucopia of dainties": Lord, *Comstock Mining and Miners*, p. 368.

83: "Choice cattle": Ibid.

83: "The newspapers and the stage": Smith, *The History of the Comstock Lode*, p. 30.

84: "This last, which never proved enough": Drury, Wells, *An Editor on the Comstock Lode*, Reno: University of Nevada Press, 1984, p. 4.

84: "hung in every broker's window": Mathews, *Ten Years in Nevada*, p. 172.

85: "Sold out of the Sierra Nevada": Doten, *Journals*, vol. 2, p. 1064.

85: "all of us dabbled": Drury, *An Editor on the Comstock Lode*, p. 24.

85: "Maybe you're goin' to Gold Hill": Waldorf, John Taylor, *A Kid on the Comstock*, Reno: University of Nevada Press, 1991, p. 132.

85: "If it's a temprance community": Ward, Artemus, "One of Mr. Ward's Business Letters," in Bradley, Scully, et al., eds., *The American Tradition in Literature*, vol. 2, New York: Norton, 1962, p. 185.

86: "Everything can be done nowadays": Smith, *The History of the Comstock Lode*, pp. 120–121.

87: "At the first filling of the pipe": De Quille, *The Big Bonanza*, p. 171.

87: "The crowd were as wild with joy": quoted in Shinn, Charles Howard, *The Story of the Mine as Illustrated by the Great Comstock Lode of Nevada*, Reno: University of Nevada Press, 1980, p. 103.

87: "the whole town was as inflammable": De Quille, *The Big Bonanza*, p. 428.

88: "wrapped in fire": Ibid., p. 429.

88: "a constant roar": Ibid., p. 430.

89: "Damn the church": quoted in James, *The Roar and the Silence*, p. 113.

90: "In sixty days": De Quille, *The Big Bonanza*, p. 435.

90: "the great work of rebuilding": Ibid., p. 436.

5. Capitalists Behaving Badly

91: "People who live in mining regions": Drury, Wells, *An Editor on the Comstock Lode*, Reno: University of Nevada Press, 1984, pp. 62–63.

93: "he had a heart": Mathews, Mary McNair, *Ten Years in Nevada or Life on the Pacific Coast*, Lincoln: University of Nebraska Press, 1985, p. 202.

93: "Sharon, some years, perchance": Bierce, Ambrose, *Black Beetles in Amber*, vol. 5 of *Collected Works*, New York: Neale, 1911, p. 37.

93: "scrawny little Midas": quoted in Makley, Michael J., *The Infamous King of the Comstock: William Sharon and the Gilded Age in the West*, Reno: University of Nevada Press, 2006, p. 36.

94: "bewildering bluffs": Ostrander, Gilman M., *Nevada: The Great Rotten Borough 1859–1964*, New York: Knopf, 1966, p. 46.

94: "He sounds like the very man": quoted in Makley, *The Infamous King of the Comstock*, p. 25.

95: "The hours were long": Ibid., p. 27.

96: "he owns too much": Ostrander, *Nevada: The Great Rotten Borough*, p. 48.

96–97: "Everybody speculates": quoted in Makley, *The Infamous King of the Comstock*, p. 32.

98: "To feed [Sharon's] mills": Ibid., p. 64.

98: "Everybody was at its mercy": Ibid., p. 35.

99: "The great game is this": Sutro, Adolph, *Closing Argument of Adolph Sutro on the Bill Before Congress to Aid the Sutro Tunnel*, Washington, DC: M'Gill & Witherow, 1872, p. 45.

101: "all sorts of electrical novelties": Muscatine, Doris, *Old San Francisco: The Biography of a City*, New York: Putnam, 1975, p. 292.

101: "9,000 Haviland plates": Ibid., p. 293.

101: "When a bell is rung": Satty, *Visions of Frisco: An Imaginative Depiction of San Francisco During the Gold Rush & the Barbary Coast Era*, Berkeley: Regent Press, 2008, p. 206.

103: "the equivalent of seventeen complete circles": Stewart, Robert E. and M. F. Stewart, *Adolph Sutro: A Biography*, Berkeley: Howell-North, 1962, p. 72.

103: "undoubtedly the crookedest": De Quille, Dan (William Wright), *The Big Bonanza*, New York: Thomas Y. Crowell, 1969, p. 165.

104: "built that road": Smith, Grant H., *The History of the Comstock Lode 1850–1997*, Reno: University of Nevada Press, 1998, p. 124.

104: "Bejabers!": quoted in Makley, *The Infamous King of the Comstock*, p. 71.

106: "the darkest year": Smith, *The History of the Comstock Lode*, p. 126.

107: "hogging game": quoted in Makley, *The Infamous King of the Comstock*, p. 86.

107: "You are probably aware": quoted in Lyman, George, *Ralston's Ring: California Plunders the Comstock Lode*, New York: Ballantine, 1971, p. 205.

108: "William Tecumseh Sharon": quoted in Makley, *The Infamous King of the Comstock*, p. 92.

108: "many of which proved disastrous": Stewart, William M., *Reminiscences*, New York: Neale, 1908, p. 261.

108: "You know I can't take my money": quoted in Smith, *The History of the Comstock Lode*, p. 163.

109: "only sought him": Bierce, *Black Beetles in Amber*, vol. 5, p. 33.

109: "if Sharon asks for back pay": quoted in Makley, *The Infamous King of the Comstock*, p. 151.

109: "[Sharon's] record of inaction": Elliott, Russell R., *History of Nevada*, Reno: University of Nevada Press, 1987, p. 164.

110: "In the entire history of Nevada": quoted in Smith, *The History of the Comstock Lode*, p. 211.

110: "I hardly knew which party": quoted in Ostrander, *Nevada: The Great Rotten Borough*, p. 71.

110: "says he is an actual resident": quoted in Makley, *The Infamous King of the Comstock*, p. 154.

110: "during his term": Shuck, Oscar T., *History of the Bench and Bar in California*, Los Angeles: Commercial, 1901, p. 337.

111: "Of all her public possessions": quoted in Lyman, *Ralston's Ring*, p. 199.

111: "It was carried to completion": quoted in Makley, *The Infamous King of the Comstock*, p. 106.

112: "If this be true": quoted in Lyman, *Ralston's Ring*, p. 249.

113: "The almighty": Brechin, Gray, *Imperial San Francisco: Urban Power, Earthly Ruin*, Berkeley: University of California Press, 1999, pp. 85–86.

114: "We are afraid": quoted in Lyman, *Ralston's Ring*, p. 266.

115: "Using the remnants": Makley, *The Infamous King of the Comstock*, p. 116.

115: "for I this night enter": quoted in Lyman, *Ralston's Ring*, p. 286.

115: "I do not expect to leave much": quoted in Makley, *The Infamous King of the Comstock*, p. 119.

116: "perfect self-possession": Ibid.

116: "like a schoolboy": quoted in Lyman, *Ralston's Ring*, p. 295.

116: "His was the vast vision": Brechin, *Imperial San Francisco*, p. 90.

116: "Mr. Ralston, in the hour of his extremity": quoted in Makley, *The Infamous King of the Comstock*, pp. 121–122.

116: "We all know the result": quoted in Lewis, Oscar, *Silver Kings*, New York: Ballantine, 1971, p. 210.

116–117: "No one, whose coin": quoted in Makley, *The Infamous King of the Comstock*, p. 120.

117: "Commerce commemorate his deeds": Drury, *An Editor on the Comstock Lode*, p. 119.

117: "All I have": quoted in Lyman, *Ralston's Ring*, p. 302.

117: "Best thing he could have done": quoted in Makley, *The Infamous King of the Comstock*, p. 121.

117: "Facing the bank's imminent failure": Ibid., p. 124.

118: "He appealed to the public spirit": Ibid., p. 128.

118: "a conservative estimate": Ibid., p. 131.

119: "Not a man drew coin": Ibid., p. 133.

119: "In the crowning hour of victory": quoted in Paine, Swift, *Eilley Orrum: Queen of the Comstock*, Palo Alto, CA: Pacific Books, 1949, p. 266.

119: "first and foremost": quoted in Makley, *The Infamous King of the Comstock*, p. 134.

120: "an ornament to the city": Ibid., p. 138.

121: "the Rose of Sharon": Ibid., p. 167.

122: "single hair": Ibid., p. 177.

122: "Dodging about the corridors": Ibid., p. 194.

123: "I spoke of her": Ibid., p. 182.

123: "Secondary skirmishes": Muscatine, *Old San Francisco*, p. 299.

124: "comparatively obscure": Brechin, *Imperial San Francisco*, p. 92.

124: "a bribe-taking judge": quoted in Makley, *The Infamous King of the Comstock*, p. 202.

124: "the best thing to do": Ibid.

125: "The Supreme Court has reversed": Ibid., p. 204.

125: "perceptible lapse of time": Ibid., p. 206.

6. The Pooh-Bah Effect

127: "Through the middle and late eighties": Lewis, Oscar, *Silver Kings*, New York: Ballantine, 1971, pp. 189–190.

129: "Not a cent": Smith, Grant H., *The History of the Comstock Lode 1850–1997*, Reno: University of Nevada Press, 1998, p. 15.

131: "a snug bit of money": De Quille, Dan (William Wright), *The Big Bonanza*, New York: Thomas Y. Crowell, 1969, p. 403.

131: "I'll help those Irishmen": quoted in Makley, Michael J., *The Infamous King of the Comstock: William Sharon and the Gilded Age in the West*, Reno: University of Nevada Press, 2006, p. 107.

131: "Anxious days followed": Lewis, *Silver Kings*, p. 111.

132:   "A blind man": Ibid., p. 127.

132:   "The lid, so to speak": Lord, Eliot, *Comstock Mining and Miners*, San Diego: Howell-North, 1980, p. 311.

132:   "Its walls": quoted in Lewis, *Silver Kings*, p. 115.

133:   "The stockholders owned an interest": Ibid., p. 122.

134:   "Who are the owners": Ibid., p. 125.

135:   "I always got $4 a day": Peterson, Richard H., *The Bonanza Kings: The Social Origins and Business Behavior of Western Mining Entrepreneurs, 1870–1900*, Lincoln: University of Nebraska Press, 1977, p. 80.

135:   "Lick, Latham, Sharon, and Hayward": quoted in Smith, *The History of the Comstock Lode*, p. 173.

136:   "Here and in San Francisco": Ibid., pp. 178–179.

137:   "simple rule": De Quille, *The Big Bonanza*, p. 116.

138:   "Boys, this running around": quoted in Smith, *The History of the Comstock Lode*, pp. 195–196.

138:   "The Bonanza Kings": Ibid., p. 218.

139:   "except in Utopia": Lord, *Comstock Mining and Miners*, p. 331.

139:   "Fair is crazy": quoted in Smith, *The History of the Comstock Lode*, p. 225.

139:   "offered at forty dollars less": Marye, George Thomas, Jr., *From '49 to '83 in California and Nevada*, San Francisco: A. M. Robertson, 1923, pp. 202–203.

142:   "For the next quarter century": Lewis, *The Silver Kings*, pp. 72–73.

143:   "He never came": Ibid., p. 45.

143:   "How much for the bunch": Waldorf, John Taylor, *A Kid on the Comstock*, Reno: University of Nevada Press, 1991, p. 62.

143:   "That is why we never envied": Ibid., p. 63.

143:   "God-damned old windbag": Lewis, *The Silver Kings*, p. 82.

143:   "He'll be the one who says nothing": Ibid., p. 40.

144:   "I don't suppose he knew": Ibid., p. 91.

145:   "send Flood back": Ibid., p. 191.

147:   "crammed with Nevada bank paper": Ibid., p. 212.

148:   "those kindergarten bankers": Ibid., p. 214.

148:   "Old Jimmy Fair": quoted in Smith, *The History of the Comstock Lode*, p. 187.

148:   "I wouldn't go through": quoted in Lewis, *The Silver Kings*, p. 143.

149:   "Flood should be popular": Ibid., p. 140.

149:   "John Mackay's a great admirer": Ibid.

150:   "Look at me": Ibid., p. 145.

151: "I think I ought to know": Ibid., p. 157.

152: "in the marriage contract": Shuck, Oscar T., *History of the Bench and Bar in California*, Los Angeles: Commercial, 1901, p. 344.

153: "cost us at least three votes": quoted in Lewis, *The Silver Kings*, p. 162.

154: "When a husband and wife died": Ibid., p. 172.

155: "the movement of the foot": Ibid., p. 173.

7. Challengers

158: "singularly pure and gentle": quoted in Makley, Michael J., *The Infamous King of the Comstock: William Sharon and the Gilded Age in the West*, Reno: University of Nevada Press, 2006, p. 58.

158: "unmerited kindness": Ibid.

158: "Wiegandish": Ibid.

158: "[a] pygmy" and following quotations: Twain, Mark, *Roughing It*, New York: Penguin, 1985, Appendix C.

158: "not only Wm. Sharon": quoted in Makley, *The Infamous King of the Comstock*, p. 59.

161: "in whom loftiness and purity": Berkove, Lawrence I., ed., *The Sagebrush Anthology: Literature from the Silver Age of the Old West*, Columbia: University of Missouri Press, 2006, p. 284.

161: "grieved to have so failed": Ibid., p. 286.

162–163: "He became a prey to remorse": Ibid., p. 292.

163: "in spite of repeated protests": Ibid., p. 287.

164: "I can't": quoted in Mathews, Mary McNair, *Ten Years in Nevada or Life on the Pacific Coast*, Lincoln: University of Nebraska Press, 1985, p. 200.

166: "The mine-working is done": quoted in Stewart, Robert E. and M.F. Stewart, *Adolph Sutro: A Biography*, Berkeley: Howell-North, 1962, p. 5.

167: "Sutro is insensible": Ibid., p. 39.

168: "Mr. Sutro, the originator": Twain, *Roughing It*, p. 384.

169: "*Too much cannot be said*": quoted in Lyman, George, *Ralston's Ring: California Plunders the Comstock Lode*, New York: Ballantine, 1971, pp. 50–51.

169: "say $400,000 or $500,000": quoted in Stewart and Stewart, *Adolph Sutro*, p. 56.

170: "the owls would roost": quoted in Smith, Grant H., *The History of the Comstock Lode 1850–1997*, Reno: University of Nevada Press, 1998, p. 110.

171: "He made what he called": Stewart and Stewart, *Adolph Sutro*, p. 63.

171: "We are opposed": quoted in Lyman, *Ralston's Ring*, p. 92.

172: "caused . . . smoke-filled": James, Ronald M., *The Roar and the Silence: A History of Virginia City and the Comstock Lode*, Reno: University of Nevada Press, 1988, p. 85.

172: "Sir, the Bank has waved its hand": quoted in Lyman, *Ralston's Ring*, p. 114.

173: "expose some of the doings": quoted in Stewart and Stewart, *Adolph Sutro*, p. 78.

173: "the vampires": Ibid., p. 79.

173: "His first pick": quoted in Lyman, *Ralston's Ring*, p. 149.

174: "not a necessity": quoted in Stewart and Stewart, *Adolph Sutro*, p. 97.

174: "the miners with whom we conversed": Ibid.

174: "not quite up to the rascalities": Sutro, Adolph, *Closing Argument of Adolph Sutro on the Bill Before Congress to Aid the Sutro Tunnel*, Washington, DC: M'Gill & Witherow, 1872, p. 37.

175: "the Bank of California rules": Ibid., p. 12

175: "Now, I say": Ibid., p. 87

176: "Early in the history": Stewart and Stewart, *Adolph Sutro*, p. 109.

176: "send your substitute": Ibid., p. 140.

177: "Shylock Sutro": Doten, Alfred, *The Journals of Alfred Doten: 1849–1903*, three volumes, Reno: University of Nevada Press, 1973, vol. 2, p. 1222.

177: "Mine friends": Ibid., p. 1234.

177: "Sutro on the brain": Ibid., p. 1229.

178: "Sutro Annihilated": quoted in Smith, *The History of the Comstock Lode*, p. 112.

178: "On one occasion": Stewart and Stewart, *Adolph Sutro*, p. 142.

179: "[He] sat down": Ibid., p. 147.

179: "Should your men succeed": quoted in Lyman, *Ralston's Ring*, p. 254.

180: "there is no difficulty": quoted in Stewart and Stewart, *Adolph Sutro*, p. 157.

181: "If the mining companies": Smith, *The History of the Comstock Lode*, p. 108.

182: "adopted the code": Ostrander, Gilman M., *Nevada: The Great Rotten Borough 1859–1964*, New York: Knopf, 1966, p. 65.

182: "Who could blame him": Stewart and Stewart, *Adolph Sutro*, p. 167.

182: "got out just in time": Ibid., p. 169.

183: "He passed his term": Ibid., p. 207.

183: "I have always been master": Ibid., p. 209.

184: "California fever": Baur, John E., "Early days and California years of John Percival Jones, 1849–1867," *Southern California Quarterly* 44 (1962), pp. 102–103.

184: "ruddy-cheeked": Ibid., p. 109.

185: "taking it easy as a clam": Ibid., p. 110.

185: "If I had answered you": Ibid.

185–186: "I was the very man": Ibid., p. 127.

186: "[the pair] worked for fifteen minutes": Lord, Eliot, *Comstock Mining and Miners*, San Diego: Howell-North, 1980, p. 275.

188: "Jones is very good natured": quoted in Ostrander, *Nevada: The Great Rotten Borough*, pp. 95–96.

189: "Dressed in a long black coat": Schlup, Leonard, "Nevada's doctrinaire senator: John P. Jones and the politics of silver in the gilded age," *Nevada Historical Society Quarterly* 36 (1993), p. 252.

189: "[restore] silver to its constitutional place": Ibid., p. 258.

8. Washoe Giants

191: "Perhaps none of the younger members": quoted in Elliott, Russell R., *Servant of Power: A Political Biography of Senator William M. Stewart*, Reno: University of Nevada Press, 1983, p. 46.

192: "wisest, kindest, most impartial": Stewart, William M., *Reminiscences*, New York: Neale, 1908, p. 201.

192: "I am engaged": Ibid., p. 190.

192: "Washington was anxious": Ibid., p. 166.

193: "held exercises at Athletic Hall": Doten, Alfred, *The Journals of Alfred Doten: 1849–1903*, three volumes, Reno: University of Nevada Press, 1973, vol. 2, p. 1087.

193: "The freedom of the public lands": 31st Congress 2nd Session *Congressional Globe*, Appendix, p. 136 (1851).

193–194: "large estates": *Atlantic Monthly* XLIII, p. 336 (1879).

194: "Why, undoubtedly it is acceptable": 39th Congress 1st Session *Congressional Globe*, pp. 4049–4054 (1866).

196: "under any circumstances": quoted in Elliott, *Servant of Power*, p. 76.

196: "one of the most remarkable deposits": Spence, Clark C., *British Investments and the American Mining Frontier 1860–1901*, Ithaca, NY: Cornell University Press, 1958, p. 141.

196: "are crazy about the mine": Ibid., p. 142.

196: "Dedicated to William M. Stewart": Lyon pamphlet.

197: "That [Stewart] has ever been of any service to me": Ibid., p. 36.

197: "one of the boldest": Spence, *British Investments and the American Mining Frontier*, p. 167.

197: "Yankee Doodle sold a mine": Ibid., pp. 160–161.

197: "I was not for both at the same time": quoted in Elliott, *Servant of Power*, p. 78.

198: "In spite of Stewart's testimony": Ibid., p. 79.

198: "an inspirational monument": Lingenfelter, Richard E., *Death Valley & the Amargosa: A Land of Illusion*, Berkeley: University of California Press, 1986, p. 123.

199: "It was an admirable place for outlaws": Stewart, *Reminiscences*, p. 261.

200: "unethical and dishonest behavior": Eliott, *Servant of Power*, p. 273.

200: "His hair and luxuriant beard": Smith, Grant H., *The History of the Comstock Lode 1850–1997*, Reno: University of Nevada Press, 1998, p. 53.

200: "The house you have built": quoted in Elliott, *Servant of Power*, p. 79.

201: "five-story central entrance tower": Goode, James, *Capital Losses: A Cultural History of Washington's Destroyed Buildings*, Washington, DC: Smithsonian Institution Press, 1979, pp. 77–79.

201: "For three days": Wilson, Neill C., *Silver Stampede: The Career of Death Valley's Hell-Camp, Old Panamint*, New York: Ballantine, 1974, pp. 234–235.

202: "Stewart is a *trump*": quoted in Ostrander, Gilman M., *Nevada: The Great Rotten Borough 1859–1964*, New York: Knopf, 1966, p. 93.

202: "He has always stood by us": Ibid.

203: "The purpose now": Worster, Donald, *A River Running West: The Life of John Wesley Powell*, New York: Oxford University Press, 2001, p. 477.

203: "Hold the waters": Ibid., p. 481.

203–204: "He wanted a West": Worster, *Rivers of Empire: Water, Aridity, and the Growth of the American West*, New York: Pantheon, 1985, p. 136.

204: "a very competent and enthusiastic man": quoted in Worster, *A River Running West*, p. 474.

205: "the whole country" and following exchanges: quoted in Stegner, Wallace, *Beyond the Hundredth Meridian: John Wesley Powell and the Second Opening of the West*, New York: Penguin, 1992, pp. 335–336.

205: "I have made some inquiry": quoted in Worster, *Rivers of Empire*, p. 137.

205: "either of utter recklessness": quoted in Worster, *A River Running West*, p. 502.

205: "Apparently [Powell] underestimated": Stegner, *Beyond the Hundredth Meridian*, p. 336.

205: "another half century": Ibid., p. 338.

206: "the long-winded silver orator": quoted in Elliott, *Servant of Power*, p. 205.

206: "Stewart rules": Doten, *Journals*, vol. 3, p. 2018.

206: "The 1898 campaign": Elliott, *Servant of Power*, p. 215.

207: "Though fortune forsake him": Ibid., p. 252.

207: "The Comstock did much": Stewart, *Reminiscences*, p. 340.

207: "At the present time": Ibid., p. 358.

207–208: "Once a man": Dwyer, Richard A. and Richard E. Lingenfelter, *Dan De Quille, the Washoe Giant: A Biography and Anthology*, Reno: University of Nevada Press, 1990, p. 41.

209: "It never rains here": in Benson, Ivan, *Mark Twain's Western Years*, New York: Russell & Russell, 1966, p. 26.

209: "I said we are situated": Ibid., p. 27.

210: "hard and long and dismal": Twain, Mark, *Roughing It*, New York: Penguin, 1985, p. 262.

211: "It is popular to admire the Arno": Twain, Mark, *The Innocents Abroad*, New York: Signet, 1966, p. 182.

212: "If I had been asked": Dwyer and Lingenfelter, *Dan De Quille: The Washoe Giant*, pp. 3–4.

212: "I was sired by the Great American Eagle": Fatout, Paul, *Mark Twain in Virginia City*, Bloomington: Indiana University Press, 1964, p. 5.

213: "When the stage lumbered by": Stewart, *Reminiscences*, p. 221.

213: "the scaredest man": Ibid.

213: "the 'livest' town": Twain, *Roughing It*, p. 309.

213: "the first twenty-six graves": Ibid., p. 346.

214: "the desperado stalked": Ibid., p. 350.

214: "If Bill Stewart had been down here": Smith, Henry Nash, ed., *Mark Twain of the Enterprise*, Berkeley: University of California, 1957, p. 63.

215: "Now—let us remark in parentheses": Twain, *Roughing It*, p. 337.

216: "All modern American literature": Hemingway, Ernest, *The Green Hills of Africa*, New York: Scribner, 1935.

216: "that Irresistible Washoe Giant": quoted in Sanborn, Margaret, *Mark Twain: The Bachelor Years*, New York: Doubleday, 1990, p. 217.

216: "to aid a Miscegenation Society": quoted in Kaplan, Fred, *The Singular Mark Twain*, New York: Doubleday, 2003, p. 117.

218: "His cravat was untied": Twain, Mark, *Sketches, New and Old*, New York: Oxford University Press, 1996, p. 149.

218: "What the mischief": Ibid.

218: "Leave the house": Ibid., p. 152.

218: "the most lovable scamp": Stewart, *Reminiscences*, p. 220.

218: "disreputable-looking": Ibid., p, 219.

219: "I was confident": Ibid., p. 224.

220: "The person and property of a Congressman": Twain, Mark and Warner, Charles Dudley, *The Gilded Age*, New York: Meridian, 1985, p. 178.

220: "forward part of his bald skull": quoted in Powers, Ron, *Mark Twain: A Life*, New York: Free Press, 2005, p. 225.

221: "Cling to the land": quoted in Sanborn, *Mark Twain: The Bachelor Years*, p. 63.

221: "one more little cog-wheel": Twain and Warner, *The Gilded Age*, p. 29.

221: "invention for making window-glass opaque": Ibid., p. 62.

221: "to build a road, or open a mine": Ibid., p. 117.

221: "as naturally as a sugar hogshead": Ibid.

222: "the heavy curse of prospective wealth": Twain, Mark, *The Autobiography of Mark Twain*, New York: Harper & Brothers, 1959, p. 22.

222: "the Shakespeare of mechanical invention": quoted in Kaplan, Justin, *Mr. Clemens and Mark Twain*, New York: Simon & Schuster, 1966, p. 284.

223: "a crazy tangle": Ibid., p. 304.

224: "For a whole year": Ibid., p. 306.

224: "He could persuade": quoted in Kaplan, *The Singular Mark Twain*, p. 472.

225: "In America, nearly every man": Ibid., pp. 306–307.

225: "Well, what would become of the poor people": Twain and Warner, *The Gilded Age*, p. 118.

226: "a large turreted three-story building": Kaplan, *The Singular Mark Twain*, p. 288.

226: "one of the wealthiest grandees": Ibid., p. 439.

226: "The continent spills its riches": quoted in Jaffe, Mark, *The Gilded Dinosaur: The Fossil War Between E. D. Cope and O. C. Marsh and the Rise of American Science*, New York: Crown, 2000, p. 142.

227: "He was almost immediately hit": Ibid., p. 266.

228: "There are two times": Twain, Mark, *Tales, Speeches, Essays, and Sketches*, New York: Penguin, 1994, p. 204.

228: "almost compulsive drive to invest": Elliott, *Servant of Power*, p. 219.

9. The Big Borrasca

231: "too much was known": Doten, Alfred, *The Journals of Alfred Doten: 1849–1903*, three volumes, Reno: University of Nevada Press, 1973, vol. 2, p. 1449.

232: "Capital, no longer generally distributed": quoted in Lewis, Oscar, *Silver Kings*, New York: Ballantine, 1971, p. 208.

233: "Where are the customers' yachts?": quoted in Smith, Grant H., *The History of the Comstock Lode 1850–1997*, Reno: University of Nevada Press, 1998, p. 209.

234: "Politics red hot": Doten, *Journals*, vol. 3, p. 1646.

234: "Why you poor sucker": quoted in Smith, *The History of the Comstock Lode*, p. 283.

235: "not purchasing & filling orders": Doten, *Journals*, vol. 3, p. 1650.

235: "At 7 this evening": Ibid., p. 1651.

235: "Men had almost reached": Smith, *The History of the Comstock Lode*, p. 269.

236: "For sufficient reasons": quoted in James, Ronald M., *The Roar and the Silence: A History of Virginia City and the Comstock Lode*, Reno: University of Nevada Press, 1988, p. 241.

236: "Wreck, decay": Shinn, Charles Howard, *The Story of the Mine as Illustrated by the Great Comstock Lode of Nevada*, Reno: University of Nevada Press, 1980, p. 263.

237: "In mining stocks": Doten, *Journals*, vol. 1, p. 733.

237: "I hoisted my name": Doten, *Journals*, vol. 2, p. 1150.

237: "shut [him] off": Ibid., p. 1341.

237–238: "All people are fond of treasures": Ibid., p. 1370.

238: "the great depression in business interests": Ibid., p. 1413.

238: "poorer financially than I ever was": Ibid., vol. 3, p. 1735.

238: "You never amounted to much": Ibid., p. 1798.

239: "About a dozen": Ibid., p. 1658.

239: "to wager from $100 to $500": Ibid., p. 1795.

239: "There was much betting": Ibid.

239–240: "[He] is racked with it": Ibid., p. 1959.

240: "I'm as inspired": quoted in Benson, Jackson J., *The Ox-Bow Man: A Biography of Walter Van Tilburg Clark*, Reno: University of Nevada Press, 2004, p. 238.

241: "I have become": Ibid., p. 325.

241: "real stinker": James, Ronald M. and C. Elizabeth Raymond, *Comstock Women: The Making of a Mining Community*, Reno: University of Nevada Press, 1998, p. 268.

242: "[The journal] presents": Doten, *Journals*, vol. 1, p. xiv.

242: "His books are on the permanent shelf": Stegner, Wallace, *Where the*

Bluebird Sings to the Lemonade Springs: Living and Writing in the West,
New York: Penguin, 1993, p. 189.

244: "I'll stand on C Street": quoted in Waldorf, John Taylor, *A Kid on the Comstock,* Reno: University of Nevada Press, 1991, pp. 186–187.

245: "Money for nothing": Taylor, Robert Lewis, *The Travels of Jaimie McPheeters,* New York: Signet, 1969, p. 325.

❦ BIBLIOGRAPHY ❦

Baur, John E., "Early Days and California Years of John Percival Jones, 1849–1867," *Southern California Quarterly* 44 (1962).

Benson, Ivan, *Mark Twain's Western Years*, New York: Russell & Russell, 1966.

Benson, Jackson J., *The Ox-Bow Man: A Biography of Walter Van Tilburg Clark*, Reno: University of Nevada Press, 2004.

Berkove, Lawrence I., "'Assaying in Nevada': Twain's Wrong Turn in the Right Direction," *American Literary Realism* 27 (1995).

Berkove, Lawrence I., ed., *The Sagebrush Anthology: Literature from the Silver Age of the Old West*, Columbia: University of Missouri Press, 2006.

Bierce, Ambrose, *Black Beetles in Amber*, vol. 5 of *Collected Works*, New York: Neale, 1911.

Bradley, Scully, et al., eds., *The American Tradition in Literature*, vol. 2, New York: Norton, 1962.

Brechin, Gray, *Imperial San Francisco: Urban Power, Earthly Ruin*, Berkeley: University of California Press, 1999.

Browne, J. Ross, *A Peep at Washoe and Washoe Revisited*, Balboa Island, CA: Paisano Press, 1959.

De Quille, Dan (William Wright), *The Big Bonanza*, New York: Thomas Y. Crowell, 1969.

————, *A History of the Comstock Silver Lode & Mines*, Virginia City, NV: F. Boegle, 1889.

Doten, Alfred, *The Journals of Alfred Doten: 1849–1903*, three volumes, Reno: University of Nevada Press, 1973.

Drury, Wells, *An Editor on the Comstock Lode*, Reno: University of Nevada Press, 1984.

Dwyer, Richard A. and Richard E. Lingenfelter, *Dan De Quille, the Washoe Giant: A Biography and Anthology*, Reno: University of Nevada Press, 1990.

Egan, Ferol, *Sand in a Whirlwind: The Paiute Indian War of 1860*, New York: Doubleday, 1972.

Elliott, Russell R., *History of Nevada*, Reno: University of Nevada Press, 1987.

————, *Servant of Power: A Political Biography of Senator William M. Stewart*, Reno: University of Nevada Press, 1983.

Fatout, Paul, *Mark Twain in Virginia City*, Bloomington: Indiana University Press, 1964.

Goldman, Marion S., *Gold Diggers & Silver Miners: Prostitution and Social Life on the Comstock Lode*, Ann Arbor: University of Michigan Press, 1981.

Goode, James, *Capital Losses: A Cultural History of Washington's Destroyed Buildings*, Washington, DC: Smithsonian Institution Press, 1979.

Hittman, Michael, *Wovoka and the Ghost Dance*, Lincoln: University of Nebraska Press, 1997.

Jackson, W. Turrentine, "The Infamous Emma Mine: A British Investment in the Little Cottonwood District, Utah Territory," *Utah Historical Quarterly* 23 (1955).

Jaffe, Mark, *The Gilded Dinosaur: The Fossil War Between E. D. Cope and O. C. Marsh and the Rise of American Science*, New York: Crown, 2000.

James, Ronald M., *The Roar and the Silence: A History of Virginia City and the Comstock Lode*, Reno: University of Nevada Press, 1988.

James, Ronald M. and C. Elizabeth Raymond, *Comstock Women: The Making of a Mining Community*, Reno: University of Nevada Press, 1998.

Kaplan, Fred, *The Singular Mark Twain*, New York: Doubleday, 2003.

Kaplan, Justin, *Mr. Clemens and Mark Twain*, New York: Simon & Schuster, 1966.

Lewis, Oscar, *Silver Kings*, New York: Ballantine, 1971.

Lingenfelter, Richard E., *Death Valley & the Amargosa: A Land of Illusion*, Berkeley: University of California Press, 1986.

Lord, Eliot, *Comstock Mining and Miners*, San Diego: Howell-North, 1980.

Lyman, George, *Ralston's Ring: California Plunders the Comstock Lode*, New York: Ballantine, 1971.

———, *The Saga of the Comstock Lode*, New York: Ballantine, 1971.

Lyon, James E., *Dedicated to William M. Stewart, My Attorney in the "Emma Mine" Controversy in 1871: Sad Commentary on the Honesty and Conscientiousness of a Lawyer and Ex–United States Senator*, undated pamphlet in Bancroft Library, University of California at Berkeley.

Makley, Michael J., *The Infamous King of the Comstock: William Sharon and the Gilded Age in the West*, Reno: University of Nevada Press, 2006.

Mathews, Mary McNair, *Ten Years in Nevada or Life on the Pacific Coast*, Lincoln: University of Nebraska Press, 1985.

Mayre, George Thomas, Jr., *From '49 to '83 in California and Nevada*, San Francisco: A. M. Robertson, 1923.

Muscatine, Doris, *Old San Francisco: The Biography of a City*, New York: Putnam, 1975.

Ostrander, Gilman M., *Nevada: The Great Rotten Borough 1859–1964*, New York: Knopf, 1966.

Paine, Swift, *Eilley Orrum: Queen of the Comstock*, Palo Alto, CA: Pacific Books, 1949.

Paul, Rodman Wilson, *Mining Frontiers of the Far West, 1848–1880*, Albuquerque: University of New Mexico Press, 2001.

Peterson, Richard H., *The Bonanza Kings: The Social Origins and Business Behavior of Western Mining Entrepreneurs, 1870–1900*, Lincoln: University of Nebraska Press, 1977.

Powers, Ron, *Mark Twain: A Life*, New York: Free Press, 2005.

Robinson, Judith, *The Hearsts: An American Dynasty*, Newark: University of Delaware Press, 1991.

Sanborn, Margaret, *Mark Twain: The Bachelor Years*, New York: Doubleday, 1990.

Satty, *Visions of Frisco: An Imaginative Depiction of San Francisco During the Gold Rush & the Barbary Coast Era*, Berkeley: Regent Press, 2008.

Schlup, Leonard, "Nevada's Doctrinaire Senator: John P. Jones and the Politics of Silver in the Gilded Age," *Nevada Historical Society Quarterly* 36 (1993).

Shinn, Charles Howard, *The Story of the Mine as Illustrated by the Great Comstock Lode of Nevada*, Reno: University of Nevada Press, 1980.

Shuck, Oscar T., *History of the Bench and Bar in California*, Los Angeles: Commercial, 1901.

Smith, Grant H., *The History of the Comstock Lode 1850–1997*, Reno: University of Nevada Press, 1998.

Smith, Henry Nash, ed., *Mark Twain of the Enterprise*, Berkeley: University of California, 1957.

Spence, Clark C., *British Investments and the American Mining Frontier 1860–1901*, Ithaca, NY: Cornell University Press, 1958.

Stegner, Wallace, *Beyond the Hundredth Meridian: John Wesley Powell and the Second Opening of the West*, New York: Penguin, 1992.

————, *Where the Bluebird Sings to the Lemonade Springs: Living and Writing in the West*, New York: Penguin, 1993.

Stewart, Robert E. and M. F. Stewart, *Adolph Sutro: A Biography*, Berkeley: Howell-North, 1962.

Stewart, William M., *Reminiscences*, New York: Neale, 1908.

Sutro, Adolph, *Closing Argument of Adolph Sutro on the Bill Before Congress to Aid the Sutro Tunnel*, Washington, DC: M'Gill & Witherow, 1872.

Taylor, Robert Lewis, *The Travels of Jaimie McPheeters*, New York: Signet, 1969.

Twain, Mark, *The Autobiography of Mark Twain*, New York: Harper & Brothers, 1959.

————, *The Innocents Abroad*, New York: Signet, 1966.

————, *Roughing It*, New York: Penguin, 1985.

————, *Sketches, New and Old*, New York: Oxford University Press, 1996.

————, *Tales, Speeches, Essays, and Sketches*, New York: Penguin, 1994.

———— and Charles Dudley Warner, *The Gilded Age*, New York: Meridian, 1985.

Waldorf, John Taylor, *A Kid on the Comstock*, Reno: University of Nevada Press, 1991.

Watkins, T. H., *Gold and Silver in the West: The Illustrated History of an American Dream*, Palo Alto, CA: American West, 1971.

Wilson, Neill C., *Silver Stampede: The Career of Death Valley's Hell-Camp, Old Panamint*, New York: Ballantine, 1974.

Winnemucca, Sarah Hopkins, *Life Among the Piutes: Their Wrongs and Claims*, Reno: University of Nevada Press, 1994.

Worster, Donald, *A River Running West: The Life of John Wesley Powell*, New York: Oxford University Press, 2001.

————, *Rivers of Empire: Water, Aridity, and the Growth of the American West*, New York: Pantheon, 1985.

Young, Otis E., Jr., *Western Mining*, Norman: University of Oklahoma Press, 1970.

✑ INDEX ✑